Counselling and He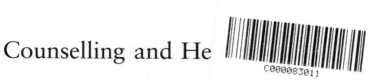

Counselling and Helping

Based on the original book by Steve Murgatroyd

Second edition

Richard Velleman and Sarajane Aris

 The British Psychological Society **BPS BLACKWELL**

This second edition first published 2010 by the British Psychological Society and Blackwell Publishing Ltd
© 2010 Stephen Murgatroyd, Richard Velleman and Sarajane Aris

Edition history: The British Psychological Society (1e, 1985)

BPS Blackwell is an imprint of Blackwell Publishing, which was acquired by John Wiley & Sons in February 2007. Blackwell's publishing program has been merged with Wiley's global Scientific, Technical, and Medical business to form Wiley-Blackwell.

Registered Office
John Wiley & Sons Ltd, The Atrium, Southern Gate, Chichester, West Sussex, PO19 8SQ, UK

Editorial Offices
350 Main Street, Malden, MA 02148-5020, USA
9600 Garsington Road, Oxford, OX4 2DQ, UK
The Atrium, Southern Gate, Chichester, West Sussex, PO19 8SQ, UK

For details of our global editorial offices, for customer services, and for information about how to apply for permission to reuse the copyright material in this book please see our website at www.wiley.com/wiley-blackwell.

The right of Stephen Murgatroyd, Richard Velleman and Sarajane Aris to be identified as the author of this work has been asserted in accordance with the Copyright, Designs and Patents Act 1988.

Wiley also publishes its books in a variety of electronic formats. Some content that appears in print may not be available in electronic books.

Designations used by companies to distinguish their products are often claimed as trademarks. All brand names and product names used in this book are trade names, service marks, trademarks or registered trademarks of their respective owners. The publisher is not associated with any product or vendor mentioned in this book. This publication is designed to provide accurate and authoritative information in regard to the subject matter covered. It is sold on the understanding that the publisher is not engaged in rendering professional services. If professional advice or other expert assistance is required, the services of a competent professional should be sought.

Library of Congress Cataloging-in-Publication Data

Velleman, Richard.
    Counselling and helping / Richard Velleman and Sarajane Aris. — 2nd ed.
        p. cm.
    "Based on the original book by Steve Murgatroyd."
    Includes bibliographical references and index.
    ISBN 978-1-4051-0610-8 (pbk. : alk. paper) 1. Counseling psychology. 2. Helping behavior. I. Aris, Sarajane. II. Murgatroyd, Stephen J. Counselling and helping. III. Title.
    BF636.6.V45 2010
    158'.3—dc22
                                                                        2009023906

A catalogue record for this book is available from the British Library.

Set in 10/12.5pt Sabon by Graphicraft Limited, Hong Kong
Printed and bound in Singapore by Fabulous Printers Pte Ltd

The British Psychological Society's free Research Digest e-mail service rounds up the latest research and relates it to your syllabus in a user-friendly way. To subscribe go to www.researchdigest.org.uk or send a blank e-mail to subscribe-rd@lists.bps.org.uk.

1 2010

Contents

Foreword

This book has evolved like the profession it seeks to illuminate. It has grown into a volume which captures the sprit of engagement in the practice and process of counselling from the perspective of both consumer and professional counsellor. This book made me think; on reflection it seems somewhat strange that there are not more texts aimed at both client and counsellor. This is so because counselling involves a client and counsellor and is impotent without both collaborators. Counselling is not something that one can do to another. It requires engagement and mutual orientation. It demands a curiosity and a state of unknowing which drives us to develop a joint understanding of the uniqueness of the client, their concerns, context, resources and the capabilities and humanness of the counsellor.

People develop anticipations and expectations in order to inform choices and navigate their way in the world. Be these expectation realistic or unrealistic where they are not met they will be disappointed. For this reason texts such as this are essential in painting a reliable picture of what counselling is, what it can deliver and equally importantly, what it is not. The numerous relevant and realistic case examples or vignettes aid the reader in seeing how counselling might be useful to them as they may see elements of their own circumstances or dilemmas in these. For would-be counsellors they give a glimpse of the diversity, challenge and potential reward of working with people across a wide range of presenting problems and contexts. More texts are needed which, as this one does, explain complex concepts in readily accessible language. For too long counselling and therapy have been shrouded in the secrecy that arises from a legitimate commitment to confidentiality. This has stopped professionals talking about the process of counselling and denied potential consumers access to an understanding of what to expect. The consequence of this has been to put some people off counselling because of misunderstandings of the practice and potential of counselling. On the flip side there is of course the possibility of clients sticking at counselling that isn't working for them without awareness that there are alternatives and not all counsellors or approaches are the same.

As we move into the next decade a clear trend is emerging. That trend is the professionalisation of counselling, an increased access to training opportunities for counsellors and a widening of opportunity for consumers to choose. These choices require information and this book takes steps toward enabling a truly informed choice. This book sets out to enthuse, empower and excite and I am delighted to say that in my view it achieves this aim. Counselling is intellectually stimulating and emotionally demanding enterprise, with enormous potential rewards be you in the role of counsellor or client.

Dr Malcolm Cross
Chair of the British Psychological Society Division of
Counselling Psychology 2007–9
Chartered Counselling Psychologist
City University London

Preface

In 1985, the British Psychological Society (BPS) and the publisher Routledge produced a book titled *Counselling and Helping*, written by Stephen Murgatroyd. For the next 20 years, this was one of the key books introducing counselling to potential counsellors.

Stephen Murgatroyd has moved on to do many different and interesting things, and is no longer directly involved in the counselling world. Some years ago, one of us (Richard Velleman) was approached by the BPS to write an up-to-date version of the book. He agreed, and asked his colleague (Sarajane Aris) to join him. This book is the result.

This is not exactly a second edition of Steve Murgatroyd's book. We started off with the first edition as our foundation, because that book was so excellent and had inspired us both, as it has so many people over the years. Our resulting book, however, is very different, although some of the chapters (especially chapters 2, 4 and 15) still retain some of the elements of the original version. In other chapters, portions are based on chapters within another book which one of us (Richard Velleman) has previously written.[1]

What is This Book About?

This book is about counselling and helping: what counselling is and how it works. It introduces the core principles of counselling, and the main types of counselling that are on offer. It also looks briefly at the distinction between counselling, the use of counselling skills, and the concept of helping.

Why is it Needed?

Many people have heard the word *counselling* and may think that they'd like to help others by *becoming* a counsellor, but they actually know very little about what counselling is and what counsellors do. Others may think or have been told that they might benefit from *having* counselling, but again they may not know what counselling is. This book is for both of these sets of people.

This is a 'toe-in-the-water' book for people who would like to be able to help others through counselling, or who would like to know more about counselling, or who may be thinking of having counselling themselves, but are uncertain of what counselling entails.

It is not a comprehensive tome, covering everything in depth, and it is not a training manual. Instead, it is an introduction for people who would like to understand what counselling is and something about the practical skills associated with counselling and helping. Because it is an introduction, every statement is not referenced as it would be in a more academic book, although further reading related to all the topics covered has been included. But this is a book aimed at engaging and encouraging a wide variety of readers who might be thinking about counselling and helping.

It is timely for such a book to be written. There is no other up-to-date practical guide that explains what counselling is in clear, non-technical language. Furthermore, the past 20 years have brought many fresh insights, and many changes of attitude, towards counselling; hence there is a need for effective practice to be summarised.

This book will be of interest to a wide range of people. It is aimed mainly at interested members of the general public: people who are thinking about either becoming a counsellor or having counselling. However, it will also be of use to a wide range of existing practitioners, who need to understand what counselling is and the range of ways in which it can be approached, even if they are not themselves being employed as counsellors. These practitioners will include social workers, nurses, probation workers, and medical doctors, both general practitioners and specialists of all types. It may also include those working in the voluntory sector, education, and other training fields.

What is its Orientation?

There is a huge range and diversity of approaches to counselling. It is not the case that one clear set of ideas or one clear theory is accepted as the best or most useful way of counselling. In this book we introduce a very wide range of these ideas, but they are underpinned by our core orientations.

Our first core orientation is that the central concern of counselling and helping is to *enable people to take charge of their lives*, and to *feel empowered to make changes*. A range of possible approaches to how this can be done is examined, but all of them are concerned with enabling and empowering people to change.

A second core orientation is the importance of the *collaborative counselling relationship*. Although a very wide range of approaches and counselling techniques is introduced and outlined in this book, it is our view that the counselling relationship is at the core of all effective counselling (and see chapter 3 for a much more extensive look at this). In our view, counselling is not just a series of interventions and techniques that are used with (or on) clients. None of these interventions is likely to be very effective in the absence of a collaborative relationship between client and counsellor.

People develop problems and difficulties in very many ways, and there are often a number of different causes for these problems or difficulties. Genetic influences, brain and hormonal factors, and a huge range of psychological, social, cultural and environmental influences, may all combine to lead people to experience problems. Counsellors need to be alert to all these influences, and not assume that only one, or a few, of these factors is the key to the unlocking of all clients' difficulties.

A further central orientation of this book, then, is that *counsellors need to see clients as unique individuals* within a diverse cultural context. Counsellors need to attempt to understand each of their clients as a whole person, within an individual context. A counsellor needs to work together with a client to enable both counsellor and (especially) client to understand what this individual is doing, and why he or she is doing it, within their specific context.

Developing this understanding of each client as a unique individual does not mean that the counsellor needs to engage in a long-term counselling relationship with the client. Developing a collaborative counselling relationship *is* vital; but helping clients to reach a level of understanding, so that they know what they are doing and why they are doing it, can sometimes be achieved in only a few sessions, although in some cases many more are needed.

Nor does it mean that clients cannot begin to deal with their problems until this understanding is reached: clients can begin to change their behaviour as soon as counselling commences. Indeed, most will have started this change process before coming to see us. However, unless clients start to understand themselves better, the change will not in most cases be maintained.

We are ourselves enthusiastic about the power of counselling and the collaborative counselling relationship, and its ability to help people in this process of change. So our aim is to have written a book that will enthuse, empower and excite readers, to enable each reader to feel that they, too, can become a counsellor; that they, too, can help people from a range of diverse backgrounds, who have developed problems in their lives, to change.

However, we also want to emphasise that, although the book provides a framework for helping and introduces some of the tools used in a helping relationship, it is not a training manual. It does not provide sufficient detail for a reader to go out and become a counsellor. To do that, people need a variety of other supports and inputs such as teaching, training, mentoring, role play, supervision and practical experience.

How is the Book Organised?

We have conceptualised counselling and the skills and knowledge needed to provide it as having a number of sets of building blocks: each set of blocks rests on the one below, and if each of these is not secure, then the whole edifice of counselling cannot be secure. If they are secure, then the three together form a comprehensive approach to counselling. These are shown in figure 1.1 (chapter 1, p. 5).

There are three of these sets of building blocks, and hence the book is divided into three parts, one for each set of blocks.

The first set, in Part I, looks at the foundations and core processes for counselling and helping. These processes are fundamental: without these foundations in place, the other building blocks will not have anything to rest upon, and good counselling will prove impossible. These foundations include the forms of helping relationships that exist and how counselling fits into these; the three sets of processes of counselling, of change, and of maintaining change; how to create the right conditions for clients to be helped and to ensure that they have realistic expectations of the counselling process; the safeguards counsellors need to have in place; and the ways in which counsellors can help themselves via training and supervision.

Part II looks at the second set of building blocks: the range of styles and approaches to counselling. Separate chapters examine in some depth different forms of counselling. Each chapter focuses on one of a variety of internal processes which underlie how people react to issues in their lives: how people cope, what people do, what they think, how they feel, how their problems emerge through physical symptoms, how their unconscious processes impact on their problems, people's spiritual side, and how we can help people through coaching.

The third and final part looks at the third set of building blocks: the social processes which also influence how people react to issues in their lives. We examine these issues by looking at people's social networks, how these can be utilised to help people move on, how we can counsel couples and families, and how people can be helped within groups of different forms.

Each chapter follows a similar format where we provide background, give examples, include some experiential exercises to help you to explore the themes in the chapter further, and conclude with a summary.

We provide recommended reading at the end of the book, indicating especially which chapters the reading will be useful for, so that you are able to follow up on themes developed in the chapters and find further information. We have deliberately not provided numerous references within each separate chapter, to aid readability.

We hope that people who are considering entering counselling, either as a counsellor or as a client, and professionals who want a better understanding of what counselling actually is, find this book useful and interesting.

Richard Velleman and Sarajane Aris
February 2009

Acknowledgements

Thanks to the University of Bath and the Avon and Wiltshire Mental Health Partnership NHS Trust (AWP) for providing support and encouragement over many years for my work, to my colleagues within the Mental Health Research and Development Unit at the University of Bath/AWP for their ongoing interest and support, and to my friend and mentor Professor Jim Orford at the University of Birmingham for half a lifetime's encouragement, stimulation and friendship.

Thanks also to the University of Exeter's Clinical Psychology programme (1977–80) which taught me so much about the underpinnings of counselling, and to all the clients over the years who helped me turn theory about counselling into effective practice.

RV

Thanks to my colleagues within Avon and Wiltshire Mental Health Partnership NHS Trust (AWP) for their interest and support, particularly to my friend, colleague and co-writer of this book, Richard Velleman, for his support and encouragement over many years.

Thanks particularly go to Steve Murgatroyd for his friendship and mentoring over 30 years and as someone who encouraged my interests and skills in counselling, helping and organisations very early in my career.

Thanks also to South East Thames Regional Clinical Psychology Training Scheme (1982–6, now Salomons Clinical Psychology Training Scheme), which taught me the foundations of counselling and therapy; and to each client I have had the privilege of journeying with, who have taught me so much about the nitty-gritty of counselling and therapy.

My profound gratitude, respect and thanks for their support in writing this book to Andy Gordon, Peter Merriott, Eve Turner, Hertha Larive and many other friends and colleagues, too numerous to mention, who have shared this journey. If I have missed out naming anyone, it is by mistake: I apologise in advance.

SjA

Thanks from us both to Steve Murgatroyd, whose original version of this book inspired us both. Although this book is very different from his, the original *Counselling and Helping* is the foundation from which we wrote.

Thanks also to Linda Ewles, whose superb editing skills enabled this book to become vastly shorter, more succinct and more readable. We very much appreciate her contribution to the final product.

RV and SjA
February 2009

1

Introduction

What This Book is About

What lies behind us and what lies before us are tiny matters, compared to what lies within us. (Ralph Waldo Emerson)

The whole of this book is an introduction to understanding and working with 'what lies within us'. We are going to introduce, below, a selection of people and problems, many of whom we will meet again throughout the rest of the book. After introducing you to these people, we will outline what we hope this book will provide you with . . . and what it won't.

Toni is a 15-year old girl in a family with one elder brother and two younger sisters. Both parents are high-flying professionals, who have prioritised their careers over their children and are often away, leaving the children with a nanny for long stretches. They hold high expectations of their children, in particular Toni, and show high levels of criticism and disappointment when they 'fail' at anything they do. Toni's elder brother is very successful academically and in sport, and takes every opportunity to taunt and criticise her about both her 'failures' and her successes. Toni has developed a number of assumptions about her life. These include the following:

- significant people in her life have high expectations of her, and she should or ought to do well or she will be criticised and rejected;

- significant people will not be there to support her but will abandon her for more important matters;
- she is likely to be ridiculed and made to feel small whatever she does;
- she is not good enough, and often feels useless.

Philip is a hard-driving and ambitious middle-range executive with a large multinational computer company. From the time he started school until the present time with this company, he has been regarded as a high-flyer: his performance appraisals at university and in the company have been excellent and he always expects to be top of the class or the best among his colleagues at any time. He has been appointed lead director for a project that the company regards as risky and difficult. Philip took on the project and was confident: he expects to be thoroughly competent and to achieve in all the things he does and does not expect to fail or experience undue difficulty. Indeed, he has told his family that he must succeed in the post he now holds since it is the company's 'biggest test so far' of his ability and (he says) it will determine his future in the company. In fact, the company asked Philip to undertake the task because they think that if anyone can do it, Philip can; but they do not think that it can be done. In other words, the company has confidence in Philip even if the project is not successful.

However, the project is going badly: none of the production requirements can be met on time and the quality of the product is poor. Philip feels unhappy because external events are forcing him to be a failure. He also feels anxious that a failure on this project will lead to a bad reputation, a cessation of promotion prospects and even demotion or dismissal from the company. Because he takes the responsibility of being the lead director very seriously, he becomes increasingly anxious and starts to believe that things are 'bound to go even more wrong' and that 'they'll sack me'. He decides not to tell his superiors of the gradually worsening situation, in the hope that things will get better. Philip feels under extreme pressure and experiences this situation as 'one of the most stressful things in my life': he frequently says that he 'feels life just isn't worth living . . . it is truly awful'.

Sally's father died when she was 13. Her mother never fully explained what had happened to her father, and Sally repressed her feelings of loss and worked hard to please her mother. Later, Sally became acutely aware of the implications (personal and emotional) of not having a father, but had spent so many years repressing her feelings that she is now frightened and concerned by her anxiety about examining these feelings. These emotions are so strong that she starts to become depressed. What depresses her is the feeling that it is essential to examine what it means for her to have lost her father, but that she cannot do so without experiencing more pain than she can bear. In her words, 'I am trapped by my own emotions.'

Paula has a chronic fear of rejection. She had had a number of experiences of rejection both at home and at school. Her father had left the family home for another woman when she was 2 years old. At school she had been shunned from group playground activities. It also emerged that her best friend preferred to join these groups rather than spend time with her. When she became an adult, she still desperately wanted to be included in activities and complained that she was never invited to participate in social events by people that she knew. In fact, people she knew had in the past invited her to join in a number of activities, but she had consistently refused their invitations out of a fear that she had nothing to say and that they would find her boring and therefore not want to include her any more. Because she constantly turned down people's offers, friends gave up asking her to join them. Paula's chronic fear of rejection was leading her to create self-fulfilling situations which made her feel increasingly rejected and which fuelled her fear of further rejection.

Harry telephoned, drunk and in tears: he had come to the end of his tether. His wife, whom he loved very much, had died a year ago, and he had been drinking heavily ever since. He had tried Alcoholics Anonymous and a spell in an expensive private treatment centre, from which he had discharged himself after three days. Nothing had worked. What emerged was that Harry's heavy drinking was a far more longstanding problem than he initially realised or was prepared to reveal; and after a couple of sessions of counselling he revealed/recalled that his wife wished him to cut down his drinking long before she died. This in turn exposed his guilt about having failed her, which had contributed to his inability to resolve his grief adequately, and to even heavier drinking after her death.

Raj and **Gita** are getting married and want a western wedding, but their families come from a traditional Indian background, and they

are being pressurised by their respective families to have a more traditional and religious ceremony and celebration. This family pressure
to conform is causing a high degree of distress and tension for the
couple, and Gita in particular is becoming depressed and anxious as
a result.

What This Book Will Do

Toni, Philip, Sally, Paula, Harry, and Raj and Gita have
a range of different problems. Many of these are amen-
able to help, and many of them can be helped through
counselling.

There are a number of main building blocks to counselling work. We introduce the main elements of them in
this book, and we summarise them in figure 1.1. This book will do the
following.

- This is a book for people wanting to dip their toe in the water. We
  want to enthuse, empower and excite you, to make you feel that you,
  too, can become a counsellor, that you, too, can help people from
  a range of diverse backgrounds who have developed problems in their
  lives. We will provide a framework for helping and introduce you
  to some of the tools used in a helping relationship. But it is important to stress that this book is not a training manual. A book of this
  nature cannot provide sufficient detail for you to go out and use the
  range of skills described here, nor can it be a substitute for the role
  play, supervision, training and experience a prospective counsellor
  will need in order to become a practitioner.
- Once you have read this book, you should know enough to be able
  to decide whether or not you want to go further, whether or not
  counselling is for you. If you decide that it is, you will then still need
  to undertake some proper training and supervision.
- Having said that, it is important not to reify training, or the skills to
  be discussed in this book, important though they are. We do not share
  the views of some counsellors and practitioners that only extensive
  professional training and the acquisition of qualifications are a prerequisite for the practice of some of the skills described later in the
  book. Helping through counselling is primarily a process of engagement and relationship, where one person is helped by the presence,
  genuineness, intention, commitment and active listening of another.

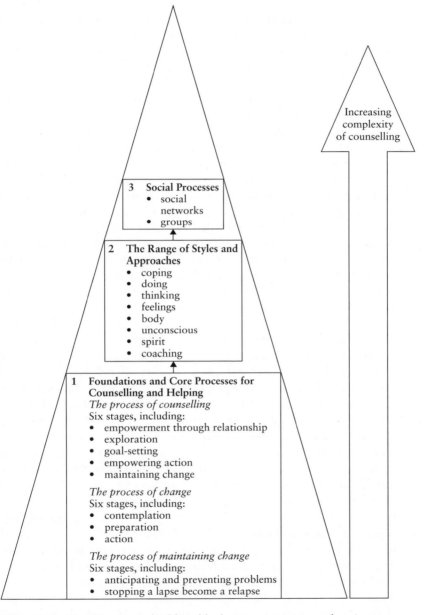

Figure 1.1 The three main building blocks to a more comprehensive counselling approach

Many of the skills used in counselling, although powerful, are relatively straightforward. While most people who help and counsel others may need guidance, and most will need supervision or mentoring, it is quite possible for many people to become skilled practitioners without extensive training, and certainly without qualifications.

- Nevertheless, there are many skills which can be learnt, and there are many issues of professional practice which anyone who counsels others must address, such as taking out professional insurance, being part of a professional body so that clients can seek redress if things go wrong, adhering to a professional ethical code and ensuring that competent supervision of practice occurs and that support is available for times when things go wrong. These suggest that qualifications may be very helpful, particularly in today's world of legislation and scrutiny. Accordingly, some suggestions of how to gain further training and qualifications are included at the end of this book.

- All books have an underlying approach, and this book is no different. Our overall ethos, and the view of counselling and helping which we advocate within this book is one based on *enabling people to take charge of their lives, and to feel empowered to make changes*. There is a wide range of possible approaches to this, many of which are explored in the book; all of them are concerned with enabling and empowering people to change. This ethos of empowerment, using a range of approaches, is different from an ethos which is overly directive or overly linked to any one theoretical perspective, though NICE guidelines are advocating particular approaches for particular problems based on research evidence. Although we introduce a range of different approaches in the book, we do not think that there is a 'right' approach to helping and counselling. Each helper needs to find an approach which is right for him or her and for the person they are working with. The way we look at many different approaches in this book is intended to help you to explore your own preferences and decide on which approach or combinations of approaches most fits your interests and orientation and works best for the person you are helping.

- A second core orientation to this book relates to *the importance of the counselling relationship*. Although a wide range of approaches and counselling techniques are introduced and outlined in this book, it is our view that creating and maintaining an effective counselling relationship is at the heart of all counselling interactions (and see chapter 3 for a much more extensive look at this). In our view, counselling is not just a series of interventions and techniques that are used with (or on) clients. None of these interventions is likely to be very effective in the absence of a collaborative relationship between client and counsellor. This strong collaborative relationship is the essence of effective counselling and helping.

- It is also important to stress that, while we do look over the course of this book at a very wide range of possible interventions, we are not suggesting that a massive amount of technical knowledge is required in order to be an effective helper. There are lots of skills, techniques and ideas which can all help in counselling, and the more skilled and experienced one becomes as a counsellor, the more helpful one can potentially be. But the key set of skills (the foundations in our model in figure 1.1) do not require extensive technical knowledge, and these key skills are at the heart of all the other interventions outlined in later chapters. These foundation skills are in essence about creating a strong collaborative counselling relationship, and using that relationship to work through the core processes described in chapter 3, to empower clients to change.

- In many communities within the UK and across the world there is an increasing diversity of peoples: cultures, races, religions, classes, sexual orientations, backgrounds. We are not examining this diversity specifically within this book, primarily because we believe that all of the approaches we describe in this book will have some relevance for, and be applicable with, peoples from all backgrounds. That is not to say that different people from different cultures or orientations will not have specific counselling or helping needs: of course they may do, but this book is an attempt to describe a set of general and generalisable ideas. We make suggestions in the Further Reading section at the end of the book about where to follow up these more specific areas.

- In the following chapters, we will pose and then answer a number of questions. This is to help clarify what is involved in a particular approach, process, skill or technique. By the time you have read all our answers, what counselling is (and isn't) will be much clearer.

- The key questions which the remainder of the book will answer include:
  - What is counselling, and how does it differ from other helping relationships?
  - What is the difference between counselling and advice?
  - What are the key counselling skills, and are they teachable or does one have to be born a 'counsellor'?
  - Why do some people find it very difficult to be helped – why can counselling be a difficult process?

○   What are the various ways in which one can be helped within a counselling relationship?

○   How is counselling different in group or family settings?

○   How does a counsellor help a person to maintain the gains they have made?

○   Does counselling simply provide social support to people who are lonely?

We are going to answer many of these questions by using the building blocks to more comprehensive counselling outlined in figure 1.1.

Part I: Foundations and Core Processes for Counselling and Helping

Our first set of answers to these questions comes from looking at the foundations and core processes for counselling and helping:

• what forms of helping relationships there are and how counselling fits into these;

• the process of counselling and the process of change.

As figure 1.1 shows, there are some aspects of counselling which are core or fundamental: without these foundations being in place, the other building blocks will not have anything to rest upon and good counselling will prove impossible.

We conclude Part I by looking at two related aspects of counselling:

• how to create the right conditions for clients to be helped and to ensure that they have realistic expectations of the counselling process;

• the safeguards counsellors need to have in place, and the ways in which counsellors can help themselves via training and supervision.

Part II: The Range of Styles and Approaches

We then look at the range of styles and approaches to counselling, examining in some depth different forms of counselling, each of which works via concentrating on one of a variety of internal processes which underlie how people react to issues in their lives. Chapters focus on helping people by concentrating on:

- how people cope;
- what people do;
- what they think;
- how they feel;
- how their problems emerge through physical symptoms;
- how their unconscious processes impact on their problems;
- people's spirituality;
- how we can help people through coaching.

Part III: Social Processes

The final part of the book looks at the social processes which also influence how people react to issues in their lives. We will examine these issues by looking at:

- people's social networks, and how these can be utilised to help people move on;
- how people can be helped within groups of different forms.

Integrating the Building Blocks

Dividing our building blocks up between core processes, individually focused and then socially focused counselling could imply that these are all separate. The reality is that most of us as counsellors use elements of a wide variety of approaches: whatever we consider is in the best interests of our client(s) at the time. Hence, with any one client, we may use a group approach, or work with a couple or a family, or work to develop our client's social networks, at the same time as we employ elements of the eight more individually focused approaches, all the while bearing in mind the core foundations of the collaborative counselling relationship and the core processes of counselling.

A key task for us as counsellors as we become more experienced is to integrate these different approaches. However, it is easier to integrate ideas when each one is easily separable, so it is best to learn about each approach separately to begin with. Therefore, although most of us as practising counsellors use a mixture of approaches in our work with any one client, we have presented them here in this book essentially as 'pure forms'. The task of integration falls on each of us as we start to use these approaches in practice.

Format and Layout of the Book

Each chapter follows a similar format whereby we provide background, give examples, include some experiential exercises to help you to explore the themes in the chapter further and conclude with a summary.

We provide recommended reading at the end of the book, indicating especially which chapters the reading are useful for, so that you are able to follow up themes developed in the chapters and find further information.

We suggest that you get yourself a notebook which can act as your 'Learning Journal', and that you make notes on the exercises in each chapter (and maybe also on important elements in the book), as part of a personal developmental plan, a way of noting down your journey into understanding counselling.

A Note on Terminology

The words we use to describe both ourselves as helpers (counsellors, therapists, practitioners, analysts, psychologists, etc.) and those we help (clients, patients, customers, service users) are each loaded with many cultural overtones and implicit messages. If we refer to someone being helped as a patient, are we using a 'medical model', which suggests that the person is ill and in need of medical care and attention, and so on? If we refer to them as a client, does this mean that money changes hands? If we call them a customer, are we likening them to people who buy goods in the local supermarket?

There are no simple ways out of the dilemmas posed by this multitude of terms and the meanings attached to them all. We could of course develop a new set of terms (helper and helpee, maybe) but we will not. Instead, we will use *counsellor* and *client*. We know that this may not be to the liking of some readers, and for this we apologise.

What This Book Won't Do

This book is *not* a comprehensive account of counselling, nor (as we have said above) is it a training manual, nor is it an academic text, with every sentence and statement referenced. It will not, therefore, provide you with skills to go out and practise as a formal counsellor. Those skills come from training, supervision and associated practice.

Part I

Foundations and Core Processes for Counselling and Helping

Introduction

It is important for prospective counsellors to realise that there is no single 'right' way to counsel all people, and (we believe) that there is no one theoretical perspective which has all the counselling answers. Each prospective counsellor needs to find an approach which is right for him or her and also be able to modify this depending on the needs and problems of the person with whom she or he is working. We do, however, believe that there are some fundamentals which all counsellors need to understand, and core skills which they need to learn. These are discussed in Part I and summarised in the figure below.

First, in chapter 2, 'Counselling and Helping', we look at what we mean by *counselling* and *helping*. We outline that, although it is a complex process, with many different approaches, counselling as we define it is primarily about *enabling* individuals: enabling them to overcome obstacles, to take control of their own lives and to learn how to take

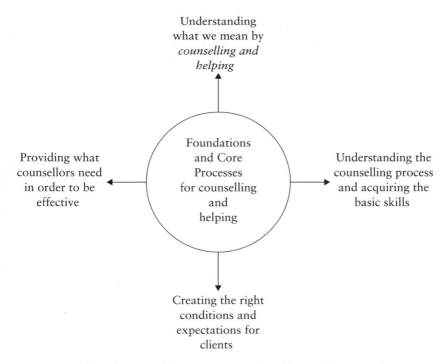

Overview of foundations and core processes for effective helping and counselling

maximum responsibility and decision-making power for themselves and their futures.

Chapter 3, 'The Basic Features of Counselling Relationships', focuses on Building Block 1 of the three-block model outlined in chapter 1. We show that, in order to deliver effective counselling, we need to understand three core processes: the process of *counselling*, the process of *change*, and the process of *maintaining change*. It is through these processes that we use a range of basic counselling skills. This chapter also shows that developing the collaborative counselling relationship is the most important of these core skills.

In chapter 4, 'Being Helped: Creating the Right Conditions and Expectations', we discuss what counsellors need to put in place in order for people to be helped. This includes being sensitive to clients' needs, putting them at their ease, having a clear framework of how client and counsellor will work together, and ensuring that clients have a realistic expectation of what will happen, with no illusions about a quick, easy solution to their problems.

Part I ends with chapter 5, 'Helping the Helpers', where we cover the safeguards counsellors need to have in place, and the ways in which counsellors can help themselves through training, support and supervision; working in teams; and taking care to recognise their limitations and avoid burn-out.

2

Counselling and Helping

If you can truly listen and be with another person, then change and transformation can take place. (Sarajane Aris)

In this chapter we:

- outline various forms of helping and helping relationships, and clarify the similarities and differences between some of these and counselling as an activity;
- examine the major styles of helping and counselling, including the directive and the facilitative styles;
- look at some contexts within which counselling and helping is offered, and some issues that may arise;
- introduce the notion of counselling and helping as a process, as a bridge to the next chapter;
- conclude with a practical exercise, key points and a summary.

The Forms of Helping

Everyone seeks help from others at some point in their lives. Here are some brief illustrations:

- **Sarah** was unsure whether she was entitled to maternity leave. A friend within the company explained women's legal rights and the company policy to her.

- **Jack** is ill, lives alone and is unable to cook for himself. Mary, his neighbour, cooks him a meal each day and makes sure that he has some groceries for a snack whenever he feels hungry.
- **Simon** is so stressed before his monthly meetings with his supervisor that he develops headaches and stomach upsets, even though the supervisor has nothing but praise for his work. Dennis shares some techniques for relaxation with Simon. This helps Simon to control his stress and the physical symptoms soon stop.
- **A team of social workers** has a high staff turnover because they have an excessive caseload. An outside consultant helps the team to secure a change in the distribution of responsibility which reduces the caseload.
- **Sue**, a nurse, feels that she is not being regarded as eligible for promotion because she supported a walk-out by cleaning staff in the hospital. Her nursing officer acts as advocate on her behalf.
- **John** feels that he is unable to make relationships and that few people show any appreciation of his work. One of his colleagues, Barry, starts to provide John with feedback on what his behaviour looks like and how something he has said is received by others. John uses this to improve his relationships. As time passes, Barry provides increasingly direct, challenging and specific feedback which makes John think carefully about how he might improve his social skills.
- **Abdullah** has moved to a new, predominantly white, neighbourhood and has been receiving offensive notes and mail through his letterbox which he finds distressing and alienating. His local community support worker and a counsellor help him to find ways of tackling this and of integrating into his new community.
- **Mike and Angie** have been married for 12 years. Mike says that he is bored and Angie says that she feels like having fun and excitement, but is not sure that Mike is able to provide it. A Relate counsellor helps them identify their situation in more detail and encourages them to explore ways of changing it.

All of these are different forms of helping. Are all of them also counselling?

There are a number of different types of helping going on here. One important point is that these forms of helping are not described in terms of *who* provides the help but in terms of the *kind of help* it is. The eight forms of helping briefly illustrated here imply that:

- helping and counselling can take place in a variety of settings and in a variety of circumstances, and will often include working with issues concerning diversity (culture, gender, ethnicity, religion, race);
- helping and counselling can be concerned with an individual, a group or a particular kind of problem;
- helping and counselling can involve helpers working at the level of an individual, a family, an organisation or a community;
- there are a variety of forms of helping (not one right and several wrong ways), and providing help may involve using a variety of helping approaches or methods;
- listening, creating a rapport and relationship building are at the core of any form of helping, and are a key part of our Building Block 1, introduced in chapter 1.

We therefore need to recognise that our work will involve choosing an approach, and skills and techniques, to suit the circumstances in which we are working; and that if we do not have the skills to help in the circumstances we are faced with, we need to access expert supervision or know how to pass the problem on, and to whom.

For the purposes of this book, we will be looking at helping as being concerned with *enabling individuals to change*, in small or major ways, and take more control of their own lives.

Which forms of helping are included in counselling?

Some of the forms of help outlined above are clearly within the realms of counselling, others are less so. Much depends on the type of counselling offered:

- some approaches to counselling argue that the only form of help which counts is a *non-directive, person-centred* approach, which consists primarily of *focused listening, exploration and discussion*;
- other approaches to counselling include the *provision of information*, the *provision of feedback*, skills development, and *teaching and coaching*;
- others again are very *insight-oriented*, concentrating on helping people access their *deep feelings* or *unconscious motivations*;
- yet others would include *advocacy, systems change* and even *direct action* (i.e. doing things with and for someone else);
- some approaches would encompass a number of these forms of helping, and term them all *counselling*.

What makes counselling different from 'just helping people'?

In some ways, nothing. Helping is a continuum. At one end is the ordinary human activity of offering help to someone who needs or asks for it. And, certainly, the wish to help people who have problems is a prerequisite for anyone wishing to train as a counsellor.

However, it is possible to provide help to people without using counselling skills, and certainly without being in a counselling relationship with them. Many people, when asked for help, respond by telling (or suggesting to) the person asking for help what to do, or by telling them what we (the helper) have done in the past, or by being critical of what they have done themselves so far. It is our view that these interactions, while they may prove helpful, are not part of counselling.

In the middle of the continuum of helping is the use of counselling skills. People can offer all types of help to others, but only some of this help will utilise the sorts of counselling skills that we describe in detail in the next chapter and throughout the rest of the book. Hence some of the helpers in the illustrations above offered help without using counselling skills, whereas others used the same skills as a professional counsellor: seeing the problem from the viewpoint of the person asking for help (as opposed to offering an 'if I were you' response), and helping the person to work out what they really wanted and what was best for them.

There is nothing magical about these counselling skills, and the others that will be described throughout the book. Although some people are naturally better than others at the skills used in counselling, most of these skills can be learnt and, used in everyday situations, they make our social lives and relationships easier.

However, using separate and discrete counselling skills is only halfway along the continuum of helping. At the other end to the ordinary human activity of offering help is a much more formalised set of activities which together make up counselling and (in even more formalised ways) psychotherapy. The difference between using these counselling skills in our normal human interactions and more formalised counselling lies in the extent to which someone is consciously using these counselling skills and techniques in order to help someone else.

Most of the rest of this book is about this more formalised set of activities. But we called this book *Counselling and Helping* in order to emphasise the continuum and the informal underpinnings of counselling. The provision of help through more formal approaches such as counselling or psychotherapy does not mean that these are a different class of activity to that of helping, just that a number of these informal underpinnings and a number of discrete counselling skills have been brought together and formalised.

So, on the one hand, there are few differences between counselling and 'just helping', but on the other the formalisation of these activities mean that counselling is different from 'just helping'. The general human activity of helping does not have a specific set of skills associated with it; but the formalised activity of counselling does. This book is about making explicit this set of skills and how they blend together to constitute counselling.

We said above that there was nothing magical about counselling skills. Counselling is often viewed as a highly skilled and professional activity, requiring substantial training and a great deal of emotional maturity on the part of the counsellor. Our view is that counselling *does* indeed involve competences and skills and *can* involve professional training, particularly in more formalised settings. But a great deal of competent counselling is practised by people who have developed their skills through experience, reading and sharing their ideas and concerns with others. The key in our view is not primarily a person's qualifications, though these do of course have their place: it is the skills and personal characteristics they utilise (which are examined in chapter 3, and in chapters 6–15 which cover Building Blocks 2 and 3), and the ethical and practice safeguards they have in place (see chapter 5). And, as we have said above, the most important element is the counselling relationship, not someone's competence in applying their technical knowledge of how to deliver various different counselling techniques.

So, counselling:

- involves knowing how to develop a helping relationship;
- involves using particular competencies and skills;
- is oriented around understanding the person's problem or issue from *their* viewpoint;
- aims to enable the person with the problem to take whatever action is needed or appropriate (for them, not for us 'if we were in their shoes') to resolve the problem.

As such, counselling *is* rather different from 'just helping people'. Our view is that counselling is primarily about enabling individuals, as far as possible, to overcome obstacles, to take control of their own lives, to learn how to take maximum responsibility and decision-making power for themselves and their futures. Counselling can thus be regarded as a particular form of helping.

Styles of Counselling

We will look at many approaches in more detail in chapters 6 to 13, when we look at Building Block 2. But approaches can in general be grouped into two major styles of helping:

- a more directive or prescriptive, training or skills oriented, external-action oriented style, where the helper directs, instructs or guides the person in need to an appropriate action;
- a more facilitative, internal, insight oriented, personal-exploration oriented style, where the helper is less directive and seeks to encourage and support the person in need to work with and discharge emotion and to reach their own realisations of appropriate actions.

We can illustrate these styles by reference to some case material:

- **Susan** says she is very shy. She gets anxious meeting new people and avoids it if she can; she rarely initiates conversation even with people she knows well. Her friend encourages her to seek help from a counselling service. The counsellor provides some routines which Susan can use whenever she starts to feel anxious – routines which reduce the stress and enable her to function in the social situation. She trains Susan to initiate conversations with strangers in shops and cafes and accompanies her as she *rehearses* these techniques. Essentially, she trains Susan to develop social behaviours. Over six months, Susan becomes more confident and is pleased to begin a more active social life.
- Another counsellor is working with **Len**, who has the same problem as Susan. Rather than offer Len a training programme, this counsellor encourages Len to explore the history of the problem in his life and to associate the problem with the way he feels about other people, especially his mother, father and brother. During counselling sessions Len gets upset and the counsellor works with Len to identify these feelings and give them meaning. Gradually, Len becomes increasingly confident in disclosing more about himself to the counsellor.

This increase in self-disclosure is accompanied by a greater willingness to talk to others. After five months, Len stops coming to the counsellor – he feels he is making enough progress on his own.

It is not difficult to identify the first approach as more directive and the second as more personal-exploration oriented. Notice, though, that both approaches produced results which those being helped felt happy with.

Different kinds of counselling and helping services in the community will use one or other of these different approaches at different times. For example, lawyers and doctors often provide information which directs a person to a particular course of action and are generally more directive than facilitative. In contrast, Relate counsellors who offer help with relationship difficulties, or Samaritans workers who offer telephone counselling services for people feeling suicidal, tend to be more facilitative than directive. We discuss the different skills one might use with these different approaches in later chapters. The point is that there are different methods and approaches for helping, and an individual helper should be conscious of the particular method they use most frequently. In addition, helping agencies ought to be aware of the predominant approach used within their organisation.

We have deliberately not suggested that one method or approach is better or more common than another; rather, that as helpers and counsellors we need to be conscious of the methods and approach we use.

We also need to be conscious of the effect that our approach has upon those we are seeking to help. Clients may become frustrated with more facilitative strategies when they feel the need for more direction; and equally they may feel that their counsellors are directing them towards action too much when what they really want is some space to reflect.

All this means that it is in everyone's interest for us to be explicit about the ways of working that we tend to use and to try to match our style with the client's needs. A failure to achieve this matching can lead to confusion, unrealistic expectations, possible unnecessary conflicts within the helping relationship and even the premature ending of a counselling relationship.

A further important point is that many individuals seeking help do not know that there *are* different styles of counselling. Even if they are aware of this, many people will not know what style of counselling an agency or organisation offers, or what style is used by the particular counsellor they are assigned to. Again, this simply means that it will be in both the counsellor's and the client's interests to be explicit about the way of helping on offer, and to check whether it fits with the needs and the wishes of the client.

Another point is that counsellors, commonly, find themselves moving between counselling styles, both with different people and with the same person on different occasions. In many senses the skilled counsellor is one who is able to make effective use of the different styles of helping according to the needs of their clients. However, both clients and counsellors will have a preferred way of being and of responding. Some will be more comfortable using thinking, or doing, or feeling; and as counsellors we need to take into account both our own natural preferences and those of our clients.

This means that counselling is a dynamic process: it changes in response to events and circumstances, to clients' needs and over time.

Some Contexts and Issues

Helping individuals

For many people, counselling is seen as a process whereby one individual (the client) seeks help from another person (the counsellor). However, there may be some problems with help-seeking that we need to be alert to.

Help and coercion

The idea of *seeking* help implies that the process is voluntary but this is not always the case. For example, many people receive counselling help because a third party wants them to. They may have been sent by someone in authority, or been asked to come by a family member or chosen to receive counselling because it is a route to get something that they want: for example, many people with drug problems accept counselling in order to obtain methadone, a prescribed opiate drug which they receive if they attend drugs counselling.

Because the motivation of the person in need is crucial to the success of any helping enterprise, it may seem self-evident that the voluntary or involuntary nature of help-seeking is going to be of considerable importance. In one way this is true: a person sent for counselling is less likely to hold the counsellor in positive regard than a person who seeks help. However, increasing evidence from a way of working termed *motivational interviewing* (see chapter 3) suggests that it *is* possible to work successfully with people who, when first referred, are not motivated to be there. Indeed, it is also self-evident that counselling cannot start unless a person attends; and if their motivation is low, the early part of our work may concentrate on developing their motivation to receive help.

Help as avoidance

Sometimes people seek help to *avoid* making a decision or changing. For example, a couple may seek relationship counselling not so much because they want to change their relationship, but because going to relationship counselling is a way of putting off a decision to get divorced.

So counsellors need to examine people's motives for seeking help. Failure to do this can lead counsellors to undertake work which is unlikely to lead to any positive outcome.

Help from many sources

The counsellor needs to know whether others are involved in the helping process. For example, say we are working to help a person with sexual problems who is also seeking help from a doctor, a psychologist and a sex therapist. One of their problems may be that they are receiving too much contradictory advice or using one of their helpers to counteract the helping activities of another. Of course, it is unlikely that a client will see two people labelled as counsellors at the same time for the same problem, but many people utilise counselling skills as a part of their work. In the example of the person with sexual problems, to what extent are the doctor, the psychologist and the sex therapist all using counselling skills, and to what extent are they saying and doing the same things?

Some counsellors take a strong stand and refuse to counsel someone if the person in need is already seeking help from another person. In our view this is generally not helpful but it is vital that everyone seeking to help an individual works together to identify the precise role they are playing in relation to other helpers. We discuss this in more detail in chapter 14, which discusses working with people's social networks. This is what makes the discussion of how people have come to be helped and what they expect to derive from the helping process so important. It also makes it necessary for us as counsellors to be explicit at the start of the helping process about the way in which we are going to work. And it raises issues of confidentiality that we will look at in some detail in chapter 4.

Referring on

We need to be clear about where an individual can be referred to, and how to refer people on to these other forms of help, if what they need and what we can provide do not match up. Referring on, if it is needed, will ensure that:

• the person in need is provided with the help most appropriate to their needs;
• we as counsellor/helper are protected from becoming involved in a helping process which it is beyond our ability to provide;
• there are good and frequent contacts between those involved in the helping process.

The process of referring a person from one counsellor to another must be undertaken with considerable care. All helping relationships are founded upon trust and mutual respect. Many people reveal information or feelings to a counsellor which they would not like to be revealed to someone else. So obviously, if we make a referral to another person, we should do so only with the agreement of the client. We need to get their permission to brief the new counsellor as fully as possible, but without disclosing information provided in confidence which they ask us not to pass on. Most of all, we need to motivate the client to actively want the referral: they should not feel that they are being simply passed on to someone else because we are not interested in working with them.

These comments about the task of helping the person we are working with will be developed in other chapters of this book. The point here is that we as helpers have a significant role to play in determining the extent to which an attempt at helping is successful.

Helping in families and groups

Not all helping activity is concerned primarily with individuals. Some helpers work with couples or families, so as to change the way in which the couple or family interacts. Such helping may be prompted by the needs of a particular family – for example, a marriage which is in difficulties, or a teenage girl who is anorexic – but in couple or family counselling, the helper's attention is generally upon the family as a unit, rather than upon the individual who is displaying some 'symptom' of the family's problems. More details of this approach are given in chapter 14, and in the suggested readings at the end of the book. However, even if we work with a couple or a family, the core skills (the building blocks of counselling) will be fundamentally the same. The intention in this book is to present ideas about helping which can be used in a variety of contexts, including couple- and family-focused helping.

Other helpers find themselves working with groups. For example, many organisations (both statutory and non-statutory,[1] public and private) run groups for those who wish to develop skills in assertiveness or to come to terms with bereavement; others run groups which are directed at mastering some skill, such as problem-solving; yet others offer group courses on such diverse topics as managing stress or coming to terms with sexuality. These groups are composed of individuals who share a common difficulty or a common area where they would like to see change. Generally, the main reason why help is offered in a group setting is because groups are an economic and practical way of meeting the individual needs of a number of people simultaneously. An extra advantage is that people can learn from each other.

We look more fully in chapter 15 at special skills which counsellors need to undertake group work.

Helping and the community

A great deal of helping that takes place through organisations and professions is concerned with communities rather than individuals. For example, neighbourhood law centres provide individuals with legal advice but they also assist in major community developments, such as co-ownership housing, and provide legal advice on social campaigns about such matters as pensions and child benefit. In this case, a neighbourhood law centre is helping both individuals and a community. Other examples are community health and development projects which may develop a wide range of services such as a counselling service with highly trained counsellors, community counselling in people's homes, parent support schemes, outdoor activities, and legal and welfare rights advice.

A non-statutory organisation, like Age Concern, the Samaritans or a community health and development organisation, may find itself working at all three levels – individual, family and community – at different times. Helpers need to make conscious choices about these three kinds of work since the way in which the needs of a particular person are viewed will differ between them, and different skills and attitudes will be involved. All organisations (statutory or non-statutory) which work at all three of these levels – as many do – need to identify whether helping an individual is best done at the individual level, or by helping the couple or family, or by focusing instead on some community-based initiative.

Helping is a Process

Counselling is a complex, subtle and sometimes fraught process, in which two or more people are genuinely in touch with each other and are seeking to effect some change. This change may be simple (such as getting some information) or it may be change that has dramatic implications for a person's life. But it is change through a *process*. This book is concerned with illuminating the processes of helping through counselling. The next chapter will outline how all the forms of counselling we are going to introduce later in the book draw upon the same key processes.

PRACTICAL EXERCISE

Sometimes in the practical exercises at the end of each chapter, we will suggest that you note things down, as with the exercise here. As we suggested in chapter 1, you should get yourself a notebook which can act as your Learning Journal, where you can note down these things and also record some of the exercises you do. Together, these will form a record of your journey into understanding counselling.

When you listen to people in various settings, see if you can identify any of the forms and styles of counselling and helping we have mentioned. For example, if someone is trying to offer help to someone, are they providing information or feedback, or are they being person centred, or are they listening in a focused, exploratory way (as described on p. 17 above). (They may of course being using more than one form of help: note down in your Learning Journal all that you hear or see.) See if you can identify their style of counselling and helping, for example, is it more directive, more prescriptive, more facilitative or more insight oriented (see p. 20 above). Make a note of the various settings in which the forms and styles of helping occur, e.g. hospital, school, youth club, bank, hairdresser. Keep some notes for yourself as you do this exercise, either at the time or immediately afterwards. This will help you to recognise and familiarise yourself with the various forms and styles of helping

KEY POINTS

*   It is important to underline the general approach that we advocate in this book, which is very simple: we believe that we should work

with the clients who come to us for help, seeking to *develop a relationship that empowers them, so they can feel responsible for the changes they have to make.* Our task is not to tell clients what they should do.

- Anyone who has practised as a counsellor will be familiar with this idea, yet it is often undermined for two quite dissimilar reasons.
  - First, new counsellors often feel it is their duty to give advice. It is not. In most cases, our task in counselling is to draw out our clients and *enable* them to reach a greater level of understanding or a greater commitment to take action.
  - Second, new counsellors often want to tell clients what to do because they are sure that they know what the client *should* do. It often happens that we feel we know exactly what clients should, ought to or must do in order for them to start or continue to change. The temptation is very strong to say, 'If I were you, I'd . . .' or 'What you've got to do is . . .'.
- While it is impossible always to resist these feelings, such an intervention runs counter to the approach of this book, which suggests that clients will be far more likely to change, and that this change is far more likely to be maintained, if *they* decide to make the change and if *they* decide what that change is going to be. If we as counsellors direct our clients' choices, they can easily interpret these decisions as being ours, not theirs. This in turn can lead to their being less committed to making or maintaining any changes.
- Strangely enough, another difficulty that new counsellors sometimes have is the opposite of what we have just outlined! Although we should not tell people what to do, this does not mean that we can never make suggestions to clients. In fact, our clients often need help and hints to get them thinking. What is all-important is *how* we make these suggestions. Telling clients what to do generally is a bad idea, but enabling clients to realise that alternatives exist, and helping them to clarify what some of those choices are, is an important part of counselling.

SUMMARY

This chapter has:

- covered a range of different ways of helping, and raised questions about where the limits of counselling are to be found;

- argued that counselling is best defined in terms of what sort of activity it is, as opposed to who is providing the activity;
- suggested that, while counsellors can be people with professional qualifications, they do not need to be;
- argued that counselling is a process that can be (and is) widely used and available within a community, provided by a wide range of people;
- suggested that counselling can:
  - take place in a variety of settings and in a variety of circumstances;
  - be concerned with an individual or a group, or with a particular kind of problem;
  - involve working at the level of an individual, a family, an organisation or a community;
- suggested that there are a variety of forms of helping, not one right and several wrong ways, and that providing help may involve using a variety of helping approaches or methods;
- argued that listening, creating a rapport and relationship building are at the core of any form of helping and are a key part of our Building Block 1;
- stated that counselling therefore involves choosing an appropriate approach and appropriate skills and techniques to suit circumstances, alongside the knowledge and skills to know how, and to whom, to pass the problem on to, if necessary;
- stated that the aim of counselling is to enable someone to take more control of their own life, and presented a general (and very simple) approach advocated throughout this book: that we should work *with* the clients who come to us for help, seeking to develop a relationship that empowers them, so they can feel responsible for the changes they will have to make. Our task is not to tell clients what they should do.
- introduced, as a bridge to the next chapter, the notion that a set of common processes underpins all counselling.

3

The Basic Features of Counselling Relationships

When we truly listen, something truly powerful occurs that enables a shift to take place. (John Welwood)

You can't get to where you want to be by remaining where you are. (Charles Handy)

This chapter looks at the key and fundamental processes which, we suggest, underpin all forms of counselling; these are the ones listed under Building Block 1 (foundations and core processes) in figure 1.1 (page 5).

Foundations and Core Processes for Counselling and Helping

This chapter introduces the counselling processes model which contains three coexisting processes, shown in table 3.1 (the processes of counselling, change and maintaining change). Our view is that counselling must go through all these stages for it to be effective, and that these processes apply to all schools of counselling. All three processes are important and go hand in hand. This chapter looks at them in turn.

Table 3.1 The counselling process model

Process of counselling	Process of change	Process of maintaining change
The 6 stages through which counselling sessions go	*The cycle of change which a person goes through when they change their behaviour*	*The process of sustaining any changes which a person has made*
1 Developing trust and engagement, including 'presence' and empowerment through relationship	1 Pre-contemplation	1 Anticipating and preventing problems
2 Exploring the problem	2 Contemplation	2 Stopping the triggering of a return to problematic behaviour
3 Goal-setting	3 Preparation	3 Monitoring and analysing high-risk situations
4 Empowering action	4 Action	4 Teaching coping responses
5 Maintaining the change	5 Maintenance	5 Stopping a lapse become a relapse
6 Ending counselling	6 Termination or lapse or relapse	6 Dealing with helplessness; reducing expectations of old patterns of thinking and behaving

Process 1: The Process of Counselling

This process model draws together, through the six stages shown in table 3.1, various concepts developed over the years, for example:

- the importance of *warmth, genuineness, and empathy* (the 'developing trust and engagement relationship' stage);

- the ideas which many schools of therapy (including both psycho-analysts and behaviourists) see as central: the clear and deep analysis of *what the problem is*, where it comes from and why it has developed (the 'exploring the problem' stage);
- the importance of *goal-directed interventions*, which behavioural and cognitive-behavioural theorists introduced (the 'goal-setting' stage);
- the importance of *action following goals*, again introduced by beha-viourists and cognitive behaviourists, and also by other psychother-apeutic schools such as Gestalt (the 'action' stage);
- the importance of *support and other techniques to enable clients to maintain changes*, emphasised by many (the 'maintenance' stage); and
- the emphasis on the whole process (including the *ending of coun-selling*) being directed by the client rather than the counsellor.

We will briefly examine each of these stages.

Stage 1: developing trust and engagement

Trust and engagement underpin all counselling relationships and all counselling stages. A client's sense of being understood lies at the heart of the helping relationship. If this stage is not successfully completed, counselling will be ineffectual. Developing the counselling relationship is the most important of the core skills.

Prospective clients often arrive feeling anxious and negative about them-selves, and apprehensive about their first appointment with us. Our job as counsellors is to develop trust and engagement and, through that, alter such anxious thoughts so that the client is thinking: 'What a relief to talk to somebody'; 'She seems to understand me'; 'He seems to know what he's talking about.' If we can successfully show our clients that we are people who can be trusted, who will take them seriously, who will listen to and understand their problems, doubts, fears, and aspirations, they will feel positive about seeing us and will be more likely to come back.

Of course, like the client, we as counsellors have concerns too, espe-cially if we are new or are insecure with a particular client or type of client. The counsellor's concerns may include: Can I help? Am I talking too little, or too much? Am I in control? Am I good enough? Do I know enough? What does the client think of me? Some of these concerns will decrease as we become more experienced in counselling. But even after such security is achieved, some concerns will always remain.

We communicate the possibility of trust and understanding by how we act towards our clients. We start to allow trust to develop between our client and ourselves by using a number of important skills, including:

- listening and showing we are listening actively, and engaging with the client;
- showing respect by looking interested, creating the space for the client to talk, not interrupting;
- reflecting both the verbal and emotional content of what has been said;
- asking for clarifications, and focusing, which enables the client to be specific;
- allowing silences;
- demonstrating warmth, understanding and genuineness by the use of non-verbal behaviour such as nods and the use of our hands and our posture, and by what we say and the way we say it;
- summarising by expressing briefly and simply the difficulty the client has described, and asking the client whether or not that is correct;
- making explicit some of the goals that can perhaps be achieved in the counselling session;
- providing clarity via such things as telling the client how much time there is, what the agency does, what counselling is, how many sessions we might offer;
- allowing time at the end of the session to look at what has been covered and what is possible in future sessions, in order to offer hope and to plan for future sessions if they are wanted.

All of these are important skills, but the most fundamental are that the client must perceive us as being *warm, empathic, and genuine*, an idea first put forward clearly in the 1950s by Carl Rogers, a key figure in the counselling world. Rogers argued that the client perceiving the counsellor in this way was an essential condition for positive change.

Warmth

Clients and prospective clients need to see us as being open, friendly and approachable. We show this by communicating openly, both verbally and in terms of our body language (smiling, eye contact and open body posture). If we model such open communication, we encourage the client to communicate in this way too. Even the way we greet people shows warmth – 'Hello, I am glad you could come today' (or, depending on the person we are seeing, 'Hi, good to see you'), accompanied by a smile, and said as if it was meant, not as if it was a routine greeting at a restaurant.

Warmth is a frame of mind as well as a practical skill. Showing warmth to others comes from developing relationships with others in which both we and they feel that we are there to learn from each other: we both want to gain each other's respect and acceptance; they will learn how to become more empowered; we will learn more about how to help other people.

Empathy

Carl Rogers defined empathy as 'the ability to experience another person's world as if it were one's own, without ever losing that "as if" quality'.

Empathy is not the same as sympathy: sympathy involves offering another person support and emotional comfort because they are in some distress or pain; empathy involves entering and understanding the private world of another person *as if one were them*, irrespective of whether sympathy is offered, so that we can better understand what it is like to be that person in need of our help. The key is understanding, and being able to let the client know that we understand: empathy is about understanding and sharing, not judging or supporting.

This has some practical implications for helping. First, it implies that we should check out our understanding of what the client is saying and show that we recognise its meaning for the person. This is known as *reflection of content*. Here is an example:

> SALLY: I get really angry when I think of just what is happening at work. I am really upset that I have been passed over for promotion, and then I have been asked to take on additional duties as well, and without extra pay! Well, I tell you, I am not going to stand for it . . . I am not going to be pushed around like a rotten egg in a salad.
>
> SARAJANE: You say that you feel angry, passed over, asked to take on extra responsibilities with no extra pay. You mentioned a 'rotten egg in a salad': is that how you feel – angry, pushed around, used, as unwanted to everybody as a rotten egg in a salad?

This both summarises the content and checks out whether things have been understood before proceeding.

But if we want to achieve and communicate empathy, we also need to *reflect feelings*, to check that the underlying and often implicit emotions that accompany the expression of content are also understood. Here is an example:

> SARAJANE: You've told me that you're concerned about what you'll feel like after the operation to remove your breast.
>
> MARY: Yes, I mean all sorts of complications could set in, but . . . well, will I look ugly, you know to my husband, you know, er . . . will he still want me . . . Will it affect me in any way other than physically

> . . . you know, you hear so much about hysterectomy affecting women
> – they get depressed and anxious . . . will this, this operation do the same
> . . . ?
>
> SARAJANE: It seems to me that I'm hearing you say 'Will I be the same
> emotionally and sexually after the operation . . .'.
>
> MARY: Well, yes that's it . . . what on earth is it going to do to me?
>
> SARAJANE: And not surprisingly, I also hear a lot of anxiety in your
> voice . . .

The counsellor uses both the content of what Mary says and the way in which Mary says the words as a basis for her reaction. Often the tone of voice, or the way the person fidgets or looks, can reveal as much as (and sometimes more than) the words that are used.

Genuineness
Clients need to perceive and experience us as being genuine and authentic, really wanting to help and empower them. We need to put across a fundamentally simple idea: that we respect people for who they are, for their uniqueness and individuality. We need to begin our relationship with a new client by directly communicating that we accept them, no matter how they might speak or what they might have done. By doing so, we create a climate within which our client can feel safe and change can take place.

Like warmth, genuineness is a statement of how we choose to *be* in our relationships with others.

Other basic features of helping
There are three other features of helping which we will mention here. These are referred to as:

- *concreteness*: getting the person we are working with to be specific;
- *immediacy*: getting our client to focus on the 'here and now' and not the past or the imagined future;
- *challenge*: pointing out discrepancies between our client's view of themselves or their world, and how it seems to us as a counsellor.

Summary of stage 1: developing trust and engagement
To recap at this stage, the skills we use to develop trust and engagement include:

- listening, and showing we are listening;
- showing respect by looking interested, creating the space for our client to talk, not interrupting and so on;

- reflecting both the verbal and emotional content of what has been said;
- asking for clarifications, and focusing, which enables our client to be specific;
- allowing silences;
- demonstrating warmth, understanding and genuineness by the use of non-verbal behaviour, such as nods, the use of our hands and our posture, and by what we say and the way we say it;
- summarising by expressing briefly and simply the difficulty our client has described, and asking our client whether or not that is correct.

We can also develop trust, and engage our client fully in the counselling process by:

- making explicit some of the goals that can perhaps be achieved in the counselling session;
- telling our client:
  - how much time there is;
  - what the agency does;
  - what counselling is;
  - how many sessions we might offer;
- allowing time at the end of the session to look at what has been covered, and what is possible together, in order to offer hope and to plan for future sessions, if they are wanted.

Case example: Philip (see chapter 1)
Early in the first session with Philip, we said:

> Hello Philip, it is good to meet you. I'm very pleased that you came today.
>
> Let me explain a little about what is going to happen. This is a one-off session for us to start to get to know each other, and to see whether or not you feel I might be able to help.
>
> At the end, we'll discuss whether or not you want to see me again. If you do, we'll meet for, say, five sessions, and spend the fifth session with you reviewing what you have got from the sessions so far, what (if any) work remains to be done, and if there is more work to be done, whether you want to do it with me or move on.

This let Philip know that this first session was an exploratory one, to see whether or not he liked this way of working. At the end of the first session he said he wanted to continue, and so we arranged a series of five more.

Not only do such statements provide a structure and framework for our client early on, so they can understand the first session and how it might fit into subsequent sessions, but being open about the agenda helps the development of trust, which is so necessary.

Stage 2: exploring the problem

Because clients often arrive for counselling feeling confused, it is important to help them to clarify exactly what the problem – or, more likely, the range of problems – is. The sorts of questions which should be in our minds during this exploration phase include the following:

- *What is the problem the client comes with initially?* No matter what the initially presented problem is, we should always be aiming to get a clear understanding of its dimensions: what, when, where, with whom, for how long, with what intensity and over what period. For example:
  - *What* might be a severe anxiety or panic attack.
  - *When* might be mid-morning, most days.
  - *Where* might be at home.
  - *With whom* might be when the client is alone.
  - *How long* might be 'For ten minutes, which feels like a lifetime.'
  - *Intensity* might be severe – 'I feel like I am dying.'
  - *Time period* might be 'For the last month, which is why I've decided to come and see someone for help.'
- *What other problems are caused by or help maintain the presenting problem?* For example, if someone has a problem with depression, it is important to clarify how this is affecting life in other ways – relationships, friendships, social life, job, finances and so on.
- *What longstanding, or underlying, problems are around?* Often, during exploration or later, issues start to emerge which have a repetitive feel to them. For example, clients will report having had similar problems in previous relationships, or that they think current problems are related to past issues, perhaps connected to a relationship with a parent.

This clarifies, for both our client and ourselves, what the problem actually is. Almost certainly the picture will be complicated – if it were not, our client would have worked it out long ago – but the more information is gleaned, the more likely it is that the picture will become clearer.

There are certain areas which should not be lost sight of in exploration and after, all of which are covered in some depth in later chapters:

- *Thoughts*: what is our client saying to himself/herself, both in the session and outside of it?
- *Feelings*: what emotions are present, and how are these affecting both what is said or done in and out of the session and the extent to which our client can listen to this session?
- *Behaviour*: how is our client behaving, both in the session and outside?
- *Body*: what is happening in a person's body – has the person developed physical symptoms? Are the symptoms in any way symbolic?
- *Unconscious elements*: what might be going on about which our client might not be aware, and can we help to bring such things to their awareness? For example, 'It struck me that there are a lot of similarities between the way you describe your wife and the feelings you still have about your father – do you think that they might be connected?'
- *Spiritual elements*: what might this be calling a person to, in terms of a spiritual understanding? What might the meaning of this be in a more holistic sense?
- *Life events*: all the above are internal, but external events must also be taken into account. These range from a train being late through to a serious bereavement.
- *Life stages*: there are certain points in people's lives when particular problems are to be expected: examinations, marriage, births, early stages of child-rearing, retirement and so on.
- *External pressures and constraints*: other external issues may affect people's ability to move and change – attitudes of family, work colleagues, friends, financial issues and so on.

The emphasis on each of these elements will vary depending on our orientation as a counsellor, but each is important, and some will be more important with some clients than with others.

Clarifying the problems is not covered solely in the initial sessions. Clients will gradually give us more information about themselves and hence will, with our help, continue to learn more about themselves.

Exploration helps our client to gain new perspectives on their problems. The sorts of skills we use to enable clients to do this are *questioning, listening, and linking*. Other skills include:

- *Giving information*: 'People going through a divorce often find that . . .' or 'Some people who drink too much have found it helpful to . . .'.

- *Displaying a deeper empathy*: sharing hunches, stating things that are not explicitly expressed ('There appears to be a sadness there'), connecting themes; re-framing events or issues, and developing a sense of presence as the relationship develops.
- Helping our client to go deeper by *identifying themes*, asking our client to *draw conclusions* from what they have said so far.

Other skills may involve challenging our client more directly with issues which may be uncomfortable:

- Directly challenging issues which arise in the session: sometimes clients seem to talk only about their negative sides, or to hold self-defeating beliefs which keep them from moving forwards, and these need to be responsibly and carefully challenged.
- Using our own discomfort or negative feelings: 'I'm feeling a bit uncomfortable at the moment because . . .' or 'I'm feeling confused. I thought you were saying that . . . but now I seem to be hearing the opposite.'
- Engaging our client in a mutual exercise: 'There seems to be . . . between us at the moment; what do you think?'

Having gained a new perspective and been helped to see the problem in a different light, our client is left with the question, 'Okay, but what now?' We must then help our client to move onwards from the new perspective, by helping them to set goals.

Case example: Philip (see chapter 1)
We gave Philip the space in the first session to start to say how he felt about himself, to express his anxiety about his work and his feeling that he was failing. He trusted us sufficiently by the end of the session to return to talk some more. The developing trust in the counselling relationship, and the ensuing rapport, allowed a move to a deeper exploratory phase. He began to see that his anxieties and fear of failure were far more longstanding problems than he had initially realised. But he did not know what to change, or how to do it – that was the next stage.

Stage 3: helping clients set their own goals

The next stage is to help our client to clarify and agree upon the goals of their work. In this stage we will introduce SMART, TINA, TAAA and medium- and short-term goal-setting.

We may need to encourage our client to distinguish between realistic and unrealistic goals, and between goals which are self-defeating and goals which are self-enhancing. Goals should be:

- specific and clear (S);
- measurable and verifiable (M);
- adequate to meet the problem (A);
- realistic and achievable (R);
- timed (a specification of *when* the actions to achieve the goal will be taken) (T);
- in the client's control;
- in line with the client's values.

The first five of these are often known under the acronym SMART (as in 'Goals should be SMART'), to which we have added two relating to our focus on counselling's central role in empowering our clients. The SMART acronym can be a useful way to remember the key successful elements in goal-setting, as well as a way of demystifying the counselling and helping process.

One problem which often besets clients is TINA, or 'There is no alternative'. Clients will often get stuck by convincing themselves that only one course of action or one goal is possible, and that this goal is impossible to achieve. Much of this stage of counselling is taken up with teaching clients TAAA, or 'There are always alternatives'. Much goal-setting and action consists of helping clients to see alternatives to every course of action.

Goal-setting moves on from exploration. Having clarified the range of problems which beset the client, we help the client to select one problem area to work on first. We then help them to clarify medium- and short-term goals.

The medium-term goals can be elicited in ways such as: 'In a year's time, I will be able to do . . .' or '. . . I will be feeling . . .'. The focus of this stage is to enable the client to realise that there are alternatives, that a choice between them can be made and that each option has both advantages and disadvantages.

Having clarified some of the medium-term aims, these general aims need to be made more specific. For example, if an aim is 'to improve the quality of my relationship with my son', this needs to be refined into, say, 'Over the next two weeks I shall cut by half the number of times I have conversations with my son which deteriorate into arguments.'

So, goal-setting involves:

- clarifying the medium-term goals;
- choosing one goal to work on;
- making that goal more specific.

Skills used at this stage include:

- asking;
- summarizing;
- brainstorming;
- suggesting as a trigger;
- balancing (getting the client to think of the advantages and disadvantages of each option).

Case example: Toni (see chapter 1)
When Toni carried out this task with us, she realised that she had a number of short- and medium-term goals. For example, she wished to continue with her group of close girl friends with whom she tended to feel more equal and less of a failure, to start to be able to shut out her brother's taunting and critical remarks to her, and to continue at school and do well enough to go to university.

Stage 4: empowering into action

Action is the next stage in this process. While setting goals can make people feel more hopeful about the future, acting on those goals involves doing something. This is difficult for many people. The way forward is to have a plan of action wherein our client, supported by us as the counsellor, moves towards the agreed goal in stages, using achievable sub-goals. Having clarified the medium- and short-term goals, the next step is *empowering the client to take action* by planning a detailed and realistic strategy of how to put the goal into action.

For example, if the goal is to 'say no to people who ask me to do extra things for them, at least twice per week', we might work out with our client that the strategy between now and next week might be 'to do only things that I have agreed to do and not try and extend myself to please others'. With each goal and strategy, we and our client need to work out a route for achieving it which takes into account both opportunities and pitfalls.

An important idea to get across to our client is that these strategies are about *testing ideas in practice*, and then discussing how well or otherwise the ideas have worked. If they do not work, it is not a failure but simply more information which we and our client can use to create a further strategic plan. But the chances of a strategy working will be greatly improved if we have gone through in some detail how it may be achieved, what pitfalls may occur and how to overcome them.

Such a strategy informs the subsequent meetings with our client, in which we help them to evaluate the success or otherwise of the chosen course of action. If successful, we and our client move on to a further course of action, or choose another problem area and repeat the process. If unsuccessful, we explore why, and then help to set courses of action which will not suffer from the same problems.

Besides the ones described previously, the skills we use in this action phase include:

- brainstorming to get options;
- appraising;
- strategy planning;
- balancing pros and cons of courses of action;
- evaluating.

Stage 5: helping to maintain change

Changing ingrained and habitual patterns is often difficult and painful, so how can we help our clients to maintain changes? We say much more about this in the final section of this chapter, on the process of maintenance, which is all about this stage. We will just say two things here.

First, our clients need *support* after taking action. Support from the counsellor is important, but it is also important to help our clients to develop their own support networks. We say a lot more about social networks in chapter 14.

Second, our clients need *to learn specific skills*, which will often be different from the skills they used to take the action in the first place. Having learnt the skills to deal with a problem in the short term, many clients will also need help to deal with longer-term issues when motivation is flagging.

Stage 6: ending counselling

Ideally, counselling ends when our client has successfully worked through the various goals delineated with our help, taken action and maintained changes, and so is ready to move on.

Unfortunately, ending counselling is often not so simple. One reason is that there are always new goals to be striven for. Another is that clients may come to feel dependent upon us. Sometimes clients relapse or develop new problems seemingly in order to retain the counselling relationship. Sometimes, also, we as counsellors become attached to our clients and may find it difficult to give them up. Many of these client–counsellor issues will need to be brought to the supervisory relationship; this is discussed in chapter 5.

A summary: the nature of the six stages in Process 1

The six stages of trust, exploration, goal-setting, action, maintenance and ending describe the process that we will go through with all clients. Of course, it is not as clearly defined as this description makes out. For example, we may pass through a number of stages in a single interview, or any one stage – especially the second – may take longer than the others.

Also, the process is *cyclical* in that the action stage will almost certainly throw up new information, which will inform the whole plan that we and the client have made together, and will therefore serve as a further part of the exploration phase. Problems connected with taking action, therefore, will provide exploratory material, may cause us to revise the goals and will influence the taking of further action.

A useful way of thinking about this model of counselling is to look at *content* versus *process*.

- As counsellors we are not in charge of the *content* of counselling – to a large extent that is determined by our client and what he or she brings to the sessions. We can of course influence this, by the questions we ask and the way we respond to the sorts of things that a client says to us, but the content is primarily up to our client.
- The opposite, however, is the case as far as *process* is concerned. It is our job as counsellors to shape the process, to ensure that sessions have a structure, that there is time for us to summarise, for our clients to say what they want to, to discuss action between sessions and so on. Clients often come to sessions feeling uncertain and confused, and it is up to us to provide a framework within which they can feel safe; then they are able to start, or continue, to work on their problems. The model describing the six stages of the process of counselling helps us by providing a framework by means of which we can give our clients a structure. Content (i.e. what is talked about) is the client's responsibility; our job is to be in charge of and to enable the process.

Case example: Harry (see chapter 1)
Harry developed a goal that he wanted to abstain from drinking altogether. With our help, he worked out a plan of action for the coming week, identifying possible at-risk situations and the strategies and tactics which he was going to employ.

The following week, Harry returned saying he had failed: he went for a country walk with one of his daughters and ended up in a pub for lunch. He had two pints with his meal and had drunk nothing else throughout the week.

This information was used in a variety of ways. It added more material which was useful for exploration: Harry could successfully control his intake under some circumstances; drinking two pints did not precipitate a full-scale relapse; and so on. It also provided the possibility for reassessing the goals – perhaps some drinking, under controlled and monitored conditions, with certain people and in certain contexts, might be a desired goal? This new material altered the plan of campaign for the next and subsequent weeks.

If abstinence was still Harry's goal, new at-risk situations had been identified, and new strategies had to be developed to overcome them, such as getting his daughter to buy the (non-alcoholic) drinks.

Alternatively, if occasional controlled drinking was now the goal, the details of when, how much, with whom, where and so on needed to be clarified: risky situations relating to these actions needed to be identified and strategies to overcome them needed to be thought through.

Helping clients to change behaviour
The most fundamental thing is to help our clients to change what they do. With many problems (e.g. substance misuse, compulsive behaviour, eating disorders) one might be able to help clients to alter their thoughts and feelings about their behaviour but until our client actually decides to behave differently, the problem is likely to remain unresolved.

The three elements that are important in helping clients to change their behaviour and maintain the changes are:

- *Performance*: although clients' attitudes, ideas, wishes and so on need to be examined and addressed, talking on its own is unlikely to provide all the help. There must be a behavioural (performance) component to the intervention as well: people must *do* something different about their problematic behaviour.
- *Practice or rehearsal*: helping a client to change behaviour will almost certainly involve the development of new skills and, as with any new skills, these need to be practised.

- *Homework*: some of the practice will occur in the counselling sessions, but much of it will occur in the client's outside life. Hence it is important to negotiate some task(s) to carry out during the times between the sessions, which usually involves the client practising some of the skills or strategies discussed in the session.

Process 2: The Process of Change

The 'cycle of change' idea was initially developed by two American psychologists (Prochaska and DiClemente, 1983) in relation to people changing smoking behaviour, but it is now used with clients with all sorts of problems.

The model shows that when clients arrive for counselling, they may be at one of six stages (see fig. 3.1).

- *Pre-contemplation stage*: an individual may not be aware that their behaviour is causing problems or be concerned about it; they may have been sent for counselling by someone.
- *Contemplation*: an individual starts to think about their behaviour, and the link between behaviour and problems.
- *Preparation*: a serious commitment is now made to implement changes.
- *Action*: the client implements the proposed action and practises new skills to maintain the new behaviour. If successful action is sustained for three to six months, the client moves on to the maintenance stage.
- *Maintenance*: this stage is the one of trying to integrate the behaviour change into the lifestyle, maintaining the chosen direction.
- *Termination or lapse/relapse*: for some, the new behaviour has been successfully learnt, and the new coping methods are incorporated into the client's repertoire. For most, however, the next stage is lapse, or relapse, which is particularly common in the first six months, where the person succumbs to the pressures to resume their old ways of behaving.

We see Prochaska and DiClemente's model as being clear and commonsensical, and there are a number of useful points worth stressing.

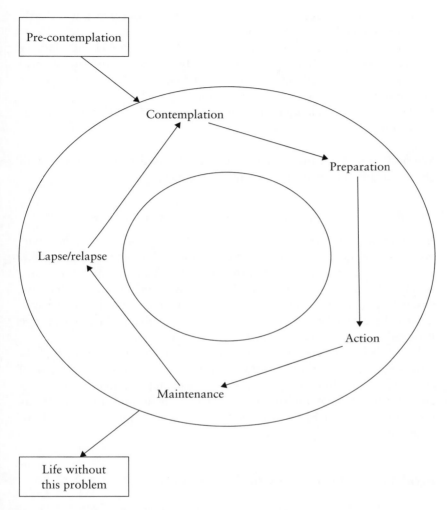

Figure 3.1 The Prochaska and DiClemente cycle of change

- The change process is a cycle: people usually make more than one attempt before succeeding; relapse is common.
- Change has various stages, and people may ask for help at any of the six stages.
- The model is not a linear one: people can re-enter the cycle at any point following a lapse.

- Motivation is not seen as a static concept, but as one which will clearly alter as people move from one position to another.
- Especially at the earlier stages, ambivalence about change is very common: not only is change difficult, but there are usually positive sides to problematic behaviours, thoughts, or feelings which people are not completely happy to give up.
- The skills and techniques used at one stage need not be the ones used at another.

We outline how all these techniques may be used when working with clients in different ways in subsequent chapters.

The process of counselling and the process of change

It is important to stress that a cycle of change model is not an alternative to the six-stage model described earlier. The two fit well together.

The six-stage model describes the processes through which our counselling sessions should travel and informs us about the tasks which we as counsellors have to carry out. The cycle of change, on the other hand, describes the processes through which the client will go when they change their behaviour: its focus is on the client's journey.

In parallel to the cycle of change model, others in the counselling field have suggested that there are three central issues involved in successful change in counselling: *readiness*, *importance*, and *confidence*. They suggest that if a change appears important to a client, and if the client has the confidence to achieve it, then the client will be more ready to have a go, and more likely to succeed.

Process 3: The Process of Maintenance

Maintaining changes that people have made is a challenging process for most people. The change is new and unfamiliar, and clients may be insecure and nervous about being able to maintain it. So this is the time when they need our help most. Lapses[1] may occur during the early parts of our intervention if our clients have moved into the action phase too soon, before they have dealt with their motivation and ambivalence sufficiently. Or they may happen later because our clients do not manage to carry out their intentions.

It is very useful to discuss lapses and relapses relatively early with clients. We often do this by *anticipating with them potential problems and their solutions*. It is important to help our clients to see that relapse is not something which just happens, but is an endpoint in a chain of decisions and events which may have started some time before the actual relapse.

There is a useful metaphor for relapse which we often discuss with our clients. If we think of the person with a problem who is trying to regain control over their behaviour as being like someone walking along the edge of a cliff, then falling over the edge of the cliff is a metaphor for a relapse. We can use the problem of depression as an example here. People who do not have a problem with depression walk quite a distance from the edge. Although they *could* fall over (they *could* become depressed), they are less likely to, because the path they are walking along is quite a distance from the edge. Clients, by virtue of the fact that they actually *have* a problem, are walking along a path which is very close to the edge of the cliff, and they could therefore more easily fall over: they could relapse into depression very easily. What can we do? We suggest two things.

- If we put railings along the edge of the cliff, they would be far less likely to fall over the edge (this prevents them from lapsing).
- If we give them a parachute, then were they to fall over, they would be able to land safely and not fall to their deaths on the rocks below (this deals with a lapse if it occurs, so that it does not turn into a full-scale relapse).

The task of helping people stay well is to discover why lapses occur for our individual clients, and to develop strategies which can act both as railings and as a parachute.

Thinking about why relapse occurs

There are many reasons why relapse occurs, but instead of listing all of them, we are going to offer an examination of the process of relapse, based on the idea that the most effective way of intervening is to change the process.

The first step in a relapse is usually an apparently irrelevant decision. Clients often tell us of little things they did which seemed to be totally harmless, but which in retrospect started the ball rolling towards the high-risk situation. An example in the problem drinking field might include accepting an invitation to a leaving-do: 'At the time, I didn't think about it, but of course, everyone else was drinking . . .'. Naturally, there is no avoiding many such high-risk situations, but what is vital is that clients are prepared for them, and have some strategies ready to deal with them. If not, they will move to the next stage: feelings of helplessness, of low self-control and of 'having been here before' and being powerless to stop it. Coupled with this is the belief that the way that they have coped in the past (by drinking, for example) will relieve these awful feelings and they think, 'But what the hell . . .', and the first drink is drunk, the first chocolate biscuit is eaten, the first numbing feelings of depression creep back in.

This of course is only a single lapse, but it can easily become a permanent relapse. After a vow to abstain – whether from alcohol or chocolate biscuits – a slip or lapse is seen as a major failure. Most people seem to react in a way where one slip is seen to have ruined everything to the extent that a person eating one biscuit or having one drink feels they might as well eat the whole packet or finish the bottle.

The process of maintenance

A central feature of helping people to prevent relapse is not to hide the possibility of relapse from clients, but to discuss it openly with them so that clients have the maximum opportunity to prepare for potential relapse-inducing situations. The following is a list of techniques that counsellors can use to prevent relapse:

- helping clients to recognise apparently irrelevant decisions;
- helping clients to monitor and analyse high-risk situations;
- teaching coping responses;
- dealing with helplessness;
- reducing clients' positive expectations about the effectiveness of previous ways of thinking and behaving which have worked in the past;
- dealing with lapse situations, which include:
  - changing a client's understanding;
  - the practicalities of dealing with a lapse, such as developing verbal and behavioural skills, and other strategies such as reminder cards;
  - programming lapses in safe situations (e.g. accompanied by the counsellor or some other trusted person, having a single drink or a single chocolate biscuit, and then stopping);
  - dealing with feelings about the lapse.

Even with all this work on lapses, some clients will nevertheless relapse. Both they and we will have negative feelings about this. Our negative feelings must be dealt with during our supervision and support, and not offloaded onto the client. It is our job to help clients work through their feelings about having relapsed, so that they feel empowered to try once more.

For our client, the important issues are to:

- learn to recognise early-warning signs;
- monitor high-risk situations;
- develop coping strategies for these situations so that they do not turn into lapses;
- set up coping mechanisms so that lapses do not turn into relapses.

Perhaps the shift of emphasis from thinking of relapse as a failure to seeing it as a learning experience is the most important issue for our client. We should expect and accept lapses and relapses, and enable our clients to learn from them.

Case example: Harry (see chapter 1)
Harry benefited from the relapse management approach. When he first came to see us, he had tried lots of different approaches and had relapsed frequently. This was discussed at an early stage, with two decisions: first, that Harry and we (as his counsellor) needed to work through possible relapse-inducing situations, and, second, that if a relapse occurred, it was vital that he return to discuss and learn from it.

Harry made many apparently irrelevant decisions. For example, one strategy to improve his social life was to invite friends round for a meal, and Harry did not think through what he would do when people arrived bearing a bottle of wine. Harry became better at recognizing when situations were likely to become risky, and he developed many skills at avoiding them. For example, he arranged with friends who came for a meal that they would take away any leftover alcohol. He rehearsed out loud in the sessions how well he was doing – and indeed, he remained abstinent for a longer period than he had ever done in the previous 30 years.

However, Harry did start to drink again. Our relationship had become strong enough so that he felt that he could continue to come to our counselling sessions following his lapse, and when he did we discussed in detail what had happened. As a result of this lapse, he decided he wanted to try controlled drinking. This went well for a time, but then

Harry had a major relapse and stopped attending counselling for two months. When he returned, we worked with Harry to enable him to see the relapse as a tremendous learning experience. Harry reverted to an abstinence goal, and continued to work on analysing at-risk situations, developing better coping skills and raising confidence and self-esteem. He also worked on dealing with any future lapses in such a way that they did not turn into relapses, and gradually he needed to attend counselling sessions less frequently.

PRACTICAL EXERCISES

Developing empathy skills

There are some practical steps we can take to develop skills in empathy.

- We can practise reflecting content with friends or relatives. Try to reflect back what they have said (paraphrase) and check our understanding.
- Try to imagine the person we are helping actually being in the various situations which they describe to us, as if we were making a documentary video. Try to create on this screen an accurate picture of the experiences they describe. Jot some notes into the Learning Journal about this, how it might feel for them and any images that arise. What might it feel like to be in their shoes?
- If we do not think visually, imagine the person as the key character in a novel – think of all the phrases to describe this person and the situations they outline to us. It may be particularly helpful to think of ourselves writing their biography.
- Work on increasing our vocabulary of emotions – use dictionaries, a thesaurus, novels and films, and any other materials we can, to enrich the way we can describe what a feeling is like.

Developing genuineness skills

There are ways in which we can improve the extent to which we communicate our genuineness to others:

- develop the ability to describe you to yourself – pay particular attention to changes in your mood, your relationships with others and your strengths and weaknesses;
- develop your ability to describe yourself to others – practise (relevant!) self-disclosure;

- read books about personal psychology, self-concept and personality, and examine your own thinking, feelings and behaviours in the light of this reading;
- try to predict your own behaviour – see just how good a judge of your own character and reactions you are, and examine why it is that you sometimes react in ways which you did not intend.

Developing concreteness skills

We can practise 'being concrete' by asking questions of others such as:

- What do you mean by . . . ?
- When you say you feel . . . can you be more specific about this feeling?
- How do others react to you when you say you are feeling this way?

Developing challenge skills

Practice non-aggressive challenging by:

- looking for discrepancies between what people say their view of themselves or their world is and how it seems to us, or between what they think and feel and what they actually do, or between the real world as seen by us and the fantasy world as seen by them;
- gently challenging some of these, in a non-aggressive and enquiring way.

Because we are implicitly given permission to do and say such things in a counselling relationship, whereas we usually do not have the same permission in other relationships, most of these exercises should be undertaken with care, and probably only with close friends!

SUMMARY

- Counselling is a process which we have described in a six-stage model. As counsellors we have the task of facilitating the process. We have to be able to take an overview, see how far we have gone and organise the sessions so that the counselling is successfully ended.
- The content of sessions is led by our client, although we influence it by our questions and responses to what is said.
- The development of trust and engagement underpins all counselling relationships and counselling stages.

- Exploring our clients' problems is a way of helping them to clarify the issues and to reduce their sense of chaos. However, helping our clients to gain clarity and a new perspective on previously inexplicable behaviour is insufficient if we do not also help them to change or manage that behaviour.
- Our clients will often believe there are no alternatives or can conceive of only one possibility. A fundamental belief expressed in our counselling is that there are always alternatives. The goal-setting and action stages are concerned with enabling our clients to realise this.
- Moving from goals to action involves having a detailed strategy of exactly how our client will put any goal into action. This strategy must involve contingency plans to deal with eventualities which will otherwise negate the overall plan.
- Our clients may need to develop new and different skills to maintain the changes. Our support as their counsellor is often crucial during this stage.
- Ending counselling is a necessary but sometimes difficult stage. Ideally, counselling ends when our clients realise they have learnt the skills which will enable them to deal with future problems successfully.
- There is a large range of skills which can be utilised at each stage. It is vital to remember the importance of helping our clients to change their behaviour. The elements of performance, practice or rehearsal, and homework, are tremendously helpful.
- Prochaska and DiClemente suggest that all clients go through a number of stages: pre-contemplation, contemplation, preparation, action, maintenance, and lapse or relapse.
- This cycle of change is not an alternative to the six-stage model depicting the process of counselling. The two fit together well. The six-stage model is the process through which our counselling sessions should develop, while the cycle of change describes the processes through which our clients go when they change their behaviour.
- Another useful way of thinking through the complexities of behaviour change is to work with our clients on the relationship between the *importance* of the proposed change to them, their *confidence* in making that change, and their *readiness* to try to achieve that change.
- We need to discuss relapse in counselling sessions, with a view to helping our clients find ways of avoiding it. Clients need to know that, even if they do relapse, we still want them to return to discuss the situation with us.

4

Being Helped

Creating the Right Conditions and Expectations

Until one is committed there is hesitancy, the chance to draw back,
always ineffectiveness. (Goethe)

The last chapter looked at the key processes that underpin counselling, change and maintaining change. This chapter looks at what else needs to be in place in order for people to be helped through counselling. What conditions do we need to create for our clients? What do they need to know? What is it that they want, what expectations do they come with and are they appropriate or realistic?

There are eight dimensions involved in creating a successful helping process, outlined in figure 4.1, six that we should deliver for our clients, and two (the last two in the list) that they may wish for but where we may have to disappoint them:

- putting people at their ease;
- giving and receiving information;
- competence;
- a clear contract or framework for working together;
- ethical behaviour;
- compatibility between client and counsellor;
- confirmation that change is needed;
- a magic solution: realistic and unrealistic expectations.

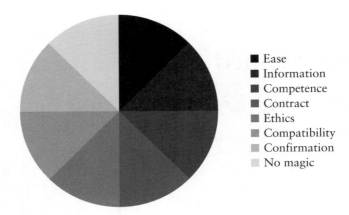

Figure 4.1   The eight dimensions of a successful helping process

Putting People at their Ease

Prospective clients often arrive feeling uncertain and apprehensive. They may be upset or irritated with themselves because they have not been able to solve their own problems. They may be unsure and troubled about what is happening ('Am I going mad?'). They will certainly be worried about how they are feeling or behaving, which is of course why they are coming for help.

But they will also be uncertain about us and about what counselling and helping is all about. Films, TV programmes and books have generated many stereotypes and myths, and so people may wonder if we will ask them to lie on a couch, or talk about their potty training, or reveal their innermost fantasies or fears.

So we need to put clients at their ease, especially at the start of their first appointment. With new clients, begin with a quiet greeting, a warm smile, maybe a coffee, and ensure that they have a comfortable seat. It is often helpful to acknowledge that many people find it difficult and get anxious when seeing a counsellor for the first time.

It also helps if we find out how clients want to be addressed, by saying, for example, 'I tend to get people to use my first name – Richard – and to use people's first names too. So is it OK for me to call you Jane or would you prefer me to call you Mrs Smith and you call me Dr Velleman?' Notice that it is important to introduce an equality immediately: either we both use first names, or we both use more formal titles: we should never call the client by their first name but then expect the client to address us more formally.

Giving and Receiving Information

A lot of our early sessions will be taken up with receiving information: we need to ask clients many questions. But in fact one of the first things we need to do is to give the new client some information. It can be useful to also have a leaflet available about counselling and how we work (frequency and length of appointments, our style of working and so on), given that lots can be forgotten after a first appointment.

In our first appointment we need to say how long the appointment will last and clarify that one purpose is to see 'whether you feel I might be the right person to help you. We need to see whether my style of working fits with what you want and whether I feel my style of working is likely to help you.'

For example, in the case of Philip, whom we met in chapter 1, early in the first session we said:

> This is a one-off session for us to start to get to know each other, and to see whether you feel I might be able to help. At the end, we'll discuss whether you want to see me again. If you do, we'll meet for, say, five sessions, and spend the fifth reviewing what you've got from the sessions. If there is still more work to be done, we'll discuss whether you want to do it with me or move on.

This let Philip know that this first session was an exploratory one, to see whether he liked my way of working. At the end of the first session he said he wanted to continue, so we arranged five more sessions.

Of course we also need to clarify (and to check many times with clients over the period we see them) what it is that they want from us, and to be clear whether we can provide it. We usually do this simply by asking them what they want: 'OK – now that you know what today is about, let's start. What is it that has brought you here today, and how can I help?'

Competence

Prospective clients will always want their counsellor to understand them and their problems, and to be able to help. This means that they will want us to have the basic counselling skills and attributes which were outlined in chapters 2 and 3.

They will also want us to be competent. Clients need to have confidence in our competence: they will expect us to know what we are doing and to be confident about our own abilities to work with clients. If we are not able to display this confidence in our own skills, we cannot expect our clients to be confident in us; and if they are not confident in us, then we will rarely be successful in helping them.

Competence (and confidence in that competence) is not primarily a matter of qualifications, although as we said in chapter 2, there is often a relationship between competences and professional training. But research has shown that many largely untrained (and completely unqualified) counsellors have obtained as good or better outcomes with their clients as more highly trained and qualified people. Competence is much more about counsellors knowing what they are doing. There are many ways in which we can gain competence, and confidence in our competence. Being adequately trained is one of them, but other ways include being well supervised, gaining (and learning from) our experience of counselling, enabling clients to feel that they are understood and being able to deal effectively with concerns which our client may raise. We discuss issues related to training in chapter 5.

A Clear Contract or Framework for Working Together

Just as prospective clients seek competence, so too they need to know about the framework within which we are going to help them and what the limits are to the help we offer. For example:

- How long is the counselling relationship – is it for one session, or 10, or 30?
- How long will a counselling session be – 20 minutes or two hours?
- Can we be contacted outside the sessions, and if so, how?
- What is our approach? What are the aims and purpose of our sessions? How might this approach help this particular client?
- How will we work together? What can the client expect from the helping relationship?
- How confidential is the relationship – is it wholly confidential or will we provide some information to others (e.g. the criminal justice system if this is a court referral), and if so, under what conditions? And what will we reveal to a supervisor of our work, and under what conditions?
- Under what conditions might the helping relationship terminate, other than those of the agreed time limit?

We need to address these questions honestly and openly. Some counsellors have a written sheet with this kind of information available to clients before the initial appointment.

One way in which counsellors can ensure that both we and our client understand the nature of the counselling relationship is to make an explicit 'contract' which gives a clear framework for working. In the example of Philip, we could give information in writing as part of a contract, and it could include the following points:

- Although we will have our sessions booked in advance, if an emergency arises you can always call and see if I have space for an additional meeting.
- If I am busy, you can leave an answerphone message and I will get back to you, or you can text me and I'll respond when I am free.
- I always discuss my work with a very experienced colleague to check out whether she thinks that the way I'm working with each of my clients is the best that can be done. But if you tell me things that you don't want me to tell her, just let me know. We can discuss why, and work out what you would be happy for me to say and not say.
- If you tell me things which imply that you are harming other people, I will not be able to keep these things confidential, and may have to inform the authorities.

The word *contract* is unfortunate because it may imply a degree of formality and even legal commitment. Nonetheless, a counsellor is making a firm arrangement with a client and a contract is one way to ensure that both parties begin a helping relationship with clarity about its purposes and its duration.

Ethical Behaviour

What do we mean by ethical behaviour? Fundamentally, it means that people seeking help do not expect to be taken advantage of (sexually, financially or emotionally), to be abused or to be be used as human subjects for some experiment without their knowledge or permission.

Abuse of trust

Clients are usually vulnerable when they come for help. Many have low self-esteem, and are therefore more open to being abused. Because of our privileged position of being party to many of their secret fears and wishes, and meeting in a private place for counselling sessions, we are in a prime position to misuse their trust. We behave ethically as counsellors when we do not take advantage of our clients and do not misuse this trust.

Unfortunately, some counsellors and other professionals *do* misuse this trust and are prosecuted for unethical conduct. Typically these prosecutions relate to the sexual or financial exploitation of clients or to breaches of professional rules of conduct.

There are, of course, different ways in which clients can be abused. The sexual one is perhaps the most obvious. Clients are vulnerable, counsellors are in a much more powerful position, and all professional ethical codes state that entering into a sexual relationship with someone while they are a client, for whatever reason, blurs roles and responsibilities and the counsellor's professional status to an unacceptable degree.

Confidentiality

The situation most commonly feared by clients is the abuse of trust by the breach of confidentiality. Clients are concerned that we will let other people know – deliberately or inadvertently – that they have sought help or that we will discuss what has passed between client and counsellor with another person.

Clients are often concerned about disclosure to a member of their family or to their employer. Obviously, telling parents what a teenager is discussing in counselling or telling an employer what an employee has told us will be seen as a betrayal of the trust the client has put in the counsellor (unless this telling was by agreement with the client), and means that the counselling then becomes part of the problem rather than part of the solution. So employees and teenagers need to be assured (if this is the case) that the details of what they tell their counsellor in confidence will not be passed to their managers or parents.

However, other issues are less clearly inappropriate. Often clients will reveal things which raise our concerns about the safety of the client or other people, or breaking the law. For example, a bus driver may reveal that he has an alcohol problem and that he frequently drives his bus while intoxicated; or a 14-year-old girl may tell us that she is going to have an abortion without her parents' knowledge. These revelations will often raise ethical issues for us (which are covered in more detail in chapter 5), but our basic rule is that issues such as these must always be discussed within supervision, and/or with our line manager: the decision to pass information on to others outside of the counselling session should *never* be made by the counsellor alone.

Disclosure to a supervisor or colleagues
Clients should always know that our work is supervised. It is vital to clarify with clients the difference between confidentiality and secrecy. The agreement we make with clients is to keep their information *confidential*, not to keep it secret. The difference is that a pledge of secrecy is made between two people, and information must remain between these two alone. But confidentiality is different. Counsellors should always have supervision (see chapter 5) when they are free to discuss anything they need to, including what clients have told them. Similarly, many counsellors work within a team setting (such as a GP surgery, or a mental health team) and, again, information must be able to be shared with other team members – not gratuitously, but to ensure that relevant team members have information so that their work with the same client dovetails with our work in counselling sessions.

Disclosure required by law
Furthermore, counsellors, like doctors and priests, may be required by law to disclose information to a court. On rare occasions, under certain circumstances, a judge can order all sorts of helpers – including counsellors – to disclose what was said during a consultation. They also have the power to require any notes or documents kept by helpers to be released to the court. Judges exercise discretion and caution in requiring these legally sanctioned breaches of confidentiality, since they recognise that the very fabric of such helping relationships is based upon confidentiality and trust.

Telling clients about confidentiality
We often say to clients in the first session:

> What you tell me here will remain confidential. But there are three things I need to say about confidentiality.
> First, all counsellors have supervisors (people with whom they discuss their work to help them think through whether they are doing the best things) and I am no different; so I may need to discuss what we are doing and what you tell me with my supervisor – who of course is bound by the same confidentiality rules as I am.
> Second, I am also a member of the team here, and I may also need to tell others in the team about what we discuss.

If you tell me things you do not want me to discuss with anyone else, please say so at the time. Then we can chat about why you feel this and see what forms of words I could use that you would be happy with.

Third, there are some things that, if you tell me, I will certainly have to take beyond our sessions. If you tell me that you are about to commit a violent crime, or that you are abusing a child or are sexually abusing anyone, or that you might be a danger to yourself or to others, then I will certainly have to discuss this with my supervisor, and we may have to tell social services or the police.

The difficulty is that this is long-winded, and seems to be telling clients that they should not tell us important things. But if we do not say it, and then a client *does* tell us things which need sharing, we will have done a serious disservice to our clients (telling them that things will be kept secret when they could not be) and to ourselves (feeling guilty that we have offered confidentiality and then broken it). As we mentioned previously, one way to deal with it is to have a written information sheet which prospective clients see before their first appointment.

In practice, confidentiality issues rarely arise. But individual counsellors and counselling organisations need a clear view about the nature of confidentiality and each of us needs to consider the ethics of breaching a person's confidence.

Other abuses of trust

Trust can be misused in many other ways. These include:

- making use of information provided by a client for our own financial or social gain;
- using information provided by a client to increase our power over them, such as by belittling them or encouraging their dependence on us;
- distorting what the client has told us to fit in with our own theoretical or philosophical framework and, by so doing, reducing our client's confidence in themselves and in us as their counsellor.

For example, suppose a female client tells us in counselling sessions about her lack of confidence in heterosexual relationships. A counsellor could use this information about her sexual vulnerability to gratify the counsellor's own sexual needs: a male counsellor could tell her that he finds her attractive and that she could have a positive sexual relationship with him, or a female counsellor could introduce the idea that she should try a homosexual relationship instead. Alternatively, we could use this information to promote our own belief about, say, how lesbian relationships are what feminist women should aim for.

Compatibility

Personality

We have said in previous chapters that, as counsellors, we must be flexible to accommodate the needs of our clients, but even with flexibility, not all clients and counsellors will 'fit'. This may be a personality issue: sometimes we simply like some clients less than others. It is important that clients feel comfortable with their counsellor, otherwise they will not be able to relax and open up about key issues which concern them.

Ways of working

Alternatively, incompatibility may be about the way we work. It may be that what clients want and what we can give are very different. So if, for example, a client wants help to plan how to behave in different ways, but the counsellor works by spending a long time looking at how the client's past has shaped present behaviour, we may need to check whether the client wants what we offer.

Gender

Sometimes matching gender may be important; for example, some people may be uncomfortable discussing sexual issues with a counsellor who is a different sex, whereas others may be uncomfortable discussing sexual issues with someone of the same sex. There is no hard and fast rule, only a need for sensitivity about what people may be uncomfortable with, and whether the client needs to see a different person or someone of a different gender. Obviously, the issue of gender matching applies more strongly in some cultures than others, and does not simply apply to the area of discussing sexual issues. For example, in some Islamic cultures, it would be very unusual to discuss any type of personal difficulty with someone of the opposite sex.

Age

Sometimes the compatibility issue is about age. A counsellor who is comparatively young (and hence is perceived to lack experience, competence, and the ability to understand) may raise doubt in an older client as to how well he or she could help. Similarly, a young client may feel that their counsellor is too old to understand their problems. As with gender, age differences do not need to prevent us from working with people, but they may make the work more difficult. It often helps to make age issues explicit and to discuss them openly.

Culture, diversity and ethnicity

There is also a more general issue of cultural and ethnic compatibility. This is where there is a need for both counsellor and client to share some of the prevailing culture and associated beliefs, or at least have some understanding of it. It may relate to relatively local issues: accent, the use of colloquial expressions, local idioms, shared knowledge and a common basis of local history; or it may relate to much wider cultural issues such as working with people of a different race or people with disabilities.

The issues of compatibility are a sort of *reverse empathy*. We described in chapter 3 how important empathy was between the counsellor and the client, so that the client can feel that the counsellor really understands them and their problems. In a similar way, our client needs to feel that *they* can understand *us* and our values and background sufficiently to be able to trust us with the details of their lives and problems.

Cultural compatibility between counsellors and clients is useful for our counselling too. One way that we help people is by modelling for them aspects of behaviour which they wish to learn. So, as outlined in chapter 3, we model open communication, warmth, genuineness and a level of competence in our dealings with the world, which we hope that clients will learn from (we are punctual, reliable and so on). But if they feel we are too different from them, even if they recognise that what we are doing is positive, they will not be able to imagine themselves doing the same things. Similarly, a client will often wish to imagine their counsellor in their situation ('What would Richard or Sarajane do?') and that is more difficult if there are big differences between us and our client.

This is not to say that clients and counsellors need to be identical. In fact, for some people, difference enables the client to feel that the counsellor is able to offer a new perspective. It can also be helpful if a counsellor does not inhabit the same social milieu as the client: you may not wish to tell someone your intimate details if you are going to see them two hours later at the pub. However, it is vital that we do not seem so different that our clients cannot see how we could possibly understand them and their difficulties; if that happens, they will not have the confidence to trust us.

Styles of working

Just as it is sometimes necessary to match the gender and social background of client and counsellor, so the style or approach of the counsellor needs to be matched to the style the potential client would like. These styles are described in chapter 2 and relate to the ways in which counsellors interact with clients. For example, one style focuses upon insight and personal exploration, while another is more directive and training oriented.

Another feature relates to the extent to which different elements of the person are the focus of our attention. Chapters 6 to 13 look at these in more detail. For example, counsellors may work by focusing largely on thinking processes (such as patterns of thought and irrational thoughts and beliefs) or on behaviour (such as developing social or assertiveness skills or reducing undesirable behaviour), or on feelings and emotions.

The final feature of style or approach is the extent to which we challenge our client's ideas, behaviours, ways of thinking and so on, when we work with them. Some counsellors seek to push the client hard to learn about themselves or explore their feelings or change their behaviour. Others are less challenging and demanding.

Research studies show clearly that counselling is most successful when the counsellor's approach matches the expectations of the client. However, many people do not have clear expectations and clients may have little or no choice about where to obtain help. Nonetheless, compatibility of working styles and approaches is an essential ingredient in the success of helping relationships.

Confirmation that Change is Needed

Although some clients come with a clear desire to change, others will be much more uncertain about whether they want to change, and whether they can even if they want to, and yet others come because they want affirmation and reassurance, not change.

This may show itself when clients seek to use their counsellor to affirm that the position they have taken is sensible or right. For example, in couple counselling, one partner will ask the counsellor to confirm that the other is being unreasonable. In such a context, we have to avoid the trap: if we agree with one of the couple, we are immediately disagreeing with the other, and taking sides will almost always lead to unsuccessful couple counselling. In one-to-one counselling, however, it is much easier to find oneself agreeing with a client's view, instead of asking the client to reflect on what *they* think about it.

Another example of uncertainty about ability to change is when a client seeks our confirmation that their situation is hopeless and therefore it is natural for them to experience depression, anxiety or fear. Or a client may argue that the counselling 'is getting me nowhere'. Such claims are commonly signs of resistance to change.

In these examples, our client is trying to prevent us as their counsellor from helping them to change. This is common because the client may find it less threatening and scary to remain with the problem than to move into the unknown. It is not necessarily unhealthy: we can use it to gently challenge the client, thus contributing positively to the helping process.

A Magic Solution: Realistic and Unrealistic Expectations

The final thing that many clients want from us is a magic solution. They want a counselling session to make all the difference, hoping that, by our saying just one thing or offering just one incredible insight, we will solve all their problems.

Such wishful thinking is, of course, not unusual: we experience it ourselves when we take our car to the garage or an ailment to the doctor. We hope that the diagnosis will be simple and that the expert will be able to put it right with minimum effort. The reality is that such simple solutions do not often exist for the sorts of difficulties that people come to counselling for: there is no instant cure and counselling is often a lengthy process.

No instant cure

Many clients will bring us their problem as if it *were* a problem with their car: some external difficulty which they hope we will remove. But problems that respond to counselling are internal and psychological, or relate to how people interact with each other. They are not external problems which can be fixed by a psychological mechanic. Sometimes a key intervention involves helping a client move from 'I have got depression. Can you cure me?' to 'I have made myself depressed. How can I change the way that I think/feel/behave so that I stop making myself feel like this?'

This relates to the client's expectations of their counsellor's style and approach (discussed above). For example, many clients utilise the medical model of helping, i.e. they assume that once they have described what is happening to them (the symptoms), the counsellor will understand or label (diagnose) their problem (illness) and give them advice (offer a cure), which will lead them to the resolution of their problem (get better) and a return to normal functioning. They expect the counsellor to undertake most of the work and to do or say something to make the problem go away. But the reality is that in counselling the client does most of the work: the medical model is not a helpful one.

Such a discrepancy between what the client expects and what actually happens often leads clients to feel that they are not getting the 'right' kind of help or that their counsellor is ineffective because he or she does not tell them what to do or how to cure themselves. As we said above, our descriptions of what clients can expect need to include guidance about the style and approach we will use. Our client information or contracts should:

- say enough about realistic goal-setting to rule out immediate 'cures';
- make explicit statements about styles of working;
- discuss the responsibilities of the person seeking help.

We will always need to underline that what we can do is help, but that the main work needs to be undertaken by the client. We have to enable a client to see that they have a choice about whether they change, and that the change has to be made by them, not by us.

A lengthy process

Another issue about unrealistic expectations is that many people come with longstanding problems which may take as long to overcome as they have taken to develop. So, for example, if we see someone who has been extremely depressed for over a year, it is unlikely that they will find their depression has gone after four or five sessions. Our clients need to know that what we can do is start a process of change that may unfold over a long period of time. Sometimes it can be helpful to see counselling as a journey, where clients acquire new skills to use for many years after they stop seeing us and often throughout their lives.

This is not to suggest that counselling is always a long, slow, tortuous process. For many people, the changes which start in our counselling sessions will continue without a counsellor. If clients learn skills about exploring their problems, setting realistic and achievable goals, taking action and maintaining change, then they can continue to change on their own.

Sometimes clients gain so much from just one or two counselling sessions that they make changes largely on their own. Many clients find that a simple idea or a new way of seeing things is enough of a nudge in the right direction for them to make the changes that they need by themselves.

Recently, one of the authors met someone with whom we had undertaken a single session of counselling help some 10 years previously. We had recalled it as a pleasant session, where we and the client had obviously 'clicked' and where we had offered a few simple suggestions about the issues that the client had brought. Recently (i.e. 10 years after this single session), when this person was holding a senior position within a neighbouring organisation, we had a drink together one evening and discovered that it had been a life-changing session for them: something that we had said had enabled the person to think about things differently, and had led to their feeling able to make some major and helpful decisions in their life. This had then changed the future course of their life, in ways that they saw as being immensely positive, and which they attributed to the nudge that had been given in that one session.

Conclusion

The overall conclusion from this chapter is that, as a counsellor, we need to make explicit our assumptions about the nature of the helping relationship with our client. We should not assume, for example, that a client is happy to be helped by someone of the opposite sex, or that they have a realistic expectation about what is likely to happen during counselling, or that they realise that their counsellor will want to discuss their problem with a supervisor. These issues, and all the others outlined above, need to be raised and clarified with each client.

PRACTICAL EXERCISES

Watch films, videos, DVDs or TV programmes that show a variety of people being helped, to see these aspects of helping in action. These can be fictional but are better if they are real or training films.

Imagine yourself going to someone for counselling for the first time, or recall it if you have experienced it yourself. What, in your view, is most helpful? What are the most important aspects for you? Record this in your Learning Journal.

SUMMARY

We have looked in this chapter at some of the things that prospective clients want from their counsellors. We have said that in order to create the right conditions and expectations for our clients we need to:

- put people at their ease;
- give and receive information;
- be competent and confident;
- provide a clear contract or framework for working together;
- adhere to ethical standards of behaviour;
- ensure at least some level of compatibility between client and counsellor.

We have also said that it is our duty to challenge two other things that our clients may want or expect but are unlikely to get:

- confirmation that they do not need to change;
- a quick, magic solution to their problems.

5

Helping the Helpers

Thatch your roof before rainy weather; dig your well before you become parched with thirst. (Chinese proverb)

This chapter focuses on the help that we as counsellors need in order to do good-quality counselling work. We need to understand the importance of our own needs for training and certification, safeguards, and support and supervision.

We cover:

- training, accreditation and certification;
- personal therapy;
- ethical and practice safeguards;
- team and interagency working;
- supervision and support;
- recognising our limits;
- burn-out – causes, prevention and avoidance;
- maintaining balance.

Training, Accreditation and Certification

We all do our jobs better if we feel competent and demonstrate confidence in how we do them. In counselling, we know that if clients feel that *we* are confident that we can help them, *they* feel more confident in us, and the more confidence they have in us the more able they are to change themselves.

Training

One major way to improve competence and confidence is through training. Some people are naturally better at demonstrating warmth, empathy and so on – the key characteristics that we outlined in chapter 3 – and some people may never be able to learn them, but the majority will benefit from training.

There is a huge range and variety of training courses available, lasting from just a few hours to several years. Some require previous training; others are for people just starting. Some may deal with specific features of counselling such as listening skills, interviewing skills or assertiveness training; others may be more generic, for example dealing with stress or massage and body work; others may look at one approach to counselling such as cognitive behavioural therapy or psychodynamic counselling; others cover all types of counselling. The organisations and websites listed at the end of the book provide details of a wide range of training.

The quality of training is more important than the qualifications acquired but, of course, it may be difficult to know what the quality will be. Good ways to assess the quality of any training on offer, as with the assessment of quality in other similar areas, include gaining personal recommendations, taking up references (i.e. looking at testimonials from people who have undertaken the training), looking at alternative (student-developed) prospectuses and looking on the Internet.

Arrangements for the training and certification of counsellors in Canada, the United States, New Zealand, Australia and Europe differ considerably from the British pattern. On the whole it is expected that the counsellor will be a certified professional who has completed an approved academic programme with predominantly psychological and practical components. Most countries have national organisations for counselling, for example:

- the British Association for Counselling and Psychotherapy (BACP) and the British Association for Behavioural and Cognitive Psychotherapies (BABCP);
- the Canadian Counselling Association (CCA)/Canadian Counselling and Psychotherapy Association (CCPA);
- the American Counseling Association (ACA);
- the Australian Counselling Association (ACA) and the Australian Guidance and Counselling Association (AGCA);
- the New Zealand Association of Counsellors (NZAC);
- the International Association for Counselling (IAC).

Such bodies have details of training programmes and certification procedures.

It is useful to dispel a myth here: the idea that we can achieve the status of a 'fully trained counsellor'. Counsellors are never *fully* trained since they are always able to learn more and to develop further. Each training opportunity provides a fresh chance to renew our resources and develop as people, as well as to hone our skills.

Accreditation and certification

Having said that a professional qualification is not a prerequisite to be a good counsellor, it is worth looking at the advantages of some form of accreditation or certification.

In Britain, *counselling* is not a restricted term protected by law. Anyone can call themselves a counsellor, and set themselves up in private practice or seek employment as a counsellor. Some form of accreditation can therefore be helpful for clients, employers and counsellors. Furthermore, much more attention has been focused on governance and quality control in recent years, certainly within the NHS and other organisations which might employ counsellors, and accreditation and certification have become much more necessary. The British Association for Counselling and Psychotherapy (BACP) and the British Psychological Society websites (at the end of the book) provide useful information on accreditation.

Personal Therapy

There are a number of reasons why many prospective and practising counsellors themselves engage in personal therapy or counselling. We highlight three key ones here.

First, there is a view that in order to help others effectively, one needs to really know oneself. Everyone has personal issues (maybe related to current family or other relationships, or to past problems, or to 'blocks' or distress of one sort or another). If these personal issues are not understood and dealt with, they can interfere with our own ability as counsellors to focus on the client and not on ourselves. Undergoing a form of personal therapy is a key way of dealing with these personal issues.

Secondly, engaging in personal therapy or counselling gives us as counsellors first-hand personal experience both of being counselled and of a particular counselling approach. This can lead to the development of deeper empathy, insight and understanding within the helping relationship, as well as a much deeper understanding about the particular counselling approach used in our own personal therapy.

Thirdly, undergoing personal therapy oneself is a potentially powerful source of support, insight, learning and ongoing personal development.

It is for these reasons that a number of counselling training courses, and training in other related areas, such as psychotherapy, make personal therapy a requirement for those on their courses.

Our view is that having personal therapy can be both extremely helpful and useful for prospective and existing counsellors, but that it is not a necessity.[1] As we shall see below, having supervision and support *is* a necessity, and personal therapy can provide some of the same elements. Nevertheless, personal therapy is not a substitute for supervision. The emphasis in personal therapy is on ourselves and on deepening our understanding of ourselves, whereas the emphasis in supervision is on our clients and on how we can use ourselves to help and support them, and enable them to change.

Ethical and Practice Safeguards

We said a lot in chapter 4 about ethical behaviour and confidentiality which we will not repeat here. But a further advantage of certification is that the organisation who has vetted us may also have useful guidelines about practice.

For example, if we are thinking about breaching confidentiality (e.g. if we are worried that our client may be suicidal, and we are thinking about asking relatives to keep a watchful eye on them), most national professional organisations have guidelines. For example, the American Personnel and Guidance Association (APGA) states: 'When the client's condition indicates that there is clear and imminent danger to the client or others, the (helper) must take reasonable personal action to inform responsible authorities . . . consultation with other professionals must be used where possible.'

So when we are faced with a person who seems to be endangering themselves or others, we need to exercise sound judgement as to the extent and nature of the risk and the consequences of disclosing information to others. We also need to consider how to inform our client about this breach of confidentiality and what support we can offer if the client then loses confidence in us.

Ethical safeguards can sometimes be limiting. The growing number of accusations of sexual harassment has led some organisations to develop guidelines to safeguard both counsellors and clients. Some organisations suggest (or even state) that males should not see female clients unless a third person is present, or have a policy of actively discouraging counselling staff from physical contact with clients. These are intended as helpful limits to the counsellor's behaviour, although they may seem unworkable on occasions, and indeed may be counter-productive. For example, it may be better for a male counsellor to see a female client than for her not to receive help at all; and sometimes the best way of responding to a client's distress is to hold their hand. Certainly such rules make it somewhat difficult to use many of the techniques outlined in chapter 10 (on helping people with their bodies).

There are two points here. First, it is always important to think about what we are doing and why – a form of *reflective practice*. Are we thinking about touching a client because of their distress, or because it gives us the opportunity to do so? Our golden rule is that what we do must be in our client's best interests, not in ours, nor in the interests of our organisation if what it tells us to do is contrary to our client's best interests.

Secondly, however, we should not disobey our organisational limits. If the organisation we work for has rules which are not sensible, they should be challenged rather than simply disobeyed, which could put us in a disadvantageous position if things go wrong subsequently. It may also provide us with a measure of the organisation: an organisation devoted to helping people to change and overcome difficulties should itself be able to change and overcome difficulties.

Team and Interagency Working

Many counsellors work within a team, sometimes alongside other counsellors (e.g. in Relate) and sometimes alongside other professionals as part of a multidisciplinary team (e.g. within primary care).

There are many advantages to team working. We do not feel or become isolated; it is possible to share training and supervision events; and sometimes supervision is offered in group settings. There are like-minded people from whom to gain support and with whom we can discuss issues. Multidisciplinary teams may also include those whose skills complement our own, to whom we can refer clients and from whom we can receive advice.

Working with others outside our team is also increasingly vital. We discuss interagency working in chapter 14 (on social networks), where we outline the importance of knowing other agencies so that we can refer clients to them if appropriate. Each organisation, such as the police or social services, has its own procedures and regulations, and it is vital to know at least something about these so that if we need to make contact (e.g. over a suspected child abuse situation) neither we nor our clients are taken by surprise.

Supervision and Support

Counselling people often feels difficult for many reasons, including the following:

- We may put a lot into it, yet the client may still not change.
- The client may say things which link into our own problems and conflicts.
- We may feel unskilled, owing to the particular difficulties a client is experiencing.
- We may lose our way and be unsure where to go next.
- We may develop a cosy relationship with a client such that we meet regularly and talk well together without realising that we are failing to help the client to move on.

For these reasons, most agencies insist on counsellors receiving frequent, high-quality supervision. The word *supervision*, unfortunately, can imply management and control, direction and authority. But here we use *supervision* as it is used in psychotherapy, to mean guidance and support provided in a helpful and facilitative way. Most national organisations require it before granting accreditation to counsellors. For example, the British Association for Counselling and Psychotherapy lists standards in its ethical framework, including those relating to the provision of a good standard of practice and care, to which counsellors are expected to conform. One standard states: 'All counsellors, psychotherapists, trainers and supervisors are required to have regular and on-going formal supervision/consultative support for their work in accordance with professional requirements. . . . supervision is defined as the reflexive exploration and development of helping practice, in a supportive yet challenging context, involving individuals in the role(s) of supervisee and supervisor.'

Characteristics of supervision

Two key characteristics of supervision are:

- *It is formal.* It is not an ad hoc chat when we feel like it or when there happens to be someone around. It is a scheduled time with a supervisor who has the skills and experience to offer a high-quality service.

- *It is regular.* If we see a number of clients on a regular basis, issues will certainly arise which need to be dealt with. Some agencies insist on one hour of supervision for every four hours of counselling; others use a minimum amount of, say, two hours per month. Whatever the frequency, regularity must be ensured.

Content of supervision

A third characteristic of supervision is that it deals with important issues. It provides an opportunity for us as counsellors to use reflective practice – our ability to stand back from our work and think about it. It enables us to:

- develop skills and understanding of our counselling work;
- develop self-awareness, in so far as this affects the quality of the counselling work;
- explore issues and difficulties for us as counsellors, or for clients, as they arise in sessions.

Supervision also provides protection for the client and the agency we work for, by monitoring our work.

Two particular types of issue need to be raised in supervision. The first is that being a counsellor can bring our own emotions into play. For example, if our client is experiencing deep grief from the recent loss of a spouse or child, our hearts may go out to them and we may feel upset; or we may relive our own personal losses, or question how well we will cope with the loss of a loved one when it happens. Alternatively, we can share moments of real joy and discovery with our clients. We can take pleasure in providing emotional support and comfort.

Often, however, clients do not want their counsellors to share so fully in their emotional experiences: they want us to be stable so that they can bounce their emotions off us. If we find ourselves getting too caught up in their emotions, we need to discuss this in supervision.

Secondly, sometimes our clients react towards us in ways that are related to how they have reacted in the past, or to their current unresolved conflicts, rather than to what we are currently doing with them. We use the term *transference* for that. And sometimes we react to clients in ways that are not about them but about us and our own issues – this is known as *counter-transference*. (These are further discussed in chapter 11, on the unconscious.) Again, these need to be discussed within supervision.

So, for many reasons, supervision is important. It is not about describing to our supervisor our client's history and problems in detail: it is focused on us, not the client, and on what we did in our counselling session or sessions. Our supervisor needs to ask us challenging questions about what we have done or said so that we can change any unhelpful reactions and become more effective in helping our client.

Process of supervision

Supervisors should utilise the same process model in supervision that is so useful in counselling itself (outlined in chapter 3): developing trust, exploring the problems, enabling us to focus on the issues and set goals, and empowering us into action. The key points are:

- Effective support and supervision is based on trust. As counsellors we must feel able to disclose things during supervision that we might not tell other people – for example, feelings of incompetence, mistakes made, annoyance with our employing agency.
- Supervisors need to explore the counsellor's issues and concerns, rather than imagining that they know what those concerns are.
- Supervisors need to help us as counsellors to focus on issues, rather than skirt around the edges. For example, many supervisors wrongly allow counsellors to recount a client's case history at great length, as opposed to focusing on the important issues by:
  - asking questions such as, 'What are you actually doing with this client?' or 'What are the difficulties which have emerged for you in the sessions so far?'
  - focusing on our understanding of the problem as opposed to the client's achievement of their goals;
  - focusing on our feelings for the client and how these might interact with the work.
- The supervisor needs to help us to implement the strategies and ideas which emerge during supervision in future counselling sessions with our client.

Forms of supervision

There is no one right way of supervising people. Some supervisors see counsellors in one-to-one sessions. Others also go through our notes of what we said at the time, and comment on the note-taking. Yet others will see counsellors in a group setting, maybe finding out from everyone if there are issues which need discussion, and then focusing in detail on one or two counsellors.

Others offer mutual supervision and support. This might involve two counsellors regularly meeting up and each supervising the other for half of the time. Mutual supervision can happen in a group context: being associated with an informal network of helpers (as we outline in chapter 14) can be a way of creating self-support opportunities for counsellors. Other people in the network can provide suggestions, advice, information, guidance and contacts which continually enrich our work.

All these forms are useful, yet they potentially suffer from the fact that all the information about the counselling is provided via the counsellor. Ways around this which enable a supervisor to get a client's-eye view include:

- audio or video taping sessions to use as the basis for supervision;
- live supervision, using a one-way screen through which a supervisor can watch work without being observed. Feedback can be provided after (and sometimes during) the counselling session;
- a supervisor sitting in on a counselling session.

Our view is that all of these methods have advantages and disadvantages, and that we need to select the way that suits us and our clients best. But the bottom line is that frequent high-quality supervision is essential.

Who should supervise?

Supervisors are generally experienced counsellors. Their experience is usually a positive attribute because they will be familiar with issues that are likely to confront us, but it can lead to problems. One is that many supervisors have had little training on how to supervise: being a good counsellor does not necessarily mean that one would be a good supervisor. The second problem is that counsellors are interested in clients, and when they become supervisors they can easily get waylaid into becoming more interested in the counsellor's clients than in the counsellor.

Many organisations lay down minimum standards of qualification and experience for supervisors. For example, the BACP requires that supervisors have a minimum of five years' experience of supervised practice as a counsellor/psychotherapist, having undertaken at least 600 hours of supervised practice during that time.

Research shows clearly that the quality of the counselling we provide is enhanced when we are receiving supervision. This work also suggests strongly that receiving feedback immediately after actual sessions is the most effective way of developing our skills. In addition, the absence of supervision and peer support is seen as a major cause of burn-out (see below).

Recognising our Limits

Part of the function of supervision is to help us recognise our limits, and not become too involved with our clients. All counsellors have to learn the major skill of not taking clients home: not literally, but mentally. We need to compartmentalise them in our minds, so that their distress does not spill over into our lives outside the counselling sessions.

Another issue which affects our helpfulness is about how our own lives impact on us as counsellors. For example, we may:

- be going through a stressful time or crisis ourselves;
- be trying to help a client with a problem which is similar to one of our own, now or in the past, such as trying to cut down on drinking;
- have a blind spot which we find it difficult to counsel people about: it may be death, sex, violence or addiction – each of these is sometimes regarded as a difficult area for many counsellors;
- be trying to provide counselling either as part of other work (e.g. nurses, teachers, and social workers spend a lot of their time counselling) or on a voluntary basis; often the time we are able to put into counselling is inadequate.

We have to think carefully about the ways in which *our* needs and problems interact with those of our clients. If we are in any doubt about whether we have handled things in the best way, we should take it to supervision.

Burn-Out: Causes, Prevention and Avoidance

The term *burn-out* is well used. Although there is nothing inevitable about burn-out, in many jobs people do gradually lose interest, and counselling can of course be the same.

Burn-out occurs when we as counsellors feel tired, drained and without enthusiasm for a sustained period of time, such as six months. We may feel that the work we are doing is neither appreciated nor effective, that there are too many competing pressures on our time, that we are unimportant and that we are performing our counselling work in a mechanical way. When we look at our work we find it difficult to recognise any concrete results or achievements. Often we feel oppressed by the organisation within which we work. Because we feel so ineffective we can be afraid of seeking support and this in turn can feed a feeling of isolation.

The result is that we can become increasingly ineffective (thereby confirming our own evaluation of our poor abilities) and disillusioned.

Causes of burn-out

It has been suggested that there are a number of causes of counsellor burn-out which we need to understand and anticipate so that they can be prevented:

- giving a great deal of our emotional and personal energy to others whilst getting little back in return;
- being under constant pressure to produce results in an unrealistic time-scale;
- working with a difficult group, for example, those who are highly resistant to change, who have been unwillingly sent for help, or for whom the chances of change are small, such as people who are terminally ill;
- the absence of support from immediate colleagues and an abundance of criticism;
- lack of trust between us as counsellors and our managers or the organisation for which we work;
- not having the opportunity to take new directions, to develop or experiment with new models of working: being unnecessarily constrained;
- having few opportunities for training, continuing education, supervision or support;
- having unresolved personal conflicts beyond the counselling work which interfere with our ability to be effective, for example marital or health problems.

This is not an exhaustive list – many of us could add more factors which, had we not done something about them, might have led us to experience burn-out.

Preventing burn-out

Burn-out can be pre-empted or avoided by taking personal responsibility for our own well-being. Rather than blaming the system, the organisation or the lack of local training opportunities, we need to help ourselves to avoid burn-out.

Some or all of the following may be useful:

- Take the initiative in bringing variety into our work or starting new projects which do not need us to wait for the system to sanction the steps we take.
- Seek a joint project with a colleague to increase the variety of work.
- Attend to our own physical health through rest, sleep, diet and exercise.
- Develop new friendships that are characterised by both giving and receiving.
- Make our own arrangements for support and supervision – and use the time to develop our own awareness rather than to moan about the system.
- Stop taking on more responsibility for other people's problems – we have to be able to switch off, and not take clients home.
- Take pleasure in planning our own reading programme about helping – this book is a good start!
- Make our own arrangements to attend training and workshop events in our area – and if there aren't any, we could organise some ourselves.
- Keep the counselling part of our life in perspective, and cultivate hobbies and interests outside work.

Here is a brief description of how Ray, a full-time counsellor, seeks to avoid burn-out:

First of all, I control my workload. I know that I cannot see more than five clients a day and adequately report on my contacts with them. As I am most effective between 8 am and 2 pm and between 6 and 9.30 pm, I schedule my client contacts during these times. I also do my documentation then, keeping 2 to 6 pm to myself, when I usually have a brief rest or a swim. I eat well in the evenings and at breakfast, so I have a light lunch and never miss meals.

Next I make sure that I only talk about my work to two people I am close to and to whom I can comment about mistakes as well as successes. I also know that I can learn from them, since they share their own experiences of helping with me, honestly and warmly.

Most important: I do not talk about my work to my wife and family (unless something quite extraordinary has happened). My family is a source of activity, interest and amusement to me.

Finally, I pursue my hobby relentlessly . . . I collect comedy materials. Tapes, records, videos, joke books . . . anything that can give amusement. I also keep a written logbook of jokes I hear – there's a special section on humour in counselling sessions.

This description illustrates that Ray's strategy for avoiding burn-out involves monitoring workloads, resting, having an active interest outside work, not letting work invade other activities, eating regularly and properly, and keeping work in perspective.

Maintaining Balance

Helping people through counselling can be both a demanding and a rewarding experience. Because the demands it makes can be considerable, we need to keep reminding ourselves of basic truths about the helping process. We list below six truths, which we look at whenever we begin to feel that all is not well:

Truth 1:   I can do no more than my best.
Truth 2:   Being anxious about my work as a counsellor is normal.
Truth 3:   Counsellors cannot be perfect: they can just do their best.
Truth 4:   Instant results are usually impossible.
Truth 5:   I will not succeed with everyone.
Truth 6:   People are in charge of their own lives.

These six truths are important reminders of our limits as helpers, helpful both to those just starting out and to those with more experience.

PRACTICAL EXERCISES

Progress diary

We have written about recognising our limits as counsellors. Keep a brief progress diary in your Learning Journal, in which you list the strengths and weaknesses you feel you have in relation to each client. This need not be long and detailed – the shorter and more succinct the better. It is a way of recording what you see happening and, over time, your development as a counsellor. In addition, the diary may show a pattern – for example, what kind of person you feel confident about helping, whether you are more confident after a training event or supervision session, or whether you seek support about particular kinds of problem. Make a note of when you are feeling out of balance and what helps to restore this.

Use others

Another way of assessing our limits and strengths is to seek a regular meeting with another counsellor where you both explore what is happening to you as counsellors. This is a form of reflective practice – diary keeping with the additional benefit that the diary talks and ask questions or asks us to elaborate.

Use tape recordings or videos

A final way of assessing our own limits and strengths in what we have done in a counselling session is to tape-record or videotape a series of sessions. We then need to listen to or look at them, and provide a critique of them, where we reflect on and evaluate what we have done. (Obviously we must obtain our client's permission, making it clear that the tapes are for our own use – or perhaps used with a supervisor – and will not be shared with anybody else.)

Questions to ask ourselves when listening to or viewing the tape are: 'What is happening at this point?' and 'How does it relate to my own actions as counsellor?' These questions will help us to see more clearly the processes we are using and enable us to recall the situation we were in and the thoughts we had as it was happening.

The *what* and *how* questions are much more useful than the simplistic question 'Was this piece of counselling good or bad?' And if we become good at asking these questions when we listen to or view tapes, we develop the ability to ask ourselves *what* and *how* when the counselling sessions are actually taking place: our skills in reflective practice increase.

Be warned: this process takes a considerable amount of time and often produces some discomfort, since things which seemed good at the time sometimes do not seem so good a few hours or days later!

Summary

This chapter has covered:

- *Training,* and how it allows us to feel both competent and demonstrate some confidence in our work as counsellors. Training can be helpful in learning about other methods and different techniques which people have found helpful.
- Training also relates to *certification and accreditation,* which allow others to judge our skills and competence as a counsellor.
- A further advantage of certification is that the organisation that has vetted us may also have useful guidelines about *ethics and good practice,* relating to issues such as confidentiality or the use of physical therapies. Such matters need to be considered very carefully, and are related to our duty to use reflective practice. We emphasise that whatever we do must be focused on what is in our client's best interests, not ours. We also stress that if the employing organisation has set rules which we consider not to be sensible, they need to be challenged within the organisation, not simply disobeyed.
- We discuss *personal therapy,* and some of the reasons why this can be very helpful to both prospective and practising counsellors; we also highlight that this is different from and in no way a substitute for good-quality supervision.
- We discuss the advantages of *team and interagency working*: we do not feel or become isolated; we can share training and supervision events; there are other like-minded people from whom we can gain support; there are others whose skills complement our own. Knowing other organisations' procedures and regulations is useful if we wish to discuss cases or to refer clients on.
- *Supervision and support* are discussed in some detail, and a range of issues are covered.
  - *What is supervision?* It is formal and regular.
  - *The content of supervision*: it is about developing our skills and understanding of our counselling work; exploring issues and difficulties for counsellor and client; and monitoring our work. Supervision involves reflective practice – our ability to stand back from our work and reflect upon it, both in the session and outside of it. This includes discussing transference issues.
  - *The process of supervision*: utilising the same process model that is so useful in counselling itself: developing trust, exploring the

problems, enabling us to focus on the issues and set goals, and empowering us into action.

- ○ *Forms of supervision*: from one-to-one through group to video and live supervision.
- ○ *Who should supervise?* People who are experienced counsellors, with some training as supervisors.
- We discuss how our abilities to help effectively will often be impaired by factors such as whether we can mentally separate our lives from those of our clients and how our own lives affect us as counsellors. It is important to learn to *recognise our limits*.
- We look at the causes, prevention and avoidance of *burn-out*, and how monitoring our workload, resting, having active interests outside work, not letting work invade other activities, eating regularly and properly, and keeping work in perspective can all help.
- We list some *truths about counselling* which help us to maintain a balance in our lives.
- We end with some practical exercises.

Part II

The Range of Styles and Approaches

Introduction

In chapter 1 we set out a model of counselling (fig. 1.1) which identified three sets of building blocks to comprehensive counselling. The first was *the foundations and core principles* outlined in Part I. In Part II, we now turn to the second set of building blocks: *the range of approaches, styles, and specific techniques* which counsellors use. Eight chapters focus on eight different approaches.

We start with 'Helping People to Cope' (chapter 6), and then move on to look at counselling which focuses on different aspects of a person, as outlined in the figure below. Each of the six points of the figure identifies a different and essential feature of ourselves, all of which are inextricably linked and interconnected. Chapters 7 to 12 look at counselling approaches which focus on these. Coaching, in the centre of the diagram, is the eighth approach, discussed in chapter 13, which draws together many of the elements in the chapter on coping and in the previous six chapters on specific approaches, and is a somewhat different approach to helping people. In each chapter, we examine the rationale, underlying assumptions and some of the key techniques used in each approach.

We do not discuss in each chapter the importance of the foundation and core processes of Building Block 1. This is not because they are no longer important – they *are* – but because we are taking them as read.

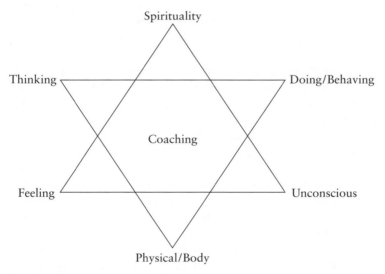

The focus of a range of counselling approaches

Each of the styles and approaches in the chapters in Part II rests upon these foundations: simply applying the skills and techniques in these chapters without using the collaborative counselling relationship and the core processes outlined in Part I will lead to ineffective counselling.

Chapter 6, 'Helping People to Cope', looks at ways to help people when they feel they cannot cope with life events such as bereavement, or stressful life stages such as new parenthood, or external pressures such as work or money worries. The counsellor's task is to enable clients to use their internal and external resources in such a way that they *do* cope.

Chapter 7, 'Helping People to Do Things Differently', is based on the assumption that people have learnt to behave in ways that lead them into problems such as phobias, anxieties and depressions. The counsellor's task is to help them learn how to change their behaviour – to 'do things differently' – so that they are, for example, less fearful, anxious or depressed.

Chapter 8, 'Helping People with their Thinking', is based on the notion that feelings and thoughts are linked. Counselling focused on thinking aims to change those thoughts and beliefs people have about themselves that lead them to feel bad; thinking more positively leads to more positive feelings.

Chapter 9, 'Helping People with their Feelings', is also based on the idea that feelings and thoughts are linked to each other, and that both are linked to behaviour. Helping clients to recognise, understand and change their feelings enables them to think and act differently and in this way helps them to overcome their problems.

Chapter 10, 'Helping People with their Bodies', looks at enabling people to recognise and work with the relationship between their bodies and their psychological symptoms. This includes working with the body's signs and symptoms ('What is your headache telling you?'), and using the body as a channel for helping, by using, for example, relaxation techniques, massage or meditation.

Chapter 11, 'Helping People with their Unconscious Processes', is based on the premise that psychological processes of which clients are unaware may be having a major impact on how they behave, think and feel. The particular focus of this area of counselling is on helping people to become aware of and to understand their inner unconscious life, and to exert some control over it.

Chapter 12, 'Helping People with their Spirituality', recognises that people have a spiritual (although often non-religious) dimension. It is about helping clients to find their inner self, to link with something greater than themselves, and to find purpose and meaning in life, even in their pain and distress.

Chapter 13, 'Helping People by Coaching', outlines a newer, practical approach to developing and unlocking a person's potential to maximise their performance. A coach guides and facilitates the client towards goals which the client has identified. Goals may concern relationships, career, self-confidence, problem solving, financial matters, team building or a realisation that 'there must be something better than this' in a client's life.

Finally, a few key points are important.

- Although we do look over the course of Part II at a very wide range of possible interventions, we are not suggesting that a massive amount of technical knowledge is required in order for someone to be an effective helper. It is true that there are lots of skills, techniques and ideas which can all help in counselling; and it is also true that the more skilled and experienced one becomes as a counsellor, the more helpful one can potentially be. But the key set of skills (the foundations in our model in fig. 1.1) do not require extensive technical knowledge; and these key skills are at the heart of all the other interventions outlined in later chapters.

- We cover a large number of skills and techniques in the chapters in Part II. We do not suggest that all counsellors need to learn all the skills and techniques outlined in these eight approaches. Our view is that counsellors need to find an approach or a number of approaches which is right for them.

- As we emphasised earlier, there is no one right approach. A key message of this book is that we as counsellors should choose the explanations and techniques that we feel happy with and that our clients generally feel comfortable with.

- Although in practice most counsellors use a mixture of techniques and ideas from a number of these approaches, we present them in the next eight chapters essentially as pure forms. It is useful to look at them in isolation first and to integrate them later, once we understand what the approach is and how it may be used.

- When we work with one aspect of our client, this work will have an impact on other aspects of the person too. So, for example, working with a client's behaviour will also affect how the client is thinking and how they are feeling about themselves and others. The work may well impact on their bodies (in terms of muscle tension or headaches, for example), on their unconscious processes and on their spirituality. Each aspect of a person is interconnected with all the others, and therefore each aspect is affected by changes in any other aspect.

- Finally, it is important to stress again that the most important element in counselling is the collaborative counselling relationship, not someone's competence in applying their technical knowledge of how to deliver various different counselling techniques. Counselling is not about the application of technical knowledge, although this is important of course; it is primarily the use of the core skills outlined in Part I of this book, and especially the use of the counselling relationship.

6

Helping People to Cope

To overcome difficulties is to experience the full delight of exist-ence. (Arthur Schopenhauer)

People have to cope with many things in their lives. These include:

- *external life events*, ranging from a late train to a serious bereavement;
- *life stages*: points in people's lives which are particularly stressful, such as starting school, major examinations, marriage, births, early stages of child-rearing, starting, leaving or losing a job, and retirement;
- *external pressures and constraints*: many other external issues create challenges, including the attitudes of family, colleagues and friends, and financial issues.

Sometimes people find these difficult to deal with and often clients will say that they 'can't cope'. Our task as counsellors is to enable people to use their internal and external resources in such a way that they *do* cope.

The ensuing chapters in Part II of this book look at a wide variety of ways in which we can help people, with each chapter focusing on a particular approach. This chapter looks at the overall nature of coping, focusing on how we can help people to cope more effectively with their lives and problems.

As counsellors, we do three things to help people to cope:

- We help people to learn new coping skills, e.g. through training in assertiveness or social skills.

- We reinforce existing coping skills and enable people to understand their relevance to current events, e.g. by encouragement or by providing new information which activates the person's own coping repertoire.
- We help restore the person's ability to cope and confidence in their coping skills.

The Stress–Strain–Coping–Support (SSCS) Theory

One influential theory we use a lot is the Stress–Strain–Coping–Support (SSCS) model developed by Jim Orford, Richard Velleman, Alex Copello and Lorna Templeton.

Stress and strain

The SSCS model suggests that there are certain sets of circumstances that people face in their everyday lives, some of which are short-term and immediate (such as the life events mentioned above) and some of which are long-lasting (such as war, long-term unemployment or chronic illness). These sets of circumstances are the *stress* component of the model.

These stressors lead to *strain* – a person undergoing stress, especially if it is long-lasting, will often respond by becoming ill or developing physical or psychological symptoms. In fact, when stress is not satisfactorily dealt with, it may affect them in a variety of ways:

- The way people see themselves:
  - They feel that their self-esteem is threatened.
  - They lack confidence in themselves.
  - They deprecate their own abilities.
  - They question their self-worth.
  - They defend idealised versions of their own behaviour.
- The way people experience the world:
  - They find reality both complex and overwhelming.
  - They see that their position in the world is determined by other people.
  - They experience the world as a place in which they have to use tactics like denial, wishful thinking or helplessness in order to

survive, even though they can recognise some of the implications of such tactics.

- The way they experience their own emotional world:
  - Anxiety and feelings of panic predominate.
  - They feel helpless and overwhelmed.
  - They feel indifferent.
  - They cannot accept praise or compliments.
- The way in which they think:
  - Their thinking is disorganised.
  - They feel unable to make decisions or to take responsibility for their actions.
  - They lack the ability to stand outside their situation and review their predicament with any objectivity.
  - They are resistant to change.
- Their physical state:
  - They do not attend to their physical needs.
  - There is a loss of appetite.
  - Sleep patterns are disturbed.
  - Psychosomatic illness may occur, e.g. muscular tension, gout, ulcers.
  - Prolonged experience of crisis can exacerbate existing symptoms, including heart disease and cancer.

Not everyone going through stress, even if it is not satisfactorily dealt with, will experience all these features, but often many will be present.

Coping and support

Thus the first two steps of the SSCS model are that *stress* (adversity) leads to *strain* (symptoms). However, a key idea within the SSCS model (backed up by a lot of research evidence) is that people respond to stressful conditions in different ways, with some of these ways leading to more (or less) strain, and some being better for their health than others.

Research evidence suggests that two key areas influence the amount of strain that stress may lead to: how the person copes, and how much (and the quality of) social support they have. Issues related to social support are considered in some detail in chapter 14 (on social networks); in this chapter we focus on coping.

The main components of the SSCS model are shown in figure 6.1.

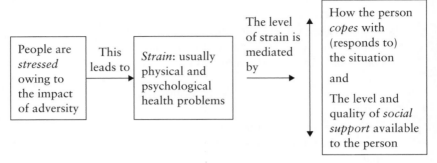

| People are *stressed* owing to the impact of adversity | This leads to | *Strain*: usually physical and psychological health problems | The level of strain is mediated by | How the person *copes* with (responds to) the situation and The level and quality of *social support* available to the person |

Figure 6.1   The Stress–Strain–Coping–Support model

The Nature of Coping

 The central idea behind *coping* is that when people are trying to deal with adversity and the resultant signs of strain, they are faced with a large, difficult life task: how to understand what is going wrong in their lives, and what they might do about it. The ways of understanding and the ways of responding are what we mean when we talk about *coping*.

Coping is certainly not limited to well-thought-out strategies. It includes ways of understanding or responding that the person believes to be effective as well as those they think have not worked. It includes feelings (e.g. of anger or hope), philosophical positions reached (e.g. 'This is a personal failing within me'), and stands taken (e.g. 'I've got to sort this out by myself').

The point for us as counsellors is that people facing adverse conditions have the capacity to cope with these conditions, and that this capacity is open to change. Coping therefore incorporates the idea of being active in the face of adversity, of effective problem solving, of *not* being or feeling powerless.

A lot of people see coping as 'all or nothing'. People think of themselves or others as having coped either well or badly with some event: 'She coped well with that' or 'I coped badly with the stress of all that.' But as counsellors we see coping as a process, not a single act but a *series* of activities which a person uses when faced with stressors. When a person uses a tactic from within a coping strategy – for example, seeking to change the situation – then they also affect the situation itself.

A change in the situation may then require a new and different coping tactic, and so the process continues.

Consider this case:

> **Dave** and **Mike** have both been divorced recently and have children in the care of their former wives.
>
> Dave sees divorce as a release from a difficult situation: he and his wife had spent the last two years of their married life arguing, being depressed and being unfaithful. They agreed on a divorce for their own sakes as well as their son's.
>
> Mike's experience is very similar, with one important difference: Mike outwardly agreed to a divorce but inwardly experienced this as a failure rather than a release.
>
> Dave is living in a flat and copes with the experience of divorce by treating it as a problem to which he and his former wife found a rational and logical solution. Mike copes with the experience of failure by drinking and taking drugs. So serious has Mike's drinking and drug-taking become that the courts have recently refused him access to his child and former wife. This development confirms Mike's feelings of failure and leads him to drink even more.

This example illustrates that:

- People adopt different coping strategies when faced with events which they regard as stressful.
- These different strategies contribute in different ways to the experience of stress, that is, *the coping strategy adopted is a part of the experience of stress*, not something separate from it.
- The coping strategy or tactic a person adopts can be *part of their problem* rather than part of the solution. Mike's coping strategy ends up reinforcing his feelings of failure.

That a coping strategy or tactic can contribute to making a situation *more* stressful rather than less is seen frequently, especially when people use *displacement* coping. This occurs when a person, for example, seeks to deal with their anger or frustration about work by expressing anger or frustration at home.

Ways of coping

As suggested above, some ways of coping are more effective than others. Some ways involve changing the situation to reduce the stress that it causes. Other ways help people to redefine the situation so that they see it as being less stressful, or they may cope with it in ways that mean that it affects them less severely.

There are a number of broad ways that people respond to stress: in the SSCS model these are summarised as *engaged, tolerant* and *withdrawal* coping. There are different elements to each way of coping, and each has advantages and disadvantages. These are defined, examples are given, and the advantages and disadvantages of each are shown in table 6.1 below. This is helpful to us as counsellors because:

- It provides a framework for understanding the coping experience of our clients.
- It shows that there are many different ways to cope within each of these major areas, each with advantages and disadvantages. Many people will come bringing with them the TINA belief ('There is no alternative' to the way I am feeling, thinking, reacting, coping, behaving, etc.), which we discussed in chapter 3. These coping strategies show us that this is not the case; there is a wide range of ways in which people can and do cope.
- We can use these descriptions as ways of encouraging our clients to identify their own preferred approaches to their stress problems, and to look at alternative possibilities.

Are some of these strategies more effective than others?

The answer to this question is interesting. The people who cope with stressful life events most effectively – those that find few situations stressful or threatening, or who deal with them in ways that do not cause them problems – are those who:

- are able to move between these three strategies with ease;
- have a variety of coping tactics available to them.

Counselling and Coping

Coping and self-concept

When faced with some stressful situation people generally go through two stages. They ask themselves whether this situation is a threat to them: 'Am I OK or am I in trouble?' Then, if the answer is that they are in trouble, they ask: 'Can I cope?'

Table 6.1 Engaged, tolerant and withdrawal coping: definitions, examples, advantages and disadvantages

Engaged coping is when people get involved in trying to control the stressful situation that they are in. They can do that in a number of ways, including:	*Tolerant* coping is when people cope by doing nothing or by tolerating the situation. They can do that in a number of ways, including:	*Withdrawal* coping is when people cope by withdrawing from the source of stress. They can do that in a number of ways, including:
Controlling the source of stress This may be by trying to *control* the situation • I try to have more control of our finances so we do not get into debt so much. • I make my son promise not to take drugs any more. • I make threats and ultimatums to stop my wife leaving me. • I agree with my boss that I will work more productively. Or by trying to *change* the situation • I look for a compromise between my own needs and those of others. • I talk abut the situation with those most involved in it, to see how we can change it. • I agree to learn new skills which will make this stressful situation different. • I confront my relative and argue, telling them how I feel, to try to make them stop the drinking or drug-taking. *Controlling the effect that the stress has on the person* • I relax and calm down: things will get better when I feel in control.	*Not doing anything* • I don't know what to do so I think it is better to do nothing at all. • I don't even want to think about the situation. I'm sure it will take care of itself, given time. *Putting others' needs first* • I clear up the mess my wife makes when she has been drinking and don't mention it when she wakes up. • It is such a pity that my employer's business is going so badly: I'm sure they are only making me redundant because they have to.	*Avoiding the stressful situation* • I don't go and visit my brother now he's got cancer. • I don't open letters which look like bills. • I won't say much to my partner, so there is no chance of a row. *Being independent* • I have my own life to lead and don't want to drag myself down with my relative. • I spend more time with my friends. • I have taken up a new hobby and spend as little time at home as possible.

Table 6.1 (Cont'd)

- I create a positive 'spin': there must be something positive in this situation which I'm missing right now, so I'll search for it.
- Time will heal – this feels bad right now, but I know from experience that it will look different in a few days' time.

Redefining the meaning of a stressful situation after it has occurred
- I rationalise the experience: it could have been much worse, or worse things have happened to me before.
- I turn a negative experience into a positive one: although I hated it at the time, I did learn a lot about myself, or these things are sent so that we can learn.
- I make a positive comparison with others: I felt I wasn't doing too well until I looked at how Fred was doing!

Advantages
- I feel that I am doing something, and this gives me hope.
- Expressing how I feel makes me feel a lot better and much less stressed.
- Confronting the stressful situation gives me hope – I feel that I cannot give up trying to change things.

- Not having to go to work will allow me to do all of those things that I have been putting off.

- I give money to my son, even though I know it will be spent on drugs.
- I am sure that it is my fault that he gets so angry with me: it must be what I say.
- I ring up and make excuses for my husband's absenteeism.

Advantages
- There seems to be less tension and conflict, but often this lasts for only short periods of time.
- If I accept the situation, I can avoid conflict.
- Doing nothing makes me feel more independent

Advantages
- Avoiding my relative means that there is less tension.
- It makes me feel more in control of the situation.
- Avoiding my relative makes me feel detached from the situation and I can hide a lot of what I really feel.

Table 6.1 *(Cont'd)*

	and I suffer less from my relative's behaviour.	• I want to look after my own needs and put myself first. I want to be independent and not have to rely on anyone else.

Disadvantages
- Trying to control this situation is very stressful in itself!
- Expressing how I feel can annoy or be upsetting for my family and colleagues.
- When I try to control the situation, it does not always work. This is frustrating and upsetting.
- I feel sure that I *should* be able to change this situation. I feel angry and hurt and responsible for it: I am desperate to find something that will work and change the situation.
- Responding in these ways makes me feel that I am doing something positive to try and change the situation, but it makes me frustrated and stressed if it doesn't work.

Disadvantages
- Doing nothing makes me frustrated because nothing changes.
- Putting my family's needs first makes me feel that I am being taken advantage of and that the situation is not changing.
- Being tolerant makes me feel powerless over the situation and guilty that I can't do anything to change it.

Disadvantages
- Doing nothing makes my relative feel rejected and unloved. This can make the situation worse and there can be more tension.
- My relative complains if I try to be more independent. I feel that there is nothing I can do to help the situation. This makes me feel sad, bitter and hurt and I worry that my relative will feel rejected and that I don't love them any more.

Source: adapted from A. Copello *et al.* (2000), *Responding to Alcohol and Drug Problems in the Family: A Guide for Primary Health Care Professionals using a Five-Step Approach* (2nd edn), Birmingham/Bath: University of Birmingham/Bath University; L. Templeton *et al.* (2003) *Responding to Alcohol and Drug Problems in the Family: A Guide for Workers in Specialist Drug and Alcohol Services using a Five-Step Approach*, Bath: University of Bath.

The first question ('Am I in trouble?') is important, because whether the person feels a sense of threat from the situation relates to their beliefs, the way in which they see themselves, their self-concept and the goals which they regard as important. In effect, then, the answer to this first question is as much about how the person sees themselves as it is about their situation.

This then leads to an important element in our counselling: we often need to explore (and challenge) the assumptions which our clients are making about themselves, as well as about their situation. Just because a person's appraisal of themselves is negative, it does not follow that the situation *is* threatening or hopeless; it may equally be the case that the person is *regarding* the situation (and possibly themselves as well) as hopeless.

As counsellors, we need to understand whether our client is correctly regarding the situation they are in as threatening, and enable them to rethink this if appropriate.

Problems in coping

The second question ('Can I cope?') relates to the nature and extent of our client's coping repertoire. But 'Can I cope' is not the most helpful way of thinking; it relates to the 'all or nothing' view of coping, whicih has already been mentioned. Instead, we want to help our clients realise that it is more useful to ask 'Which ways of coping or reacting are most likely to be helpful to me (and others), and which ways are likely to be least helpful?'

When people find it difficult to cope, it may imply one of several possibilities:

- the lack of an appropriate coping response in the person's coping repertoire;
- the lack of previous experience of such a situation, for example, facing up to the loss of a close relative or friend for the first time;
- the lack of material resources (i.e. cash, mobility, social contacts and social support) to put a particular way of coping into action.

As counsellors, we need to discern which of these three situations provides the best explanation for a person's failure to cope with a situation which they correctly regard as threatening.

Techniques to help people cope

Chapters 7–13 contain many specific techniques aimed at helping people to change and to cope with difficulties. In this chapter we will take more of an overview, and suggest that there are eight steps we can take within our counselling relationship.

1   Help the person face up to the situation

Discourage denial and promote objectivity in their thinking about the current situation. Make sure that they are accurate in their appraisal. Look at the extent to which the situation is shaped by their own thoughts, actions and reactions.

2   Break up the situation into manageable steps

To prevent the person from being overwhelmed, encourage them to see their actions as a series of manageable, discrete steps which they need to take.

3   Stop them panicking and promote objectivity and accurate appraisal

People in adversity often have a poor grasp of reality; they feel panicky and over-emotional and think irrationally. We need to encourage the use of objective data and rational thinking. We need to get them to evaluate their own performance as a 'coping person' and encourage objectivity about this feature of their behaviour.

4   Avoid false reassurance

Just as we seek to promote objectivity in our clients, so we need to be objective in our own evaluations of our clients' progress and prospects. We need to be positive and encouraging, but we must avoid being *over*-optimistic and *over*-confident about the ability of our clients to take command of their situations.

5   Discourage projection

The term *projection* is covered in chapter 11 (on the unconscious), but in brief it refers to the attribution of certain qualities (e.g. guilt, anger, aggression, jealousy or fear) by one person to another when in fact these qualities are more present in the person doing the attribution than they are in the person receiving the attribution. Put simply, people who project believe that others are doing to them what they are doing to others. When a person is in crisis, projection is common and tends to make personal relationships difficult. Counsellors need to be aware of this and to help clients to see that this is what they are doing.

*6   Help and encourage clients to help themselves, especially by
linking in with their network of social supports*
As we mentioned above and discuss in greater depth in chapter 14, social
support is one of the crucial determinants of whether people develop
problems from stress. Often, clients will seek to use their counsellor as
their main social support. Clearly one of our key tasks *is* to be supportive,
but this is in order to *empower* them to gain this support from others
too, so that they do not become dependent on us.

7   Teach active coping skills
It may be that a client already has sufficient coping skills, but needs to
learn to use them more effectively. Or there may be insufficient coping
responses in a client's repertoire. We have to empower our clients to
learn new effective ways of coping. We need to be active as a counsellor, not simply a listener.

8   Changes need to be sustained and maintained
As we stressed in chapter 3, maintaining changes in the way that people
cope with adversity is challenging for most people. We need to help them
if they lapse back into old ways of coping, help them to anticipate potential problems and empower them to work out solutions.

Summary of counselling tasks

When we described the experience of stress leading to strain at the
start of this chapter, we summarised the effects of stress under various
headings. We can use the same headings to summarise the tasks of a
counsellor in helping people to cope. We need to work with:

- The way people see themselves:
  - re-establish a sense of self-worth;
  - stop self-deprecation and promote a positive view of self;
  - turn negative defences into positive prescriptions for action.
- The way people experience the world:
  - promote objectivity in thinking about their situation;
  - ensure that they take responsibility for their own part in the
    creation of the problem;
  - increase their feeling of control of their situation;
  - encourage them to think of the present and future more than the
    past and present;
  - discourage wishful thinking and encourage rationality;

- ○ teach coping skills where appropriate;
- ○ discourage dependence on us.
- The way they experience their emotional world:
  - ○ encourage them to identify more accurately their own emotional experiences;
  - ○ discourage projection;
  - ○ reduce the level of anxiety;
  - ○ encourage the acceptance of positive feelings.
- The way in which they think:
  - ○ encourage purposive thinking;
  - ○ break up the situation into manageable steps;
  - ○ focus upon specific goals;
  - ○ restore the ability to stand outside themselves and review their situation;
  - ○ enable them to envisage the prospect of change.
- Their physical state:
  - ○ seek to ensure that they eat regularly;
  - ○ seek to ensure that they sleep adequately;
  - ○ seek to ensure that their physical well-being is as important to them as their material and psychological well-being.

The list of eight techniques to help people cope and the list comprising the summary of counselling tasks suggest that helping a person to cope is demanding work. It is. Furthermore, it is often under the additional pressure of time. The tasks listed here constitute the ideal, but in practice we use these task lists as reminders of the possibilities rather than as specific agendas for action with every client.

Teaching coping skills

Mention has been made of teaching coping skills. In the main, these are techniques which will be covered as we go thought the range of styles and approaches in Building Block 2 (chapters 7–13). Again, however, in this chapter we will provide an overview of some of the ideas behind these skills.

The skills that people need to cope adequately with adversity are many and varied – some refer to these as *personal effectiveness training*. They include skills of:

- planning and decision-making;
- being assertive rather than aggressive;
- communication to enhance the quality of relationships;

- dealing with specific life events, such as marriage, becoming a parent, job interviews, bereavement and terminal illness.

The training programme is similar for all of these skills. The counsellor:

- assesses the current skill levels of the client;
- breaks down the skills to be mastered into manageable units of work;
- rehearses the person (through role-play and practice sessions) in the new skills;
- sets tasks to be completed in the real world ('homework') which involve the use of the new skills;
- helps the client evaluate their performance.

All this is undertaken within the confines of an agreed programme of work (a contract) and the client is encouraged to assume increasing responsibility for learning these coping skills. Throughout, the aim is to encourage the client to increase their repertoire of appropriate and effective coping behaviours for use in a variety of situations.

PRACTICAL EXERCISES

Previous or current responses to problems

Think about some area of your life that has been, or is currently, a problem. Use the worksheet below to note down the situation, your response(s) and how each one made you feel.

Exercise 1   How I respond

Example of a difficult situation	*How I responded*	*How this made me feel*
I knew my daughter wanted to get some drugs	I took money from her purse so that she couldn't buy drugs	Relieved and guilty but worried that she would steal from someone else
I think my husband may be having an affair	I confronted him with my suspicions	He denied it but I don't believe him, so I still feel upset and worried

Source: adapted from Copello *et al.* (2000) and Templeton *et al.* (2003).

Do it a few times, with different problems.
Reflect on what you have written:

- Did you find that you tend to respond in the same kind of way all the time? Or did you respond in different ways to different situations, or in different ways at different times?
- Were you unsure about how to respond? You may have tried lots of different ways of responding to the situation, and have little certainty about what the best thing to do is.
- You may feel unsure about what to do next: whether to respond the same way the next time something happens, or to try another way of responding to the situation.

Helpful and unhelpful responses

Some ways of responding and coping are more helpful than others. You may find (or have found) it difficult to decide on the best course of action. There is no right or wrong way and you need to find the best solution for you and your situation. Use the worksheet below to note down the situation, your response(s) and what was helpful and unhelpful.

Exercise 2   Understanding helpful and unhelpful responses

Example of a situation	*How I responded*	*What was helpful about this*	*What was unhelpful about this*
I never saw my partner in the evening – he was always in the pub	I started going to the pub and drinking more	I could see how much my partner was drinking and how he behaved	I had more hangovers myself and felt that I was doing nothing to change his behaviour or help myself
It was rumoured that they were going to lay people off at work	I worked extremely hard, putting in long hours, to make them realise that they should not get rid of me	I am pretty sure that I am safe from being laid off	I don't think I can sustain that level of work, and I may have set myself up to fail in the future

Source: adapted from Copello *et al.* (2000) and Templeton *et al.* (2003).

Changing responses

Select some of the responses which you feel have been less effective, or which you could have improved. Use the worksheet below to note down the situation, what your response(s) was and what you could do differently next time.

Exercise 3   Changing my response

Example of a situation	*How I used to respond*	*What I could do next time this happens*
I am overweight and I know I need to lose weight	I regularly start a new diet, and believe that I will keep to each one, but I always seem to fail	I could try to change the way that I eat overall, and eat 20% less at each meal
Whenever I go to pick up my children from their mother, we get into a row which upsets the kids and sours their time with me	I promised myself that I wouldn't react, but each time she said something cutting or sarcastic about me, I would rise to it	I could avoid the conflict by arranging for my mate to pick the kids up; or asking my ex-wife to drop them over to me instead. Alternatively, I could find new ways of not rising to her attacks by telling myself that I know she is not going to react differently and that her reaction is about her and not me

Source: adapted from Copello *et al.* (2000) and Templeton *et al.* (2003).

Summary

- People have to cope with many things in their lives, including external life events, various life stages and external pressures and constraints. Our task as counsellors is to enable them to use their internal and external resources in such a way that they *do* cope.
- As counsellors we help people to learn new coping skills, reinforce existing coping skills and help to restore people's ability and confidence in their coping.
- One influential theory is the *Stress–Strain–Coping–Support model*, which suggests that dealing with adversity is stressful and people often respond by showing forms of strain (physical and psychological

symptoms). The amount of strain is affected by the ways they cope with the stress, and their social support.

- People facing adverse conditions have the capacity to cope with these conditions, and this capacity is open to change: coping incorporates being active in the face of adversity, effective problem solving, being an agent in one's own destiny, *not* being powerless.
- People adopt different coping strategies when faced with events which they regard as stressful: these different strategies contribute in different ways to the experience of stress.
- The coping strategy adopted is a part of the experience of stress, not something apart from it.
- The coping strategy a person adopts can also be part of their problem rather than part of the solution: it can contribute to making a situation *more* stressful rather than less.
- How a person copes may have a direct effect on the adversity itself. Some ways of coping may change the situation so as to reduce the stress that it causes; other ways may actually increase it.
- How a person copes may mean that, while the experience of adversity is still at the same level, they may redefine the situation so that it is not seen as being so stressful, or they may cope with it in ways that means that it affects them less severely.
- There are a number of broad ways in which people respond to stress: we summarise them as *engaged*, *tolerant* and *withdrawal coping*. This provides counsellors with a helpful framework of strategies.
- The people who cope most effectively are those who are able to move between these three strategies with ease and who have a variety of coping tactics available to them.
- We need to understand whether our client is correct in regarding their situation as threatening, and enable them to rethink the situation if appropriate.
- If they decide that the situation really is a threat, we need to help our client to ask, 'Which ways of coping or reacting are most likely to be helpful to me (and others), and which ways are likely to be unhelpful?'
- There are eight steps we can take to help people cope with difficulties.
  1 Help the person face up to the situation.
  2 Break up the situation into manageable steps.
  3 Stop them panicking and promote objectivity and accurate appraisal.
  4 Avoid false reassurance.
  5 Discourage projection.

6   Help and encourage clients to help themselves, especially by linking in with their network of social supports.
7   Teach clients active coping skills.
8   Help clients to maintain changes.

- We may also need to teach coping skills, including planning and decision-making skills, learning to be assertive rather than aggressive, communication skills to enhance the quality of their relationships and skills for specific life events.

- The chapter has focused on things we can do to help our clients cope more effectively. *How* we provide this help is also vital: the core skills of developing a collaborative counselling relationship have to be at the heart of everything we do if we want to be effective as counsellors.

7

Helping People to Do Things Differently

What we have to learn to do, we learn by doing. (Aristotle)

An ounce of action is worth a ton of theory. (Friedrich Engels)

We are what we repeatedly do. (Aristotle)

We met **Paula** in chapter 1. She has a chronic fear of rejection, so she turns down invitations to social events. She fears that she has nothing to say, and people will find her boring. On the few occasions when she does go out, she finds it difficult to talk to others and is seen as shy and mousy.

One of the first things that we notice about other people is their behaviour. Helping people to change what they do and how they behave, so that they move through society more easily, are therefore central in helping and counselling.

In this chapter, we focus first on the basic assumptions that underlie this approach. Second, we look at common kinds of difficulty that our clients may have with what they do and how they relate to others. Third, we look the basis of all skills training. Fourth, we outline skills and techniques to help clients to modify or change their behaviour. Finally, we discuss when it is appropriate to work in this way.

Background to the Behavioural Approach

There are two basic assumptions which underpin the behavioural approach.

- *What people do – how they behave – defines what their problem is,* and therefore how counselling can help.
- *Psychological problems are learnt.* Some people have learnt to behave in ways that lead them into problems (such as fears, phobias, depressions) and our task as counsellors is to teach them to behave differently.

Hence, with the first assumption, if someone is anxious, some forms of helping might involve talking with them to discover why they are anxious, and to change how they think about the anxiety-provoking situation; but a counsellor following a behavioural approach will get the client to *do* things differently – to learn how to relax and then to put themselves into increasingly more intense anxiety-provoking situations, using their relaxation skills to lower their anxiety in each situation. Or if someone is depressed, instead of talking about causes and new ways of thinking, a counsellor following a behavioural approach will get the client to *behave* differently – to get out of bed in the morning and start engaging successfully in activities such as shopping, hobbies and talking to other people.

The second assumption, that psychological problems are learnt, has three parts to it:

- People learn how to behave.
    - Most people learn ways of behaving as they grow up, by copying what they see their parents and other key figures doing.
    - Some ways of behaving are learnt by association: for someone who has been in a car accident, for example, car travel becomes associated with fear and anxiety, and hence makes the person feel anxious.
- For many reasons, some people learn ways of behaving which are not helpful.
    - They may fail to learn useful skills of interaction as they grow up, or they learnt them less well, or they learnt ways of behaving which are actively *un*helpful.
    - They may have had unfortunate experiences which led them to associate a common event (such as air travel or seeing a spider) with high levels of fear and anxiety.

- People can learn how to behave differently.
  - They can learn how to acquire useful skills of interaction and/or not to behave in ways that cause them to have problems with others.
  - They can learn how to disssociate common events from fear and anxiety.

Common Problems Amenable to the Behavioural Approach

Fears and phobias

A phobia is when someone has such a major fear of a common event or thing that they cannot function when it is near. They become too anxious to think clearly, and often panic.

There are many theories of why someone develops a phobia, but the idea we use is that our client has developed an association between a particular situation or thing and an anxious reaction. So each time they come across it (or even think about it) they become increasingly anxious until it is so bad that they cannot lead a normal life.

Helping people with phobias

There are two parts to the help that a counsellor focusing on behaviour can offer.

1 The counsellor needs to enable the client to see that what they do and how they react to situations or things is a matter of choice. Our job is to help them believe that, by using the skills that we can show them, they can overcome this extreme anxiety.
2 We need to teach our client these skills.

The key skill is *relaxation*. Once a client has learnt how to relax at will, the relaxation is then paired with *exposure* to whatever the feared thing is. The basic idea is that relaxation is incompatible with fear and anxiety. If someone can learn to relax at will, then they will not be able to feel panic. The client learns to respond to their fearful thing in a different way: with relaxation rather than fear and anxiety.

So, first, we train the client in deep muscle relaxation and ask them to practise at home so that they will be able to relax at will. (This is outlined in more detail in chapter 10, on the body.)

The next step is to expose the client to whatever they are afraid of. First, we go through the relaxation procedure and ensure that our client is very relaxed. Then we gradually expose the client to their feared thing – spiders, for example. We will first ask them to think about something very slightly anxiety-provoking, such as a tiny money-spider in a locked cupboard in another room. We then get them to practise their relaxation until they are very relaxed again. This process continues with increasing levels of exposure to the spider, ensuring that we raise the level only once the client is able to become very relaxed with the previous level. Eventually the client learns to relax with a real spider in the room.

Skills of social interaction

People may lack the basic skills which enable them to interact with another person – for example, they may not have the skills of making eye contact, using facial expressions, exchanging small talk or having an introductory conversation. Alternatively, people may have these skills but not be able to assess situations in order to use them appropriately. The basic approach is that people use interpersonal skills to negotiate their way through social interactions and that these skills can be learnt.

Lack of these skills, or their inappropriate use, leads to difficulties, including avoiding people or situations, acting inappropriately or using excessive behaviour (such as extreme anger or effusiveness) when it is not called for. One of the ways in which counsellors who use the approach of focusing on clients' behaviour to help people is by training clients in the use of these skills.

Ways of Helping

Skills training (ST)

In order to help improve the way we do things and get different results, a number of skills-based training approaches have been developed, including training in social skills, assertiveness, anger management, life skills, personal effectiveness (and its offshoots, parent effectiveness, leadership effectiveness and teacher effectiveness), coping skills and coaching. All these forms of helping (and many others) are, essentially, about developing a range of skills to change what we do and how we relate to others.

In using a ST approach, two key sets of processes are used: one focuses on the client's behaviour, the other on their skills.

In terms of *behaviour*, ST uses an ABC framework as the focus:

- *Antecedents*: what led to the particular behaviour.
- *Behaviour*: what that behaviour was.
- *Consequences*: what happened afterwards.

In terms of *skills*, ST goes through the following steps:

- *Assess and evaluate* the skills of the person (e.g. looking at what behaviour they would have liked to exhibit in the above ABC scenario, and what they actually did, and what the difference was).
- *Provide coaching and instruction* to develop new skills or refine existing ones.
- Help the person *practise these new skills*.
- Provide *sensitive and appropriate feedback and support* in their use of the skills.

The key is the focus on behaviour, and on breaking down behaviours into small parts, each of which can be modified.

To take an example, Paula (who was mentioned at the start of this chapter) says: 'I end up avoiding eye contact and making excuses not to take a guest to lunch at work because I don't know what to say to them and I'm worried what they will think of me.' Some other approaches, covered in later chapters, might focus on Paula's thoughts, emotions, unconscious processes or concern about what others might think of her. In the behavioural approach, our focus would be on the behaviour (avoiding eye contact, avoiding taking someone to lunch, not having things to say). Our aim with Paula would be to reduce the incidence of her avoiding eye contact and taking guests to lunch and to increase her skills (and confidence) in having things to say.

We are most likely to do two things:

- help Paula to improve her skills so that she is well practised at having things to say in new social situations, and at making appropriate eye contact, smiling at people instead of looking anxious;
- help Paula learn to associate the act of meeting a new person with positive outcomes instead of negative ones. Hence we would encourage Paula to associate meeting and taking a work guest to lunch with positive outcomes such as learning interesting things about the

guest, and feeling competent when trusted with looking after an important person.

With all of these skills-based training programmes, our aims are:

- to provide a *safe context*, in which the client can develop and practice new skills;
- to build a *helping relationship*, whereby the client trusts us and receives accurate feedback from us, which is aimed at enabling and encouraging them to develop these skills;
- to teach the client *appropriate skills* in such a way as to ensure that they will be used in real life (as opposed to simulated situations) where it is sensible to use them.

All skills-based training programmes work in this way, whether they are about assertiveness, anger management, communication skills or social skills.

Assertiveness training

Hence, with assertiveness training, the person seeking to become more assertive is encouraged to practise phrases, techniques and ways of interacting which put their views across in a calm and natural way, without being aggressive or self-deprecating, or belittling the other person. Of course, they do not get it right immediately, and one of our tasks as counsellors is to *shape* their behaviour – to suggest slight changes in what they say and the way they say it, and help them to take small steps towards being assertive. We do this behavioural shaping by providing feedback, and by concentrating our feedback on observable behaviour (such as the statements they make, their eye contact or lack of it, the amount of smiling, the tone of their voice) rather than on what they say about their feelings about this behaviour. Assertiveness training as a specific example of skills training is examined in more depth later in this chapter.

Skills for improving communication

To take another example, in a skills programme aimed at improving and enhancing interpersonal communication, the person seeking to be able to communicate more effectively is encouraged to focus on seven sets of skills, of increasing complexity:

1 *Observation skills*: looking at people and assessing their expressions, learning how to pick up what people are thinking and feeling; also self-observation – learning to see how one is coming across.
2 *Listening skills*: learning to focus on what others are saying. Many people who are socially anxious focus so much on what *they* are going to say next that they do not listen to what others are saying to them.
3 *Speaking skills*: learning how to phrase things, and some simple (and then progressively less simple) stock phrases and topics of conversation; using non-verbal accompaniments to speech; learning how to use self-disclosure of factual and feelings information (appropriately) in conversation; learning clarity in the expression of emotions and attitudes; also learning how to match what is said and how it is said (playfully, humorously, seriously) with the mood of the situation.
4 *Interactive and timing skills*: learning how to mesh your points and ideas with those of others; timing interventions in a way that shows recognition of others; building on what others say and do.
5 *Expression of attitudes*: learning how to express attitudes and beliefs in a non-aggressive way; matching your style to that of others, or choosing a different style deliberately so as to influence others.
6 *Managing social exchanges*: greetings, farewells, making requests, gaining access to strangers; offering compliments, praise, encouragement and congratulations; showing and giving sympathy; providing explanations without becoming too long-winded; dealing with awkward situations; being assertive without being aggressive.
7 *Situation training*: the person is encouraged to act out, in role-play, situations in which they feel the skills would be useful, so that we are able to provide feedback, advice and coaching.

Very often, these skills-based training programmes are delivered in a group setting (see chapter 15, on helping people in groups). It is often more efficient to work with people in groups, which also provide a ready-made social setting where members can practise their new skills.

Although what we have described may sound quite straightforward, in fact a great deal of work and skill is required to cover all the stages of assessment, teaching appropriate skills, and providing practice and feedback. However, such behavioural skills-based training has been shown to be effective in many different situations, including reducing social anxiety, reducing alcohol consumption and improving the quality of social interaction of people with severe and chronic psychiatric disturbance.

Making skills training relevant and effective

ST programmes have to be tailored to match the individual needs of the person or the specific needs of a group. Given this, we need to give thought to the following six points.

- The rationale of ST training programmes needs to be clearly defined and explicit so that the client understands the role we are taking and the tasks they are being asked to do – a contract can be useful here.
- If we intend using video or audio as ways of giving feedback, we need to explain their usefulness and provide adequate opportunity for getting used to the equipment and feeling safe with the feedback process.
- Skills should be tailored to the current level of skill of our client and paced at the right speed.
- If we are working with a group, we need to take full account of individual differences in learning.
- Skills, practice sessions and role-play should not involve unlikely situations: they need to be appropriate and relevant.
- Feedback needs to reflect a person's skill level, intelligence and emotional state fully; we should describe actual observed behaviour sensitively and be non-judgemental.

Anger Management and Assertiveness Training

Two specific skills-based training programmes are anger management and assertiveness training.

Anger management

Not all of the ST programmes that are currently described in the literature focus exclusively upon behaviour. Some, such as anger management programmes, focus upon the relationship between thoughts, feelings, bodily reactions and behaviour.

Anger management training programmes, like all other skills training as outlined above, usually involve four main steps, which can take from one hour to several sessions.

1   We develop a *clear understanding* of the way in which the client currently responds to stress: the triggers; how they think and feel;

and the behaviour, bodily reactions and feelings that results from this way of thinking.

2   Through coaching and instruction we teach *specific coping skills*, emphasising the specific behaviours that our client needs to exhibit, and the thinking processes, feelings and bodily responses that accompany these behaviours.

3   We provide *graded practice* so that the person is able to use the new behaviours and thinking patterns which allow them to produce these new, appropriate behaviours. The graded practice also allows them to try out their expression of feelings appropriately and skilfully (often using the results of assertiveness training, discussed in the next section).

4   We provide clear *feedback* sensitively, gradually shaping their behaviour and thinking so that they deal with stressful situations more appropriately.

These are, of course, the basic steps of all ST programmes. The difference is that this particular programme looks closely at *the things people say to themselves* when they behave angrily. So we might help a client to generate alternative self-talk statements, ones that will allow them to cope with a situation and not blow up in anger (see table 7.1).

These self-talk statements are devices that can be used to interrupt the normal flow of thought when one is feeling angry. Similar self-talk ST programmes have been developed to deal with fear, anxiety, depression and stress.

Assertiveness training

In a similar way to anger management training, assertiveness training generally involves drawing the client's attention to their own self-talk patterns and ways of relating to others; it also involves teaching a related but different set of skills.

Assertiveness, in the context of assertiveness training, means the expression of one's own needs and feelings in a way that shows respect for the needs, feelings and rights of others. Some people who are not skilled in assertion use aggression to express their own needs; others simply do not express their needs at all. Hence assertiveness training works as commonly with people who are overbearing as it does with those who are excessively meek. Many clients mistake aggression for assertiveness, or fear being assertive because they think they will come across as being

Table 7.1   Alternative self-talk statements in different situations

Preparing for my anger	'This could be difficult, but I know how to deal with it. I can work out a plan to deal with this. Stick to the issues – don't take criticism personally. You've been here before and have come out OK.'
Confronting my anger	'As long as I stay calm and don't let my feelings build up, then I will be in control of this situation and myself. Concentrate on the positive and on what has to be done. Don't jump to conclusions. They don't have to like you and you don't have to like them – but you have to work together whether they like you or not.'
Coping with feeling angry	'I am getting tense . . . so *relax*! Take a deep breath and give yourself time to think. My feeling angry is a cue: I need thinking time. They want me to feel angry – so I won't let myself become angry. If I allow myself to be angry then I will just look stupid!'
Reflecting on the unresolved conflict	'Thinking about it makes me upset – so I'll stop! Relax – it beats getting angry with myself! The situation may seem hopeless – but it is not serious. I must not take it personally.'
Reflecting on a resolved conflict	'I did well there – well done . . . I deserve a treat! I could feel myself beginning to get upset, and I stopped myself! I realised that it wasn't worth it. See, I *can* keep my cool!'

aggressive. One task of assertiveness training is to enable them to see that an assertive person respects others, whereas an aggressive person shows disrespect for others.

Some common situations in which people who lack assertiveness skills have problems include:

- finding it difficult or feeling unable to say no when asked to do something;
- feeling unable to reject advances or refuse suggestions made by others;
- feeling angry with someone but lacking the skills to express that calmly;
- feeling manipulated by others, but not knowing what to do;
- wanting to ask for help or make a specific request, but lacking the confidence to do so;

- wanting to say something but not having the skills to do so, so saying nothing;
- having difficulty managing conflict at home, at work or with friends;
- dealing with criticism, sniping and nagging.

As with other ST programmes, developing an appropriate assertiveness programme involves identifying the assertiveness needs of the client, teaching specific assertiveness techniques, practising these techniques and providing feedback about their skills.

Some of the techniques we might use include getting clients to use *I* language ('I feel like going out tonight. I'd like to go to our favourite restaurant – would you?' 'I feel upset with what you have just said'); teaching them how to stick to the point and to say clearly and directly what they want and feel; teaching them that they have an equal right to speak and have their viewpoint heard.

Assertiveness training has been shown to be effective for a variety of client groups in promoting assertiveness and reducing anxiety. This includes people referred to mental health services, prisoners, nurses, managers working in public sector settings such as education and health, and staff working in benefits offices.

Problem-Solving, Goal-Setting and Action-Planning

 The final section of this chapter will look at three other useful techniques when working with people to modify or change their behaviour.

Problem-solving

Problem-solving is a simple technique, but it is a very powerful way of helping people change what they do. It includes three stages:

1 identifying the problem clearly;
2 generating a solution;
3 taking STEPs towards solving the problem:
   - *select* a solution (S);
   - *try* it out (T);

- *evaluate* what happens (E);
- *persist* until you feel better (P).

Identifying the problem

This is the most important stage. A vague feeling of unease, worry or depression is hard to get hold of and work with; a specific problem is much easier. We give below an extract from a session: it demonstrates some of the processes which lead to being better able to identify what each problem is.

Sally at first could not name her problems – they 'just all felt too much': 'Life's just awful and I am hopeless at everything.' We worked with Sally to help her identify more clearly what feels 'all . . . too much'. Sally was asked to think about problems at home:

> RICHARD: What is getting to you most at home?
> SALLY: Undoubtedly the mess.
> RICHARD: What is this mess?
> SALLY: Lots of things. Toys and half-sorted piles of clothes everywhere. The kitchen is bursting at the seams and there is nowhere to put anything down without moving a heap of other things, so things keep getting lost.

Sally was then able to identify that they don't have enough space for everything. When we asked Sally to name this problem, she called it 'lack of storage space'.

Generating solutions

The basic technique is to ask the client to choose one of the problems they have identified and to think of as many solutions as possible.

Sally tackled her problem of 'lack of storage space'. With our help (encouraging, giving some hints but never providing her with a list – it needs to come from and therefore feel owned by the client) she came up with the following:

- buy fewer things;
- increase storage space in the house;
- move to a larger house;
- stack things;
- build a storage cellar;
- use the garage for storage;
- buy a storage system (racking/boxes/baskets);
- visit a website specialising in storage solutions.

Taking STEPs (select, try, evaluate, persist)
Selecting a solution means looking through the list and deciding which one looks the most promising. Sally chose to focus on increasing storage space especially in the loft, which she decided to have boarded over. In the short term she decided to buy a stacking storage system from her local DIY store and at least tidy everything away.

Trying it out means asking the client to try it and see what happens!

It is important to encourage the client to *evaluate* the success of their chosen solution; it may not provide the complete answer. The person needs to know whether to persist with the chosen solution or to look for further solutions to supplement it. A week after Sally bought the stacking storage system she reported that the problem was much better. Even though things were not 'in their place', at least the house was no longer full of loose toys, clothes and papers. Two months after Sally started using the loft space she evaluated the effect. She had managed to get rid of a lot of clutter. The extra space in the house meant that she could start to make a place for other things. Her evaluation showed there was still one part of the house which overwhelmed her: the kitchen. She needed to be taught the last step in problem-solving.

For Sally to *persist* until she felt better meant asking her to look at the kitchen problem further. In doing so she became aware of how much space was taken up by things she rarely used, so she decided to put them up in the loft.

The process of evaluating, then persisting, is ongoing.

Having made these changes, Sally was coping better. We then asked her to think again about her problem of 'the mess' and the lack of storage in the kitchen: Was the house now normally tidy? Did the mess still get her down? This type of questioning reveals to what extent the problem has really been dealt with.

Sally's answer revealed that while she was less overwhelmed, the house was still messy. She was encouraged to use the whole problem-solving method again. At Stage 1, Sally identified two new problems: things lying around the house often had no place where they belonged, and people in her family did not have the habit of putting things away. These two problems were related: so many things had no 'home' that no one saw any point in tidying up. Sally started generating solutions to these problems and two months later, although the house was not as tidy as she would ideally have liked, it was significantly better.

The uses of problem-solving
We have used a relatively straightforward case for the sake of clarity, but the problem-solving method can also be used effectively with a range

of more complex difficulties. As with all techniques related to behaviour, problem-solving works by focusing on what people *do*, and modifying it so that they do things differently.

Goal-setting

> *One of the marks of an intelligent person is to be able to distin-*
> *guish what is worth doing and what isn't and to be able to set*
> *priorities. (Ann Wilson Schaef)*

This quotation encapsulates the essence of goal-setting. In many ways, goal-setting is a part of the 'select a solution' stage described above under 'Taking STEPs', but it involves looking at the selected step and making sure that the sub-steps needed are clear and well worked out.

For goal-setting to work well, the goals need to be SMART (as described in chapter 3), that is, they need to be:

- specific and clear (S);
- measurable and verifiable (M);
- adequate to meet the problem (A);
- realistic and achievable (R);
- timed (a specification of *when* the actions to achieve the goal will be taken) (T).

Action planning

Often, our clients will need help in moving from goal-setting to actu-ally taking action. So we usually develop an action plan with them, which specifies what they are going to do, when, what might go wrong, and how they might overcome these problems. We usually work with them to write down this action plan, using a simple pro forma, like the one in table 7.2.

> **Dawn** had constant worrying thoughts about her job which felt unmanageable. She was afraid her work wasn't up to the mark and that she would loose her job. Although her problem was with her thoughts, we sought a solution by focusing on her behaviour – things that she could actually do. We went through the problem-solving and goal-setting phases, and then she filled in the following action plan with us in order to test out these ideas.

Table 7.2 Dawn's action plan

Overall aims	Goals	Action plan	Possible problems	Strategies	Progress
Deal with faulty thoughts like 'I will lose my job'. Make my job more manageable.	Talk to my supervisor about specific problems and stresses that I have with the job, and get her to help me.	1 Arrange a specific appointment with my supervisor, within the next week. 2 Write down the top five major specific problems and stresses I have with the job, so that I don't forget them. 3 Write down her suggestions about what I should do.	Supervisor may be too busy to meet me.	Ask her ahead of time for a 15-minute meeting, and reassure her that I will not take up too much of her time.	On Monday, set up meeting. Saw supervisor on Thursday. I was anxious and cried, which was uncomfortable. But, despite that, the meeting went well! She and I prioritised my work. She reassured me about my job and the quality of my work.

The Application of Helping People by Working with their Behaviour

Working with people's behaviour is a very powerful approach, and there is an almost inexhaustible list of areas where it can be helpful. Examples include:

- training in basic communication skills, for a wide variety of people including socially anxious teenagers, long-stay psychiatric patients who have difficulty engaging in the community, and people needing anger or aggression management or assertiveness skills;
- working with people with fears or phobias;
- working with people who are depressed, who need to concentrate on their behaviour and make themselves more active, in order to kick-start their systems and provide more rewarding daily activities for themselves;
- teaching better communication skills to couples;
- coaching people for job interviews;
- dealing with conflict management within work teams;
- high-level skills training, for example, for those undergoing professional training in counselling or health visiting.

When not to work with what people do

There are times when focusing primarily on behaviour would not be appropriate. These include situations where clients need to work mainly on how they are thinking or on their emotions. So, for example, when someone has been recently bereaved, they will probably need to focus on their emotions rather than their future behaviour. We need to be sensitive too when a particular method isn't working effectively for someone, and to be prepared to change our methods.

PRACTICAL EXERCISES

Exercise 1

Aim: to become aware of the difficulties people have with what they do and how they relate

Task: Observe for a week, keeping a diary of the problems people you come across have with what they do and how they relate. Also look out for these on TV programmes. See if you can categorise them into types of problems. Jot down what kinds of skills training or other behavioural techniques might help them.

Exercise 2

Aim: to try out one of the methods of skills training
Task: Identify an area of communication you would like to improve. Try out, over a period of a week, one of the skills outlined in 'Skills for improving communication'.

Exercise 3

Aim: to give you an opportunity to practise and improve goal-setting
Task: Ask yourself what you would most like to achieve in the next week, month, six months, year and six years. Write down your goals in order of importance to you. Ask yourself how strong your desire and commitment to achieving them are. List what might prevent you from achieving each of the goals. List concrete things that would help you to achieve each goal, and concrete things that would help you *not* to be prevented from achieving each goal. Then get working on the list!

SUMMARY

This chapter has covered:

- A brief outline of the behavioural approach and some of its under-lying assumptions:
  - what people do – how they behave – defines what their problem is, and therefore how a counsellor can help them;
  - people learn how to behave, either by copying adults as they grow up or through association;
  - some people learn ways of behaving which are not helpful to them;
  - people can learn how to behave differently.
- *How to deal with phobias* using a combination of relaxation and exposure.
- The basis of behavioural, skills-based interventions (skills training), including a focus on two sets of processes:
  - *behaviour*, using an ABC framework (antecedents, behaviour, consequences);

○ *skills*, going through the steps of *assessment and evaluation* of the skills of the person, providing *coaching and instruction* to develop new skills or refine existing ones, helping the person *practise* these new skills and then *providing feedback and support* in their use of the skills.

- The importance of making skills training relevant and effective.
- Two specific skills training programmes: *anger management* and *assertiveness training*.
- Three further techniques of *problem-solving*, *goal-setting* and *action-planning*.
- Some examples of what kinds of problems this approach can be used for.
- When not to work with behaviour.
- Some practical exercises.
- As with all the chapters on different approaches in Part II, we have focused here on the techniques we can use to help our clients change what they do. *How* we introduce and help our clients to utilise these techniques is also vital: the core skills of developing a collaborative counselling relationship have to be at the heart of everything we do if we want to be effective as counsellors.

8

Helping People with their Thinking

Men are disturbed not by things but by the views which they take of them. (Epictetus)

Katie was feeling apprehensive prior to a job interview. She started anticipating the worst, imagining herself being unable to answer the interview questions, telling herself that she was not good enough. This train of thought led her to feel convinced that she had no chance of getting the job. And indeed, when she went to the interview, she became tongue-tied, did badly and was even more convinced that she was pretty useless!

Why was Katie anticipating the worst? Why did she tell herself that she was not and would not be good enough? Why did she sabotage (albeit unconsciously) her chances at her interview? One answer to these questions is provided by *cognitive therapy*, a major approach to counselling which starts from the premise that *it is the way we think about ourselves that leads us to develop and maintain problems*.

In this chapter, we focus first on clients' common negative thoughts and unhelpful beliefs, because this approach to counselling suggests that these thoughts and beliefs are often what lead people to feel bad about themselves. Secondly, we look at skills and techniques which can enable us to challenge these beliefs and help clients to see that their negative beliefs in themselves are unhelpful and incorrect. Thirdly, we outline skills and techniques to help clients to modify or change these views to more helpful ones. Finally, we discuss when it is appropriate to work with thought processes in this way.

Background to the Cognitive Approach

The approach of cognitive therapy was first developed in the 1960s and is built on three key assumptions:

- *Mood and thought are linked*: if we change one, the other starts to change automatically because feelings and thoughts are linked together all the time.
- *The way we think (and hence feel) is a matter of choice*: there is always more than one way of seeing things; the viewpoint that we choose is vital to our mood and thoughts.
- *Rethinking our thoughts and beliefs enables us to develop another perspective*: by finding another way of seeing things, we can improve our mood.

The issue of what comes first – thoughts or feelings – is not important for using these ideas to help people. A vicious cycle can easily be set up, with a bad mood exacerbating negative thoughts, which then lead us to feel worse, which in turn maintains, escalates and heightens our negative mood (see fig. 8.1). The example of Katie above shows this vicious cycle well: she was feeling apprehensive prior to a job interview; she started anticipating the worst, imagining herself unable to answer the interview questions, telling herself she was not good enough; this train of thought then led her to feel convinced she had no chance of getting the job.

Hence the assumption behind this way of working is that, if a person were able to think differently or adopt another point of view, then they

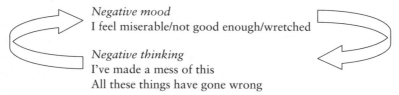

Negative mood
I feel miserable/not good enough/wretched

Negative thinking
I've made a mess of this
All these things have gone wrong

Figure 8.1   The negative vicious cycle

could start a *positive thinking cycle*, and therefore begin to feel and act differently. A major skill which our clients need to learn (and which we as counsellors need to cultivate) is looking for ways to think differently.

Four Key Steps to Thinking Differently

There are four key steps involved in helping clients to change their thinking:

1   recognize and identify negative thoughts;
2   recognise unhelpful thinking and negative self-beliefs;
3   develop techniques to challenge these thoughts and beliefs;
4   encourage practice and action planning.

Step 1: Recognizing and Identifying Negative or Unhelpful Thoughts

The Thought Record

Anna was often miserable and worried. She had moved to a new place and a job which she was not enjoying. She had left her boyfriend, Sam, and all her friends behind. She felt lonely and depressed, was finding it difficult to socialise, and could only focus on how useless she was and how bad she felt.

At the first session Anna was asked to keep a 'Thought Record', a special kind of diary to help her pinpoint her automatic thoughts and feelings (see table 8.1). Anna knew her feelings all too well, but she was barely aware of the automatic thoughts that went with them. Answers to the questions revealed the thoughts linked to the specific feelings. This example looks at recording what was going on when Anna was feeling bad, but it is also helpful to get clients to record situations when they are feeling OK.

Key questions for Step 1

Quite often thoughts are not easily put into words. The following are key questions which can help with identifying specific thoughts.

Table 8.1   The Thought Record

Situation (be specific)	*Feelings* (there may be more than one)	*Thoughts and images* (keep the different thoughts separate)
Travelling to work	Sad	I've made the wrong decision about accepting this job. There's nothing I can do to change it.
	Lonely	I've no friends here; no one is bothered.
Getting flustered talking to my boss	Miserable	I should be able to cope better than this.
	Anxious	I'm useless and feeble.
Sam telephoned when I was out	Worried Tense Upset	I'm losing touch with him.
	Confused	I'm not sure about our relationship.

- What went through my mind at the time and what images came to mind?
- How am I seeing things now?
- What is it about this that matters to me?
- What does this event or situation mean to me?
- What does it say about me?

Step 2: Identifying Unhelpful or Irrational Thinking and Beliefs

The second step is to help clients to examine the thoughts which they have recorded, and to identify, recognise and work with these unhelpful thoughts and beliefs. (We use the term *unhelpful thoughts and beliefs* in preference to the rather derogatory terms – 'crooked thinking', 'irrational beliefs' and 'faulty beliefs' – that cognitive therapy sometimes uses; we also use the less jargony term *thoughts* rather than 'cognition'.)

Cognitive therapy argues that *unhelpful self-beliefs are at the root of unhelpful thinking*, and that these two together strongly contribute to a person's experience of distress.

Cognitive therapy suggests that many of these unhelpful self-beliefs and ways of thinking are not grounded in a rational appraisal of the way the person actually is; instead, they have been acquired in some way. This is often by the ways in which other important figures in their lives – parents, partners, etc. – have interpreted their behaviour, which interpretations have then been reinforced by the person in their own right. This has then led them to interpret their own experiences in increasingly negative ways. Cognitive therapy also holds that the things that people say to themselves (their patterns of self-talk) also work to reinforce these unhelpful self-beliefs and shape a person's emotional response to a situation in a way that determines their subsequent thoughts and actions.

So a counsellor using this perspective will work with a client, trying to help the client alter their own beliefs and patterns of self-talk. We need to make a careful assessment of their thinking patterns, and the underlying beliefs that are driving that thinking.

Assessing thinking patterns and underlying beliefs

A cornerstone of the cognitive way of working is to make a distinction between *helpful* beliefs and *unhelpful* ones. (Cognitive therapy may use the terms 'rational' or 'adaptive' instead of *helpful*; and 'irrational' or 'faulty' instead of *unhelpful*.)

The following are *helpful* beliefs:

- We see ourselves and our world in relative, and not absolute, terms. For example, we express our needs as 'desires', 'preferences' or 'wishes' rather than in statements of 'musts', 'shoulds', 'oughts' or 'have tos'.
- We experience pleasure when our desires are met.
- We experience mild displeasure (sadness, annoyance or concern) when our needs are not met, but this displeasure is not extreme, nor does it overpower us – we develop further preferences and modify our thinking to take account of our recent experiences.
- We welcome (or at least accept in good spirit) feedback which is not always positive.

On the other hand, *unhelpful* beliefs include the following:

- We see and think about our world and reality in absolute, extreme or black-and-white terms rather than thinking of our needs in terms of preferences or wishes, or shades of grey.
- We think in terms of 'must', 'should' and 'ought'. This means that what begins in our thinking as a desire (e.g. to be successful) is soon translated into an imperative ('I must/have to be successful'). When we make these demands on ourselves or fail to achieve them, we experience negative emotions – depression, guilt, anxiety or anger being the most prevalent.
- We 'awfulise' our experience of the world because it has not met with our expectations (i.e. we predict the worst outcome or a total disaster if something minor goes wrong).
- We find it difficult to accept feedback which suggests that we need to change.

These unhelpful beliefs are like looking at ourselves through a hall of mirrors at a fairground: they distort reality. Most writers and clinicians in this cognitive approach would say that the tendency to develop irrational beliefs is often set up in childhood, by negative experiences and messages received from, for example, parents or schools. These are often expressed in 'should' and 'must' terms. Thus, the person learns to see the world in 'ought to' ways and hence develops unhelpful (and fundamentally irrational) beliefs about themselves.

These distorted patterns of thinking are underpinned by what some cognitive therapists describe as *core unhelpful (or faulty) beliefs*. Seven of these are outlined in table 8.2.

The point to note here is that holding one of the irrational beliefs is likely to lead to the experience of some distress or unhappiness, since it leads the person to 'awfulise' about what is happening to them. *It is not the event or other people that creates the distress; it is the way in which one thinks about the event or other people that leads to distressing experiences.*

Unhelpful thinking

Beliefs can sometimes be difficult to identify, so we find it useful to listen out for the sorts of unhelpful thinking which can arise from these unhelpful beliefs (see table 8.3). It is not an exhaustive list, but we have found it useful to learn to recognise these.

Table 8.2   Seven core unhelpful beliefs

Core unhelpful belief	Examples of expression
Uselessness/inadequacy/worthlessness	'I'm useless/inadequate/worthless/not good enough.'
Incompetence/non-achievement	'I'm incompetent/a failure.'
Avoidance	'If I don't look at this/do anything, perhaps it will go away.'
Unlovability/abandonment/rejection	'I'm unlovable – everyone leaves me.'
Vulnerability/helplessness	'I'm helpless, vulnerable, overwhelmed, have no control – it's awful, catastrophic.'
Undeserving/victim	'I never get what I want – bad things always happen to me.'
Entitlement	'I should be given . . . , I should be recognized.'

Step 3: Helping People to Change their Thoughts and Beliefs

The third step is to help the client to develop skills and techniques to challenge their unhelpful thoughts and beliefs and to look for other perspectives. There are a variety of ways in which we can do this, including:

- developing an Alternative Diary;
- using a Diary Worksheet;
- challenging by looking for evidence;
- challenging by looking for other points of view;
- asking 'What is the worst that could happen?';
- using rules to develop perspective.

All of them involve:

- helping clients to see the link between thinking and distress;
- emphasising the need to challenge unhelpful thinking and helping clients to develop more adaptive or rational thinking;

Table 8.3 Types of unhelpful thinking

Unhelpful thinking		Examples
Being absolute/ judgemental	Pressurising, often using words such as: • should • must • have to • ought	'I should have done better.' 'I must not make a mistake.' 'I have to get all this work done.' 'I ought never to lose my temper.'
Being extremist	Being extremist, often using words such as: • always • never • nobody	'I am always left to do the clearing up.' 'I'll never change.' 'You never listen to a word I say.' 'Nobody ever notices what I do for them.'
Catastrophising/ awfulising	Predicting the worst outcome or a total disaster if something minor goes wrong.	'If I make a mistake, I'll lose my job.' 'If I get angry, I'll lose control completely and hurt someone.'
Over-generalising	Assuming that because something happens once, it will always happen, or concluding that everything is always awful because of one bad experience.	'I never seem to say the right thing.' 'Politicians always tell lies.' 'We always do things your way.' 'I always get it wrong with you.'
Exaggerating	Magnifying negative aspects of oneself or giving negative events more importance than they really deserve, and forgetting or giving positive events less importance.	'I'll never get over it.' 'Any fool should be able to complete this.' 'No one enjoys my company because I never know what to say.'
Discounting/ ignoring the positive	Rejecting the good things as if they did not count, or overlooking personal strengths and good experiences, and dwelling instead on the negative.	'She only said that to make me feel better.' 'It's just that I had a stroke of luck.' 'Oh, he compliments everyone.'
Mind-reading	Believing that you know what others are thinking.	'She knows I've made a mess of this.' 'They all thought I was stupid.' 'He doesn't like me.' 'They only asked me because they couldn't find anyone else.'

Table 8.3 *(Cont'd)*

Unhelpful thinking		Examples
Fortune-telling or predicting the future	Believing you know what is going to happen.	'Everything is bound to go wrong.' 'I won't be able to cope on my own.' 'I would fall apart if something awful happened.' 'The interview went so badly I know they won't even consider me for the job.'
Black-and-white thinking	Viewing things in 'all or nothing' terms and switching from one extreme to another. Compromise is overlooked.	'If I can't get this right then I might as well not bother.' 'One mistake ruined the whole thing.' 'If you can say that then our relationship means nothing to you.'
Taking things personally	Seeing anything that happens as a personal responsibility or a personal attack.	'You are criticising me.' 'They didn't ask me because they don't like me.' 'If they don't get here, it's because I gave them such bad directions.'
Taking the blame	Taking responsibility when it is not yours.	'It's all my fault.' 'If only I'd done this, then that would have never happened,'
Emotional reasoning	Mistaking feelings for facts.	'I'm so worried I know something is going to go wrong,' 'I'm sure they've had an accident,'
Name-calling	This implies a negative judgement, usually an attack on the self, sometimes on others.	'I'm such a stupid cow/idiot,' 'You are completely heartless,' 'I'm bad,'
Scare-mongering	Focusing on the negative and potentially scary aspects of a situation.	'Maybe she's got a fatal illness,' 'What if they can't do anything about it?' 'I couldn't cope,'
Wishful thinking	Wanting things to be other than they are.	'If only I were younger . . . thinner . . . smarter . . . not the way I am.'
Magical thinking	Believing that things which need some action will magically change, without any action on one's own part.	'If I just leave things, maybe they will get better on their own.'

Source: adapted from G. Butler & T. Hope (1995), *Manage your Mind*, New York: Oxford University Press.

- being persistent in pursuing the unhelpful thoughts that lead some-one to seek help;
- providing accurate feedback to the person we are working with on the extent of the changes they are achieving as they progress.

Developing an Alternative Diary

The Alternative Diary uses two columns: one for thoughts and the other for alternative points of view. Clients take one thought at a time, write down the thought in the first column, and then ask 'Is there another way of seeing things?' In the second column they write down any alternatives they can think of, regardless of whether they seem credible. Examples are given in table 8.4.

It is crucial to do this exercise on paper so that clients have a written record to refer to when they feel too low to think of any alternatives.

Table 8.4   The Alternative Diary

Thoughts	Alternative points of view
I've made the wrong decision.	• It seemed the right one at the time with the facts I had. • It's too soon to tell. • I probably think that because I feel so bad.
There's nothing I can do to change it.	• Extremist words creeping in! • Things I *can* do are to stick with the job and think how to make a go of it; chuck it; talk it over with my friend Sue; get out and about more.
I should be able to cope better than this.	• The 'should' really puts pressure on me. • Maybe anyone would feel unsettled right now. • I *am* coping in some ways. • The facts: I *have* found somewhere to live; I *am* working things out with George; I *am* learning new things at work.
I'm useless and feeble.	• If someone else said that about me I'd think it was a complete exaggeration, and a put-down. • I know it's not true and saying that only makes me feel worse.

Table 8.5   Key questions to enable alternative viewpoints

Questions about thoughts	Questions about reality	Questions about unhelpful thinking	Questions about coping
What other points of view are there?	What are the facts of the case?	Could I be making a mistake in the way I am thinking?	What is the worst that could happen?
How would someone else think about this?	How can I find out which way of thinking best fits the facts?	Am I thinking straight?	How bad is this going to get?
How else could I think about this?	What is the evidence?	Am I using one of the ways of unhelpful thinking (table 8.3)?	What can I do when that happens/how can I cope with it?
How would I think about this if I were feeling better?		Am I pressurising myself?	How can I get help?

Many clients find developing these alternative viewpoints incredibly difficult. We can help by posing key questions (see table 8.5).

Using a Diary Worksheet

The Diary Worksheet is a tool which draws together the Thought Record and the Alternative Diary.

In order to change their unhelpful thinking and beliefs, clients will need to have an understanding of what triggered these thoughts in the first place, and to be able to make the links between their thoughts, their beliefs, their feelings and their behaviour. A simple way to do this is by using the Diary Worksheet (see table 8.6).

Challenging and modifying techniques

Having helped people (by using the Diary Worksheet or the Alternative Diary) to be clearer about how their bad feelings are caused by their negative and unhelpful thoughts, we now need to help them modify these thought and belief systems. We are going to discuss five methods of doing this:

Table 8.6　Example of a Diary Worksheet

Column 1: Questions for the client to answer	Column 2: The client fills in details for each distressing situation
Date/time: When did the event take place that gave rise to your experience of distress?	Sat. 9 pm
Situation: Who were you with, what were you doing?	Went to a social gathering alone. Knew no one.
Feelings: What did you feel? Rate each mood or feeling (1–10)	Anxious 10 Disappointed 9
Automatic thoughts and images: What was going through your mind? What images do you have of the situation? Look especially for 'musts', 'shoulds', 'oughts'.	No one wants to talk to me. I look stupid. I feel awkward I'm such a failure.
Thinking bias: What was your thinking bias or distortion?	Over-generalising. Taking things personally. Name-calling.
Irrational belief: What core beliefs underlie your thinking?	Uselessness/inadequacy
Alternative thoughts: How can you change this? Is there an alternative way of thinking about or understanding the situation?	I did talk with the host and I joined a group. They were in the middle of an intense exchange. No one treated me as if I was stupid. It was my first time. The host asked me to come again.
Feeling rating: Rate each mood or feeling again.	Anxious 9 Disappointed 7

Source: adapted from D. Greenberger & C. Padesky (1995), *Mind over Mood*, New York: Guilford.

- looking for evidence;
- looking for other points of view;
- asking 'What is the worst that could happen?';
- using rules to develop perspective;
- using other techniques.

Of course, like the other techniques we have looked at, some strategies are likely to be more suited to one person than another.

Challenging by looking for evidence

> **Marion,** a junior administrator in big firm, was depressed. She thought she was being given too many of the rotten jobs at work, and felt she was being used as the dogsbody, never being given the interesting work. She put on a brave face, but assumed she was regarded as not very able.

It soon emerged that these were all Marion's assumptions, none of which she had checked out. When she did, by talking to her colleagues and boss, she was surprised to hear that no one realised how she felt, or that she minded being asked to do these tasks. Contrary to what she had assumed, the evidence suggested that Marion's colleagues admired her abilities. After she had shared how she felt with her boss, he gave her more interesting work.

In Marion's case tackling the thoughts and checking out her assumptions resulted in a plan of action. As a result she felt much better. Getting the facts straight is crucial, although it often takes courage and we need to take this into account when we are working with our client.

Challenging by looking for other points of view

> **Jason** and his partner **Natalie** often fought. Following a recent fight, Natalie walked out of the house leaving Jason fuming. He thought 'Right, that's it. She's done with me for good.' He was angry and miserable. He did not want to lose the relationship.

Jason was encouraged to put himself in Natalie's place and to try to work out what other perspectives there might be, from Natalie's point of view. Jason came up with:

- It's her way of cooling down.
- She doesn't realize how Jason might interpret her behaviour.
- She has difficulty controlling her temper and was taught to walk away as a child.
- She is ashamed. She thinks he really means the unpleasant things he said about her during the fight and she wants to get back at him.

Jason was amazed. He had told himself that there was only one possible explanation for Natalie walking out and only one possible outcome:

the end of their relationship. Doing this exercise demonstrated for Jason something outlined in chapter 3: there are always alternatives (TAAA)! This is a useful technique for clarifying the many sides of all situations, and for bringing back perspectives that often get lost in the heat of the moment.

Challenging by asking 'What is the worst that could happen?'
Our clients often think that if their worst fears came true, it would be a catastrophe. Another challenge is to help clients *not* to see that as a catastrophe; catastrophising leads people to feel much worse, and then it becomes harder for them to cope. We can help clients by working through with them how they would deal with this difficult situation. Our task is to enable clients to tap into resources within and outside of themselves to help keep the distress within acceptable limits. How have they coped with difficulties in the past? Can they look to friends or family for support, advice or help? Do they have personal qualities, skills or abilities they can use?

Using rules to develop perspective
The following rules may help a client to find the most useful perspective and develop a more constructive view of the situation.

- *The 100 year rule*: will it matter in 100 years' time? Things that seem hugely important to us today may matter little when seen from a great distance.
- *The measuring rod rule*: is the thing that is upsetting us really the most important thing in life at the moment?
- *The middle of the night rule*: in the wakeful early hours, problems and worries assume immense and often insurmountable proportions. We have to learn to tell ourselves 'This is not the time'. The rule is: 'Think about it in the morning.'
- *The water under the bridge rule*: often things we feel bad about continue to prey on our minds long after the event. The art is to let them flow by us, imagining that they are sticks on the surface of a stream flowing speedily downstream: they are water under the bridge.

Other techniques

A few other techniques are also often useful to enable people to challenge and modify some of their thought and belief systems.

Distraction
This is a strategy for keeping problematic aspects such as fearful worrying or anxious thinking under control. Most people find that it is possible to concentrate properly on only one thing at a time. By encouraging clients to turn their attention to something which is neutral or pleasant, they may be able to distract themselves from worrying thoughts and images, and break a cycle. We outline three basic distraction techniques below.

- *Physical exercise*: doing something physical that is distracting, such as walking the dog, jogging, playing squash, or (less strenuously but still in the same vein) taking the drinks round at a party or helping with the washing up. John played squash to distract himself from his thoughts about how useless he was with girls. He realised that when he was playing and concentrating on squash, he never engaged in these negative thoughts.
- *Refocusing*: focusing attention on what is outside them, rather than on their internal state. Lorna learned to distract herself from her anxieties prior to shopping at a supermarket by reading car number plates and attending closely to her shopping list. Joan updated her diary or planned her 'to do' list instead of feeling anxious and self-conscious when waiting to see her GP.
- *Mental exercise*: creating a mental picture by generating a distracting phrase, picture or mental exercise. Thelma was asked to recall images of her last holiday as a way of dealing with her worries prior to travelling on the Tube.
- *Developing a compassionate mind*: using images and experiences to develop self-compassion.

Homework
Working with thinking involves helping people to acquire and then use new skills, and new skills need practice. So we always set some homework tasks. Examples include suggesting that clients:

- learn written statements and repeat them a number of times each day, especially in situations in which they often find themselves thinking and acting unhelpfully;
- complete diaries documenting each occasion on which they use self-talk involving 'shoulds', 'musts', 'oughts' or 'got tos';
- challenge one unhelpful belief, in writing, for 10 minutes each day on the 'alternatives' part of their diary – the aim being to encourage them to give up this one unhelpful belief and to replace it with a more helpful belief through their own efforts.

Summary of Steps 1 to 3

It may be useful to summarise where we have got to.

- There is some event or situation which results in a person experiencing unpleasant feelings of some kind: anxiety, anger, guilt, shame, tension.
- The person holds beliefs about this event which underlie or shape their thoughts and reactions to it, and some (or even many) of these beliefs and thoughts are unhelpful, such as those listed in table 8.3.
- The way a person reacts or responds to an event or situation is shaped by these beliefs and thoughts.
- The *cognitive* approach to helping is based on the idea that it is not events per se which create distress, it is a person's reactions to these events which produce distress.
- This reaction depends crucially upon the nature of the person's thinking and beliefs about themselves and their world.
- In the end, it is these thoughts and beliefs that shape their response.
- Using the cognitive way of working – working with thinking – we help clients to recognise unhelpful beliefs and thoughts, to challenge and modify them and to develop alternative viewpoints which will lead to an improvement in their experience of unpleasant feelings.

Step 4: Practising and Action-Planning

 Controlling unhelpful or negative thinking and changing beliefs is a skill which takes time to learn and may be hard work for clients. They may need reminding that:

- The main part of the change process will be carried out by themselves, outside of the sessions. It is important that they set aside enough time to experiment and practice with new ways of doing things.
- The more a person practises, the more they improve.
- Homework tasks should help clients progress at their own pace, and not be too difficult. It is also important to encourage clients to see setbacks as learning opportunities.

Such practice outside of the sessions is especially important in developing the skills of self-help, creating a strong a personal basis for changing unhelpful thoughts and sustaining the work we undertake during our sessions.

Finally, when we are trying to help someone to change their unhelpful thoughts and beliefs, we must always bear in mind the importance of past influences and previous history. A childhood history of negative experiences, for example, means that a client may be more likely to find alternative strategies harder to develop and maintain. As we all know, it is easier to fall back on familiar patterns and habits when the going gets tough!

The Application of Working with Thinking

When to work with thinking

This approach, and the range of techniques for working with thinking, have been used with a great variety of people in many different situations, including:

- coping with anxieties, fears and simple phobias;
- managing pain;
- coping with depression;
- managing and improving feelings such as anger, shame, guilt or low self-esteem;
- coping with substance misuse and other addictive behaviour;
- coping with conflicts, such as those between marital partners or staff in a workplace.

There is now an extensive literature documenting that the cognitive approach is a significant way of working with many client groups in a variety of settings.

Within Mental Health Services in the UK, cognitive approaches have been recommended as a key evidence-based practice within NICE (National Institute for Health and Clinical Excellence) guidelines, for a variety of problems. There is some limited evidence that, for many problems, individualised helping is more successful than group helping using these methods. However, cognitive work has been used in groups for assertiveness training, parent effectiveness education and stress reduction, and there is growing evidence for the effectiveness of cognitive work in groups for helping depression.

When not to work with thinking

It is also the case that there are some situations where working with thinking is *not* the best option. This includes times when clients need to work primarily on their feelings rather than their thoughts, or with difficulties related to behaviour which need to be dealt with by focusing on the actual behaviour, or on problems to do with unconscious patterns of behaviour that keep repeating themselves.

A key task for a competent counsellor is to assess which approach to use as the prime helping tool with a particular kind of person, and the right time in the process of counselling to use that approach.

Practical Exercises

Case study: Philip

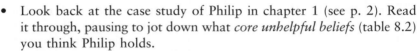

- Look back at the case study of Philip in chapter 1 (see p. 2). Read it through, pausing to jot down what *core unhelpful beliefs* (table 8.2) you think Philip holds.
- Check whether you have included at least the following, related to:
  ○ inadequacy;
  ○ incompetence;
  ○ avoidance rather than action;
  ○ helplessness.

  Philip's beliefs drive his behaviour and, unbeknown to him, create his distress, leading to his feeling anxious and awful. The situation is not as black-and-white as Philip wishes it to be, but he behaves and thinks as if it were. The beliefs he holds about the situation shape the way he behaves and his thoughts about his situation, and lead him to create his own distress.
- Look again at the case of Philip, and see what kind of *unhelpful thinking* you can identify (table 8.3).
- We think that Philip is using at least five:
  ○ absolute or extremist thinking;
  ○ over-generalising;
  ○ catastrophising;
  ○ black-and-white thinking;
  ○ fortune-telling.

Use your own experience

Identify some situations where *you* have felt bad. Work through the exercises, questions and worksheets discussed in this chapter:

- Step 1: use the Thought Record (table 8.1) and work though the key questions for Step 1 (see above).

- Step 2: use the seven core faulty beliefs (table 8.2), and the ways of unhelpful thinking (table 8.3) to analyse your own belief patterns.
- Step 3: try using the Alternative Diary (table 8.4), the Diary Worksheet (table 8.6).
- Ask yourself the key questions to enable alternative viewpoints (table 8.5) in Step 3.
- Challenge your own unhelpful thoughts and beliefs by using the five methods listed in Step 3:
  - look for evidence;
  - look for other points of view;
  - ask 'What is the worst that could happen?';
  - use rules to develop perspective;
  - use the other techniques.
- When you notice patterns in your thoughts and beliefs, ask yourself:
  - Is there a theme?
  - What is this telling me about my thoughts and beliefs?
  - What kind of thoughts and beliefs would I like to have?
  - How could I use the techniques outlined in this chapter to change my thoughts and beliefs into the ones I would like to have?
- As well as seeing if you can recognise patterns in your own thinking and beliefs, also look for these in TV programmes, dramas, plays or books. Keep a workbook or record for yourself over a set period such as one month.

Summary

This chapter has covered:

- A brief outline of the cognitive approach and three underlying principles:
  - There is a link between mood and thinking, so that if we change one the other one starts to change automatically.
  - We have a capacity to choose; the way we think (and hence feel), is a matter of choice.
  - We can learn how to rethink our thoughts and beliefs and hence develop another way of seeing things.
- The nature of our unhelpful thinking and beliefs.
- The four steps to working effectively with thinking:
  - how to identify our unhelpful thoughts and beliefs;
  - how to recognise them;

- how to develop techniques to challenge and to develop alterna-
    tives to these unhelpful thoughts and beliefs;
  - how to plan action.
- Some examples of what kinds of problems this approach can be used
  for.
- When not to work with thinking.
- Some practical exercises.
- As with the other chapters in Part II, this chapter has focused on the
  principles of this approach and the techniques we can use within it.
  It has not focused on the core processes of counselling or on the
  importance of the collaborative counselling relationship. It is worth
  stressing, however, that introducing these techniques in the absence
  of this relationship is likely to be ineffective: the relationship is at
  the heart of counselling.

9

Helping People with their Feelings

Better to express feelings than repress them. (Strephon Kaplan Williams)

This chapter will focus on how working with clients' feelings and emotions can often help them to overcome their problems. After a brief outline of the background to this approach, we look at feelings, the types of problems we can have with them, and how as counsellors we can help people to recognise and change their feelings.

Background to Working with People's Feelings

A number of approaches to counselling focus on helping people by enabling them to understand their feelings better. One major approach is the psychodynamic one, which is covered in chapter 11, on working with unconscious processes. In this chapter, we focus predominantly on the *humanistic* approaches taken by Gestalt therapy and by counsellors who concentrate on mindfulness and compassionate approaches.

There are three key assumptions taken when we work with clients' feelings in this way:

- *The way we feel (and hence think) is a matter of choice.* We don't have to be driven by our feelings: we can choose what and how we feel about ourselves, others and the experiences we have.

Figure 9.1   Thoughts, feelings and behaviour

- *Mood, thought and behaviour are linked.* If we change one, the others start to change automatically, because feelings and thoughts are linked all the time, and both are linked with behaviour (see fig. 9.1).
- *Recognising and working with our uncomfortable, distressing or painful feelings allows us to change those feelings.* If we are able to recognise, understand and change our feelings, we can then both think and act differently. Our skills as counsellors lie in helping our client to understand and recognise their feelings in order to change them.

Feelings and emotions

People experience a huge range of feelings, both positive and negative: misery, sadness, anger, depression, anxiety, fear, frustration, jealousy, humiliation, shame, guilt, loss, betrayal, joy, love, confidence, compassion, warmth, excitement, delight, playfulness. Sometimes people talk about emotions instead of feelings; some books use the word *affect* instead.

As the quote at the beginning of the chapter suggests, often it may be better to express our feelings rather than to repress them. However, the way we learn to do this, in particular knowing when, where, with whom and how to express our feelings, is the key to healthy and effective expression of them.

Common Kinds of Difficulties with Feelings

There are two common kinds of difficulties with feelings.

- Difficulty in *recognising or accepting feelings*: being unable to connect with or to discriminate between different feelings. People may experience 'not having' feelings or being 'out of touch' with them, or unable to 'own' their feelings.
- Difficulty in *coping with feelings* when they appear to be overwhelming, for example, overwhelming depression or grief. Or feelings may be

so strong that a person is pushed to act inappropriately, for example, love or infatuation leading someone to say or do inappropriate things, or humiliation leading someone to be inappropriately angry or anxious.

Our aims in counselling people so that they can deal with and change their feelings are:

- to help them to move from an ineffective or unhelpful expression of their emotions to an effective or helpful one;
- to enable clients who have difficulty accessing or recognising their repressed feelings to be in touch with, and recognise, their feelings, 'owning' them;
- to enable clients who cannot cope with their feelings, who feel overwhelmed by them or whose feelings may be expressed inappropriately, to understand and deal with those feelings more helpfully and, if relevant, to change them.

A key message is that nobody needs to be driven by their feelings: we can choose what and how we feel about ourselves, about others and about the experiences we have, as long as we can develop our capacity to be aware of and understand our feelings, know how to express them helpfully and to modify them.

Skills and Techniques to Enable People to Change their Feelings

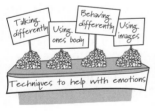

You can't stop the waves but you can learn to surf. (Swami Satchidananda)

When people are not in touch with their feelings, or when they find them overpowering or difficult to cope with, they may be functioning at a thinking and social level, but in such a way as to deny and constrain their emotional world. This is likely to give rise to tensions, anxiety and, in some circumstances, physical symptoms or problems. Once a person begins to ignore feelings in this way, those feelings can become larger than life.

We met **Sally** in chapter 1. Her father died when she was 13 and Sally repressed her feelings of loss and grief. In her twenties she started to think more about her father's death but she became very distressed and unable to explore her feelings without more pain than she could bear.

When helping Sally and others like her to accept and start to cope with their feelings, we need to be mindful of the following:

*   Avoiding lengthy discussions about past feelings because it can encourage our client *to think about feelings as historical experiences* rather than to experience emotions in the present. This prevents change.
*   Discouraging a client from talking about what *could*, *should* or *might* have been in the past, or similar speculation about the future. Such talk avoids dealing with current feelings and is a way of making feelings intellectual rather than emotional experiences.
*   Avoiding putting words into our client's mouth. No matter how empathic we might feel, we cannot be sure that we know what a person is feeling.

General ways of helping

There are some general ways of helping people to access and explore their feelings and start to change or control them:

*   Getting them to be concrete and focus on the detail when they describe incidents or conversations.
*   Encouraging them to do things in the sessions which enable them to experience and explore their feelings directly – not to just *talk* about feelings but to explore them actively, using some of the methods outlined below.
*   Encouraging them to accept responsibility for their own behaviour and their own feelings. This enables them to stop denying their feelings, or displacing their emotions, or blaming other people.
*   Encouraging and teaching them to hold a compassionate view of themselves.

Specific Techniques to Help People Change their Feelings

In this section, we turn from general ways of helping to look at five kinds of specific techniques (see table 9.1).

Table 9.1 Techniques for working with feelings

Enabling clients to talk differently	Enabling clients to behave differently	Working with images	Working with bodily sensations	Developing mindfulness
• Focusing on the here and now • Avoiding 'whys' • Owning feelings • Taking responsibility • Saying 'won't' not 'can't'	• Writing feelings down • Using the 'empty chair' • Sculpting and other psychodrama techniques • Amplification • Reversals • Rehearsal	• Using dreams and imagery • Working with imagery and artwork	• Focusing on the body	• Present-moment awareness • Befriending emotions

This is not an exhaustive list of all techniques for working with feelings. Techniques referred to in other chapters are also relevant, such as assertiveness or anger management in chapter 7 (on changing people's behaviour) and others discussed in chapters 10 (on the body) and 11 (on the unconscious). Also, developing 'compassionate mind', a relatively new approach, and techniques arising from this, would also be relevant.

Working with feelings by enabling clients to talk differently

Focusing on the here and now

We need to enable our clients to focus upon what is currently happening, as opposed to focusing on the past or the future. (This approach is often associated with the work of Eugene Gendlin, who talks about this as *experiential focusing*.) When we talk about past feelings, they are distorted through selective perception and selective remembering. Clients often recall experiences as catastrophic (fitting in with their view of themselves as failures or unworthy in some way) or exceptionally pleasant (which are felt to be more appropriate for us to hear). Similarly, statements about feelings which the client hopes to experience in the future will also be distorted. Rarely are the fantasies or worries a person has about future feelings realised exactly.

For example, **Karen**, a playschool teacher, was always worrying about terrible things happening in the future – the school burning down or she being blamed when children hurt themselves. She was over-whelmed and unable to focus on what she was doing and feeling in the present. Her counsellor kept bringing Karen back to her feelings at the current time and in the current place. Slowly Karen was able to connect with her actual feelings of anger at being overburdened with too many tasks and difficult toddlers to manage, without any back-up. Karen learned how to express these feelings and needs, assertively and appropriately, to the head teacher.

Avoiding 'whys'
This method concerns the way we deal with the 'why' questions which a client often asks, such as 'Why do I get so angry with myself?' or 'Why do I feel so depressed?'

Almost all 'why' questions of this type lead us to answer with 'because . . .', so that dealing with feelings becomes intellectualised and prevents connection with feelings.

To avoid this, we do two things:

• We focus upon the *what* and *how* of behaviour. If the client is encour-aged to be aware of what they are doing and how they do it, then they are in a good position to make wise choices about whether they are going to continue to do it.
• We encourage the client to make statements rather than ask ques-tions. For example, instead of saying 'Why am I still so angry with my son?' we encourage the client to answer with a statement like 'I am still angry with my son because I have asked him twice to do something and he has still not done it!' This encourages clients to take responsibility and develop awareness.

Owning feelings
Clients often have difficulty in 'owning' their own feelings: they treat their feelings as if they were not a part of themselves. Essentially, this relates to language, so we ask the client to stop talking about 'it' and to start saying 'I'. For example, instead of saying 'My hand is trembling', we encourage the client to say 'I am trembling'; to say 'I am hurting' instead of 'It hurts'.

Our aim is to encourage clients to connect with their feelings in a com-passionate way, and to take responsibility for those feelings and their connection with their bodies. In so doing, we enable them to become aware of how their feelings relate to the way in which they think about themselves and to what they do. In other words, we seek to ensure that they *own* their feelings.

Taking responsibility

We encourage clients to accept full responsibility for their feelings. So instead of saying that other people make them feel or act in a particular way, or projecting their feelings onto other people ('He made me angry', 'You are making me nervous') we encourage the client to accept their thoughts, feelings and actions as part of themselves. They speak as much as possible using 'I'. Statements which begin with 'I want', 'I feel' or 'I see' express what is happening and suggest that the client is willing to own these experiences.

This sounds straightforward, but many people find it difficult. For example, Joe is finding his work stressful and has difficulty accessing his feelings and taking responsibility for them. He said: 'We all know that my kind of work is demanding and stressful.' We need to encourage him to take responsibility for this feeling and to rephrase it in the first person, so that he says: 'I feel the work I am doing is stressful to me.'

Clients often blame other people or a previous experience or a poor decision. As long as they attribute responsibility for their feelings or behaviour to another person or thing ('It's just the stress of the job' or 'It's because of his temper'), they remain powerless to change their situation – they give their power to this other person or thing. We need to help the client to understand this principle, so that they learn to do their own work and accept responsibility for their own lives and actions. Through rephrasing, Joe is encouraged to see his feelings and reactions as *his* and therefore to see them as something he can work on.

Saying 'won't', not 'can't'

Another language technique is to encourage clients to stop saying 'can't' and replace it with 'won't'. For example, Rhiannon often reacts to her counsellor's suggestions by saying 'But I can't say that to my mother' (even though Rhiannon is 36 and has a lot she wants to say to her mother). Her counsellor challenges her to accept responsibility for her choice by saying 'I won't say that to my mother' (or even 'I could say that to my mother, but I choose not to'). This is a small but powerful technique; it stops clients feeling helpless and enables them to see that they have choices.

Working with feelings by enabling clients to behave differently

Another set of techniques involves getting clients to *do* things: often doing something, as opposed to simply talking about it, can facilitate clients' experience of feelings. Obviously, we need to use these techniques sensitively: they are not party games!

In each of the methods outlined below, we need to focus upon what our client is experiencing and describe it as accurately as possible. These descriptions enable our clients to become aware of their feelings and their relevance and meaning.

Writing feelings down

We routinely recommend clients to keep a journal or diary to record their feelings and monitor which skills and techniques they find useful. We have suggested using diaries in other chapters, and the format is the same, although here of course we are focusing on writing down feelings and not behaviours.

Using the 'empty chair'

This is a valuable and flexible technique for helping people to say what they feel. It can help a client to recognise and accept their feelings, to deal with inappropriate feelings and to take responsibility for these feelings.

- *Expressing an emotion*: the 'empty chair' is used is when our client needs to express some emotion to a person who is not present. For example, a client felt that she could not talk directly to her husband about her feelings about his sexual demands so we suggested that she could talk to the empty chair as if it were him. As she started to give voice to her feelings about this for the first time, she began to feel that maybe she could manage to have that conversation with him in reality. In a further development she began to occupy her husband's empty chair and to talk back to herself. The conversation soon switched from sexuality to matters concerning the degree of intimacy between them across a variety of features of their marriage. This enabled her to see what was happening to her and her marriage, and how she was letting it happen. It also showed her the way in which her own behaviour towards her husband supported her husband's behaviour towards her.
- *Dealing with inner conflict*: another way of using the empty chair technique is to conduct a conflicting inner dialogue. Frequently occurring conflicting thoughts include:
  - 'It's wrong even to think about . . . but I can see myself doing . . . – I feel really confused.'
  - 'I should feel . . . but I feel something else: isn't that awful?'

○ 'Everyone expects me to . . . but I feel like I want to . . . and then
   I end up shouting at . . .'
○ 'Part of me wants to do this and part of me doesn't.'
These inner dialogues can give rise to feelings including anxiety, guilt
and self-doubt; they may also indicate the extent to which the client
has intellectualised their own feelings. We ask the client to hold a
conversation between these two parts of themselves, one of which
will occupy the empty chair. This can help to clarify and ease feelings of anxiety, guilt and self-doubt.

- *Making difficult choices*: a further variation of the empty chair
  technique is when the counsellor occupies the empty chair, and has
  a dialogue with the client. For example, 17-year-old Stella was
  trying to make a critical choice about her career. Her father, mother
  and two of her teachers were pushing her towards four different career
  choices. We used a chair for each of these four people and Stella developed an argument with each in turn. The result was that Stella chose
  a quite different career path. It brought out Stella's need to make up
  her own mind in a way that was respectful of the other people. It
  enhanced her own awareness of herself while at the same time
  strengthening her feeling that she had to accept responsibility for
  herself and her choices.

Sculpting and other psychodrama techniques

Psychodrama is a powerful way for clients to understand predicaments
in relationships and explore new roles and relationships. This is done
by acting out a particular role or situation in their life, often from
a range of perspectives. This can be done in a group setting or in individual, couple or family counselling.

Sculpting is one especially useful tool within psychodrama. Here, the
client places people (or objects such as chairs, buttons or pebbles) into
a symbolic arrangement with the aim of clarifying their feelings about
the arrangement. All sculpting processes start non-verbally by creating
or exploring a pattern in space, with the option then to change the
pattern, and, at the end, to talk about the pattern and how it has been
changed. The sculpt can be dramatised by the client giving voice to
different parts of the sculpt, or by other members of the group or the
family taking the roles.

Sculpts can be thematic. For example, as part of a family counselling
session, the client might get family members to adopt postures which
the client feels are representative of how they are and the roles they take
in the family. Alternatively, sculpts can be without any specific theme:

the client makes a pattern and then speaks of what the arrangement shows them.

Amplification
This is a particularly useful technique when our client thinks they recognise a feeling, such as anger or guilt or excitement, but is unable to assess how strong this feeling is, or how it is influencing their thoughts and actions. We can encourage understanding by asking the client to amplify those feelings. For example, when a client says that she is angry with her husband, we might encourage her to amplify her feelings in the session – shouting and getting angry, throwing cushions at her husband (or at an empty chair), formulating the most expressive statement of her feeling that she can. This enables her to recognise the difference between her actual feeling and the extreme of that feeling, and to develop the skill of being accurate in her assessment of the level and nature of her own feeling.

Amplification serves another purpose: by acting out and dramatising their feelings a client can see and hear their own feelings as if it were a video of their inner self and can more directly own these feelings.

The expression of feelings concerns gestures and expressions too. In order to direct the client's attention to the link between what they feel, say and do, we can identify a body movement (such as wringing hands), a posture (such as crossing arms) or a phrase the client uses (such as 'I've got to') and ask the client to amplify these features and describe what this felt like.

A third use of amplification is when a client glosses over something said with feeling which appears significant to us. We ask them to repeat it several times with increasing emphasis. This enables the client to recognise the extent to which the phrase has meaning for them, while giving them space to explore how comfortable they feel with different levels of its meaning.

All these examples have a similar purpose: to enable the client to recognise the level of their own feelings, and the interaction between these feelings and their thoughts and actions.

Reversals
This technique involves asking the client to act out the feelings they want to feel. It can be useful in a number of ways.

- *When the client is unable to express or experience feelings*, for example, 'I ought to be angry/happy about what this is doing to me, but I can't be'. We ask the client to act out the feelings they think they should feel (e.g. anger or happiness) as convincingly as they can. We then discuss the impact this had and ask them to identify the blocks to feeling, thinking and behaving.

- *Where we are seeking to help a person to manage overwhelming feelings* or *where they feel out of touch with their feelings*. We ask our client to redirect their feelings in an 'as if' situation. For example, Kelly often felt overwhelmed by her anger towards her manager. She was asked to imagine herself feeling calmer and act as if these were the feelings she now held. This technique can help to de-escalate overwhelming feelings.

- *Where we are seeking to help a client to develop feelings and behaviour which are the opposite of their usual role.* For example, Brian was always inappropriately subservient and obsequious. He was asked to act aggressively and belligerently towards his counsellor whenever he felt that the counsellor was not responding to him or responding inappropriately. After a few sessions using this instruction, Brian was able to own and recognise this other part of himself. He began to learn how to express himself assertively to his counsellor, and then to behave more assertively with people in authority, which was the problem he had in the first place.

Rehearsal

Many of the techniques outlined above relate to the idea of rehearsal – providing clients with the opportunity to experience what it feels like to be in a situation before it happens, and to practise and imagine being in the situation with the desired feelings. In the context of working primarily with feelings, the idea is to minimise the use of behaviour routines and to encourage spontaneity. Rehearsal of feelings can be particularly useful in managing overwhelming anxieties about, for example, a forthcoming event such as a job interview or a confrontational conversation.

Working with images

Using dreams and imagery

This technique can be utilised for people who need to access their emotions, and for those who need help in dealing with them. Because it is gentle and unthreatening, it is particularly useful with individuals who are 'out of touch' with their feelings.

This is not about interpreting dreams but enabling the client to relive their dream in a way that illuminates and connects with feelings. Dreams allow people to access thoughts and feelings which they may not be able to access consciously. By re-living the dream and acting it out in consciousness, the client is able to get in touch with or examine their feelings more directly. This is possible because our working assumption (shared, of course, with the client) is that the people and situations we dream about are in fact aspects of ourselves and our own feelings. Here is an example of working with dreams.

> **Anna** is married and has a small child. In her dream she saw her family, her close friend and her mother walking in open country in which there was just one tree. In the distance she saw a hurricane approaching. She tried to persuade her family, friend and mother to run to the tree and hold on tight. At first no one would listen to her. Then everyone saw the hurricane and started to run for the tree. Her friend and mother fell down and the child found it difficult to get hold of the tree. Anna tied the child to the tree and went back for her mother and friend. By the time Anna had secured them both to the tree, the wind was so strong that Anna was blown away.

Anna's interpretation of her dream was that she was so busy rescuing other people from the difficulties of life that she had little time for herself. She discovered through re-enacting the dream that she had to attend to her own needs now if she was going to be 'saved' from the weariness she felt from looking after others who didn't listen to her.

We can work through dreams by asking the client to act them out in detail or by exploring each scenario and person in active imagination. The results often provide a powerful basis for revealing inner feelings. In the example, the use of the re-enacted dream made a substantial difference to Anna.

Working with imagery and artwork
By exploring and changing images, we can affect every aspect of ourselves powerfully, as the following example illustrates.

> **Daniel** is a highly successful lawyer who lives for his work. He has recently separated from his wife. After long hours at work he tends to drink excessively, and has 'no time for feelings'. He is, however, having difficulties controlling his frustration and temper with his children and his secretary, which is often uncalled for. Daniel denies that this is a problem, but wants to see how he can control himself better.

At first Daniel found difficulty putting his feelings into words and was highly sceptical of the benefits of counselling. However Daniel was asked for images of himself in the situation when he looses his temper and to create an image of how he would like to be instead. Daniel's image of himself loosing his temper was of a taut piece of fuse wire, ready to snap. He was asked to draw this. It helped Daniel to connect in a non-threatening way with his anger and hurt, and his fear of these feelings. Working with this image and the image he drew of how he would like to be (a free-flowing stream) helped Daniel to connect with his feelings and emotions in a creative and healing way. He also recognised a view of himself which he had not been aware of and had not been able to talk about.

Working with 'felt experience' and bodily sensations

Focusing on the body

Here the idea, again associated with the work of Eugene Gendlin, is to work with a person's bodily sensations or 'felt sense' as a way of connecting with their inner feelings and experience. For example, Natalie was talking with her counsellor Sarajane about the sexual abuse she had experienced. Natalie was talking about her feelings in a very detached way, as if she were talking about someone else. She was also holding her arms very tightly across her tummy. Sarajane asked Natalie what was going on in her body and whether she could get a sense of *where* in her body these feelings were.

> SARAJANE: Natalie, just take a moment to relax . . . now, pay attention inwardly, to your body . . . perhaps in your tummy? . . . see what comes there when you ask, 'What is my main feeling now when I think of that experience?' Can you just get a sense of those feelings in your body . . . ?
>
> NATALIE: Yes . . . it's kind of like a tight ball . . . like something that's heavy . . . hard to put into words . . .
>
> SARAJANE: So that something is like a tight ball – what does that feel like to you?
>
> NATALIE: Um . . . heavy and . . . stuck.
>
> SARAJANE: Natalie, just ask yourself what it is about the whole problem that makes it a heavy and stuck place . . . see what comes . . .
>
> NATALIE: It's moving . . . it's changing. . . .

This brief scenario illustrates how using this approach enables Natalie to move from discussing her feelings in a detached way (and feeling detached from them), to a sense of connection with those feelings, via her body, with a resultant felt shift in her feelings.

Developing mindfulness

Further techniques related to feelings are part of a growing area in psychology and counselling named *mindfulness*. These techniques have often developed from meditation, where the aim is to focus within oneself, and to remain *present* in oneself and not be distracted by external things. Two of these mindfulness techniques follow.

Present-moment awareness

Cultivating a present-moment awareness is a way of enabling a person to stand back from the situation that has triggered unpleasant feelings and begin to take stock from a centred or meditative perspective within them. Developing such a present-moment awareness also helps a person to stay present. This approach is particularly useful when working with inappropriate or overwhelming feelings.

Befriending emotions

This is a meditative approach to feelings in which we encourage the client to allow their feelings to be 'just as they are'. By not getting caught up in judging their feelings and just letting them *be*, they can begin to experience their emotions directly. Giving emotions their own space allows them to be experienced and hence worked with.

The Application of Working with Feelings

When to work with feelings

Work with feelings is particularly recommended when either the experience or the expression of feelings is difficult or blocked, or is unhelpful or inappropriate, and where we feel that, unless we work with a person's feelings, they will be unable to move on.

Such work can be particularly useful where a client:

- has experienced abuse, other trauma, or grief and loss;
- needs to express their feelings about themselves, another person or a situation;
- needs to explore their depression;
- needs to understand and express conflicts better, such as those within relationships;
- needs help to cope with complex difficulties such as compulsive gambling, alcohol and drug problems and eating difficulties.

It can also be useful in the initial stages of developing a counselling relationship when we assess that the client finds talking about feelings easy: working with clients in their preferred way can be useful as a starting point.

However, whether we work with feelings (as opposed to thoughts or behaviour) depends on a number of factors, such as a person's interest in and readiness to work with their feelings, the amount of support they have, their vulnerability and their capacity to work with feelings.

When not to work with feelings

While it is always important to acknowledge feelings in a helping relationship, there are situations where working primarily with feelings is not indicated. The following are instances where working with feelings is inappropriate:

- *When a client has a tendency to be overwhelmed, taken over or threatened by their feelings*, which leads to their being unable to access any of their other functions such as thinking or action. This is particularly important when the client does not have supportive relationships in their life. On such occasions it may be more effective to help our client focus on their thinking or on what actions they can take instead. For example, Leslie, an isolated mother of two, had sought help following years of violence from her husband. She was overwhelmed by anger and shame, experiencing nightmares and unable to function in her job or look after her children. While still acknowledging Leslie's feelings, we worked with her to think through what steps she could take to feel better about herself and manage her day-to-day life.
- *When a client uses discussions about feelings as a way of avoiding doing anything, or thinking about alternatives.* It became apparent when working over a number of sessions with Roger, who was depressed, that he was using the helping relationship to unload his feelings session after session, but was not processing them or wanting to move on. We made that observation explicit in the session, and encouraged Roger to think through what he could *do* differently.
- *During the first session*, particularly if a new client seems threatened or is unaccustomed to talking about or expressing their feelings. The point is about timing and the need for the counsellor to assess when to work with feelings as the focus for helping.

- *If the client's normal style of relating is through thinking or doing,* working with feelings may not be an effective way of working, at least initially.

PRACTICAL EXERCISES

Keep a journal

A good exercise to help with developing your awareness of and capacity to identify feelings is to keep a personal journal or log over a month which focuses on your own feelings. This is particularly useful to link our feelings with the situations or experiences that may have also triggered unhelpful thoughts and actions. It also helps to separate thoughts from feelings, which can be a common confusion initially. Alternatively, you could just keep a log of your feelings over the course of each day, and see what feelings arise and what triggers them.

Make feelings explicit

A good way to help develop and express feelings is to take a recent emotional experience of your own. Break it down into all the specific feelings which might have been involved. Each feeling will be positive or negative, have an attitude or belief behind it, cause a bodily reaction, express a psychological state in energy and image, and have a specific object, event or action as a focus. Some of the causes of your emotions and feelings will come from the present and may arise from past issues or experiences. Include both.

When you have done this, write down the most helpful or appropriate expression for each feeling. Feelings motivate actions.

Step back, explore and develop different feelings

Write down your feelings spontaneously on paper. Read them out and ask, 'What is the feeling behind what is happening to me? What is *under* the feeling?' (e.g. self pity). 'What might be the belief that underlies my feelings?' (e.g. if the feeling is 'being upset', the underlying belief may be 'I should not cry in public').

Ask yourself what feelings you would like to develop instead, and what strengths and qualities you possess which you might use to change these feelings. Write down both the feelings you would like to have, and the qualities you could use to help you change. Imagine yourself experiencing these new feelings. How would you be thinking if you felt like this? What would you be doing differently?

Express feelings directly

Express your feelings, even if it comes out without finesse, and express yourself in the first person: 'I feel awful/stupid', and so on.

If you keep expressing your feelings, it will become easier to do so. If you cannot come up with a direct feeling, then see if you can come up with an image of how you feel, such as:

- 'I feel like a chewed up piece of meat which has been spat out.'
- 'How does a chewed up piece of meat feel, I wonder.'
- 'Awful, good for nothing, rejected.'

The more you practice this, the easier it will become to express how you feel. You may want to draw the image too.

Imagery and visualisation

Allow an image to emerge of your current feelings. Imagine that this image leaves your body/mind and is opposite you, perhaps in an empty chair. How do you feel in its presence now that it is outside of you? Talk about your current feelings to this image, saying all the things you feel, including, for example, rage, fear, abandonment or whatever comes up.

Switch places and become that feeling, and feel what it feels like. Look back at yourself now that the feeling is no longer inside of you. How does yourself look? Respond to what yourself said, keeping the conversation going honestly. Continue with this conversation until you really acknowledge what each part of you needs; and can forgive or let go of whatever conflicting or difficult feelings you are holding. This may take more than one conversation. You may find it helpful to draw any images that arise.

Now that this feeling is outside of you, what other feelings have taken its place? Do the same thing with each of those feelings in turn – develop an image of that feeling, take it outside of you and talk to it.

Developing a compassionate image

Allow an image to emerge that represents something compassionate for you. It may be a person, object, place. Get a sense of this and when you feel this visualise any difficult feelings you have being dissolved or transformed by this compassionate image. This may take practice. Again you might find it helpful to draw your compassionate image.

SUMMARY

This chapter has covered:

- A brief outline of the approach of working with feelings and three underlying principles:
  - The way we feel (and hence think) is a matter of choice.
  - Mood, thought and behaviour are inextricably linked: if we change one, the others start to change automatically.
  - Recognising and working with our uncomfortable, distressing or painful feelings allows us to change those feelings.
- Two common kinds of difficulty that people have with feelings: difficulty in recognising or accepting their feelings; and difficulty in coping with their feelings.
- A wide variety of skills and techniques which are helpful in empowering people to change their feelings.
- When not to work with feelings.
- Some practical exercises.
- As with all the other chapters in Part II, we have taken as read the importance of the collaborative counselling relationship, and of working through the processes of counselling, which we described in some detail in chapter 3. As we have reiterated throughout, these processes are fundamental, and without working through them, it is unlikely that our counselling will be effective.

10

Helping People with their Bodies

Take a moment – or a lifetime – to appreciate your body. (Dan Hillman)

The body is an important and frequently neglected focus for helping and counselling. Counsellors working with clients through their bodies and their physical symptoms can often help them to overcome their problems.

In this chapter, we start with a brief outline of some key assumptions behind this approach, and then look at how we can help people to recognise and work with the relationship between their bodies and their psychological symptoms. We then outline various techniques which help people by focusing on their bodies.

Background to Working with People's Bodies

As with other ways of working, there are some key assumptions under-lying this approach.

- There are strong relationships between people's psychological and phys-ical states which can show in different ways.
- A person's physical state can:
  - *mirror* their psychological one: someone who is depressed may talk or move slowly, for example, or someone who is anxious may look tense, fidget or perspire;

- *reveal* their psychological one: sometimes the first signs of stress come from physical problems such headaches, stomach cramps, sweating, muscle tension, aches in the neck or lower back;
- *act as a signal* for a variety of emotions: fear, anger, frustration, boredom, lethargy, depression, excitement and guilt can all be physical as well as emotional and intellectual experiences;
- be the *actual manifestation* of a psychological problem; obvious examples are problems which impact on body shape or size such as anorexia, bulimia and obesity;
- be *symbolic* of their psychological state, representative of the emotional difficulties that they are experiencing.

- Similarly, a person's psychological state can influence the development and course of their physical illnesses. Research suggests strong links between emotional distress and physical illnesses such as cancer, heart disease and arthritis.
- As counsellors, we can enable clients to recognise the link between their body states and their thoughts and feelings, and by starting to change their bodily states, change their thoughts and feelings in turn.

Our bodies are especially important in current western culture with its emphasis on body image through advertising and the media. How people look and what they think of how they look (their body image) are hugely important, and can become a focus of distress. Obvious examples of the relationship between body image and distress are anorexia, bulimia and obesity, but most people are conscious of body image – so much so that their social behaviour can be significantly affected by a negative body image. Many single people who seek partners but find relationships difficult to sustain suggest that their body image could make all the difference to their success.

How Do We Help by Focusing on People's Bodies?

 A central idea is that we need to look at the way our clients present themselves physically with the same intensity as we assess their behaviour, thoughts and feelings. People's bodies often suggest that what they say is only a part of their story.

When we counsel using the body as a focus, our major tasks are to:

- establish the meaning the client attributes to their own body images, and to their postures and movements;

- clarify the extent to which these attributions are a focus or sign of their difficulty;
- establish the purposes and likely outcomes of body-focused helping techniques before using them, especially if the client is reluctant to see their body as a means for changing the way they think and feel.

There are two main kinds of body-focused helping techniques.

- *Techniques that work with the body's signs and symptoms.* Many people do not see the relationship between their bodies and their psychological symptoms. The key is *enabling people to recognise what their bodies are telling them* – the old adage 'listen to your body'.
- *Techniques that use the body as the prime focus for helping,* through the use of activities such as relaxation, meditation, and more hands-on activities such as massage. Similarly, it can be helpful to suggest to clients that they become physically fitter and undertake exercise. Indeed, there is increasing evidence that this can be an effective way to overcome depression, as well as help with many other psychological problems.

In this chapter, we look at a number of techniques in both these categories (see table 10.1). There are also many more suggestions for further reading at the end of this book.

Other chapters in this second building block on the range of styles and approaches (see fig. 1.1) also mention the importance of working with the body during counselling. For example, chapter 7 (on changing people's behaviour) introduces relaxation as a way of dealing with fears and phobias, while chapter 9 (on working with feelings) discusses several activities which link feelings with bodily actions.

Table 10.1   Body-focused helping techniques

Working with the body's signs and symptoms	*Using the body as the prime focus*
Mirroring	Working with symptom as symbol
Reflective questioning	Relaxation training
Exaggeration	Meditation and visualisation
Biofeedback	Massage
Humanistic (Gestalt) methods	Complementary therapies
Focusing	

A *word of caution*

A word of caution at this point. First, many books about non-verbal behaviour – for example, classics like *Manwatching* and *Intimate Behaviour* by Desmond Morris – suggest that particular gestures or postures are indicative of particular emotional states; for example, sitting upright with arms folded in front of the chest suggests defensiveness. But we need to be mindful that gestures and postures are learnt and rooted in culture. So we should treat standardised interpretations with caution.

Secondly, many books about stress and anxiety strongly recommend learning relaxation techniques. We also do this. Yet several studies have shown that some people find relaxation training stressful in itself! This is also true for meditative techniques and massage. As always, we need to assess people, their problems and their needs, before launching into one way of helping rather than another.

The Body as Sign or Symptom

 Before looking at the first category of body-focused helping techniques – those that work with the body's signs and symptoms – we discuss what a client's body can show us and why.

The body as a sign of negative or positive feelings

Gary is unhappy and depressed and feels that those around him are well and energetic. He loses weight and has little energy. He feels tense, so much so that he aches in muscles he uses regularly. A nervous tick in his left eye that he had as a child has returned. He sweats more than usual and has several headaches during a typical working week. He slumps in his chair at work and home, and drinks to dull his feelings.

Gary is acutely conscious that his body and behaviour 'give the game away'; even if people do not know why he is depressed, they certainly know that he is. In this case the body is an indicator of the unhappiness and depression Gary feels.

Sonia tries to avoid her feelings altogether, in particular her depressed feelings, by exercising excessively and restricting her eating, She is painfully thin (anorexic), but thinks she is 'fat and ugly'. She also cuts herself from time to time as a way of releasing the feelings that build up inside her.

Sonia's body is a clear indicator of the distress she is experiencing inside; people around her are alarmed at her weight loss and her apparent lack of awareness of it. However, unlike Gary, Sonia is unaware that her body and behaviour give the game away about the state of her feelings and is very 'cut off'.

Our body also reflects feelings of energy and activation, or excitement and pleasure. Reaction times and alertness are better when we feel confident than when we are stressed or depressed. An excited person shows their high energy through their eyes and sometimes their speech runs away with them. Our body is an indicator of what some psychologists have called 'emotional tone' – the overriding mood of the emotions we feel at a particular moment.

The body as an indicator of change

Since moods and emotional states can change quickly, our body can be used as a sign or indicator of change. Under certain conditions of stress, for example, some individuals produce small pouches under the eye that disappear within a moment or their skin colour changes markedly. Others produce higher heart rates which dissipate quickly.

However, we all have particular consistent styles and characteristic ways of behaving. For example, some of us are morning people ('larks') while others are more active and lively in the evenings ('owls'). It is likely that biorhythms play a part here.

Other studies suggest that there is a clear group, known as Type A, whose behaviour is characterised by speed and impatience, competitiveness and hard-driving, and high levels of job involvement. This group of people are contrasted with Type B people, who take life as it comes and are moderate in their behaviour. Type A behaviour makes special demands on the heart and cardiovascular system; studies suggest that Type A people are more at risk of heart disease than Type B. This example of behaviour indicating proneness to some types of illness shows clearly how the body can be an indicator of a possible future problem.

Summary: what the body can show

These points make clear that the body can be a *sign* or *symptom*:

- of our current emotional state;
- of what we need to be attending to: warning signs to watch out, slow down or stop;
- of our overall state of well-being;
- of the extent to which our emotional state is changing during the course of a particular encounter;
- of possible future difficulties which our client might experience.

Causes of bodily signs

Psychologically related signs and symptoms can occur for a variety of reasons, including:

- difficulties in releasing psychological and physical tension;
- an unconscious attempt to repress or bury psychological conflicts or undesirable thoughts or emotions;
- the desire to receive attention through the development of physical symptoms (being physically ill often draws more emotional support than unhappiness or depression);
- the experience of intolerable levels of stress from unanticipated or uncontrollable events;
- the symbolic nature of the person's distress.

Whatever the reason, this approach to counselling takes the view that our bodies provide an external expression of psychological issues which are somehow blocked, and which then show themselves physically.

As counsellors, part of our assessment needs to focus on the reasons for the psychologically related physical problems, because the methods we use will depend upon our understanding of these causes. The five hypotheses listed above are the most frequent ones we use when we feel that a client's physical state indicates some underlying distress.

In summary, in this approach to counselling, our task is to attend to our client's body postures, actions and symptoms with these points in mind, and then to empower our client to change. The techniques outlined below are particularly useful when focusing on the body but, as mentioned earlier, empowering our clients to take exercise and get fitter can also be effective.

Techniques for working with the body's signs and symptoms

Mirroring

By using the technique of mirroring, we draw our client's attention to the way in which their body reflects their emotions. We 'play back' the client's physical posture or movements and ask them to explore what these postures or movements mean. We examine with our client the impact their body has upon their behaviour, thoughts and feelings. Often our client is unaware that their body shows others how they feel, often even more clearly than their words.

Reflective questioning

Asking questions which enable the client to reflect on links between their feelings and body can be an effective method of helping. Questions like the following can help a client to connect more deeply to their body's message:

- 'I notice that it's hard for you to maintain eye contact with me – I wonder what might be going on for you right now.'
- 'Can you get a sense of where that is happening in your body?'
- 'Can you get a sense of what [these signs or symptoms] mean for you?'
- 'Does this [sign or symptom] remind you of anything?'

Exaggeration

Exaggeration is a technique that can be used when the client shows little awareness of the link between their emotions and their body movements and postures. For example, if a person says they are depressed, we ask them to show what depression looks like without using words. They are asked to exaggerate the physical features of depression and then show the extent to which they actually feel depressed. A person who is not fully aware of their body and its language will find this activity difficult and yet rewarding. It begins to show them that they can affect their emotional state by the way they behave. Playing a video of such activity is an additional powerful way of drawing the client's attention to the link between their body and feelings.

Biofeedback

Electronic biofeedback devices provide clients with information about their physiological levels of stress and anxiety. Biofeedback devices are usually small machines which produce a sound (often a hum or a buzz) whenever there is a change in the bodily process being monitored, such as skin temperature, rate of sweating, heart rate or muscle tension. These devices are similar to machines which monitor a person's heart rate when using gym equipment.

Because heart rate, perspiration rate, respiratory rate and so on increase with anxiety and decrease with calmness, these machines provide immediate feedback to a person about their level of anxiety. By focusing on the degree of sound which the machine is making, people can change it. In effect, although people *generally* cannot control and alter at will their physiological functioning (the level of heart rate or amount of sweating), they *can* change their skin temperature or their perspiration rate by focusing on *changing the sound* associated with those bodily functions. And because these bodily functions are associated with anxiety, by reducing (say) their heart rate the client is also reducing their anxiety level.

In this way, a client can develop skills to control their level of bodily anxiety and, in so doing, reduce their anxiety levels generally. With practice, people then become able to control these bodily indices at will, even without the biofeedback.

Humanistic techniques

In previous chapters we mentioned methods of helping which are also useful when working specifically with the body. These include the techniques stemming from Gestalt psychotherapy described in chapter 9, on working with people's feelings, such as the 'empty chair' technique, or psychodrama techniques such as 'sculpting'. By physically acting out various elements, these techniques are used to help a person become aware of and to gain control over aspects of their difficulties or feelings.

These Gestalt therapy techniques are also useful for focusing awareness in the bodily here and now – something that many people (like Sonia above) find difficult, due to their disconnection from their bodies.

Focusing

Focusing is another technique (described in chapter 9, because it enables clients to become in touch with, explore and move through their feelings) which is useful in raising clients' awareness of what their bodies are saying. By using exploratory questions such as 'Where in your body do you feel this [tension/anxiety/depression, etc.]?', we ask the client to focus on their body, and on the 'felt sense' of their experiences within their body.

The Body as the Focus and Source of Presenting Problems

 The previous section has looked at our seeing the body as a *sign* of underlying psychological problems, where it provides a clue to some of our client's underlying psychological needs. But there are also a number of situations in which our client seeks help because of direct concerns about their body. These include the client who:

- has anorexia or bulimia (although they may not be concerned about this themselves but are seeking help because family or friends are concerned);
- is overweight but feels unable to lose weight;
- wishes to overcome addiction to a substance such as alcohol, minor tranquillisers, cigarettes, solvents or glue;
- has genuine physical pain and seeks psychological ways of reducing that pain;
- has an illness such as a heart problem, cancer, arthritis or a back problem.

Physical versus psychological distress

We need to distinguish between the person who presents a physical feature as a sign of a deeper psychological need and the person who, while they may have deeper psychological needs, has a significant physical problem.

While there may be a psychological component in any physical problem (either as cause or consequence), it is also important to know at what point it is most helpful to focus on the underlying problems and when to focus on the physical problem.

The first, and vital, practical step is to ensure that our clients have consulted a medical doctor about their problems. We must not get trapped into believing that there are psychological causes and cures for every ailment, even if our client is convinced that their problem is psychological. Headaches, for example, are often caused by tension, but sometimes they are caused by brain tumours.

Secondly, we and our clients both need to be fully aware of the current local medical opinion concerning the problem. For example, if a client wants to end their dependence upon minor tranquillisers prescribed by their doctor, both client and counsellor will need to collaborate with the doctor in finding the best way forward.

The third question concerns our understanding of the medical or physical phenomena with which we are dealing. Organisations concerned with helping people overcome their physical difficulties – for example, Weight Watchers, Alcoholics Anonymous, Narcotics Anonymous, support groups for self-harm – provide detailed help (although sometimes these organisations also hold a particular view of the problem, for example Alcoholics Anonymous believe that 'alcoholism' is a disease, an approach that is not supported by many other groups and organisations). We should familiarise ourselves with the materials and information from these sources and encourage clients to seek this kind of support in addition to our own.

The fourth question for counsellors to ask themselves is: 'What can I do differently and more usefully than the organisations with expertise and competence in helping people with this specific problem (for example, alcohol problems, glue-sniffing, over-dependency on minor tranquillisers, self-harm)?' In many cases the answer will be 'very little' and the task thus becomes making a sensitive referral to the appropriate agency, continuing to offer support to the client and maintaining good collaborative contact with the agency.

Finally, if we decide to help a person with physical problems, we need to ensure that we do not add to those problems. For example, if our client is reporting high levels of pain and we suggest relaxation, we need to be aware that relaxation exercises can involve tensing muscle groups which could conceivably increase the pain. As always, it is vital that counsellors (especially new ones) engage in such counselling only with appropriate supervision and training.

Issues in working with the body as a focus for helping

Before detailing ways of using the body as the prime method of helping a person, we need to address an ethical question, particularly if the work requires direct physical contact. In chapter 4 we said that the person seeking help expects us to behave ethically. Some clients will not accept physical methods of helping as ethical. Nor will they be appropriate. For example, for massage to be effective, our client may need to undress partially, and many may find this unacceptable. We therefore need to ensure that we make our intentions clear to clients and that they accept physical methods as appropriate to their needs.

Furthermore, we need to be aware that the use of methods involving high levels of physical contact, such as massage, will also raise issues about the degree of ethical risk involved. Some organisations do not encourage (indeed, forbid) their workers to engage in physical ways of helping. We cannot overemphasise the need for caution and sensitivity when we intend to make any form of physical contact with a client, as we discussed in more detail in chapter 5.

Finally we need to recognise that helping by working with the body is more acceptable in some settings and with some cultures than others.

Techniques for using the body as the prime focus

Working with 'symptom as symbol'

As we have touched on briefly above, there is a wisdom in our bodies providing us with symptoms that are often symbolic of underlying difficulties.

> **Sam** was finding it difficult to say 'no' to his boss, who was giving him an increasing burden of work. Sam got on with it resentfully, but never told his boss how he felt. He was experiencing increasing shoulder and neck pain and heart palpitations.

We focused on these symptoms together and slowly Sam made the connection between his shoulder and neck pain and the sense of responsibility and resentment that he was not expressing. (In some situations, it might be helpful to encourage Sam to see that his pains related to his having to *shoulder* more and more work, and to his boss being a *pain in the neck*.) As his counsellor, we helped Sam to learn to talk assertively with his boss, who had no idea what Sam had been feeling, and who subsequently eased Sam's workload. Sam's symptoms then disappeared.

This example shows that the symptom can also be the route to healing. We can help a client to make the link between a physical symptom and an underlying problem by asking what the symptom might mean and if there might be any link with their current difficulties.

Hence it is important to make sense of the symbolic message of the body, particularly if there is a persistent body problem. As we said earlier, often illness can be seen as a symbolic message from the body to get attention concerning some important conflict, or some state of emotional, mental or spiritual imbalance, that needs to be faced. It is often a warning sign to watch out, slow down or stop. Useful questions are, for example, 'How might the symptom(s) relate to what is happening in your life?' or 'Are there similar things happening to your attitudes, thoughts or emotions as those that are happening to your body?' These may help our client to tune in to their body's distress signal. As a counsellor, we may also want to draw particular attention to our client's language, such as 'I can't stomach that' or 'That (behaviour) is hard to swallow', as ways of understanding and providing a way into our client's emotional distress.

Relaxation training
Relaxation training can help a variety of difficulties. It is most commonly used to:

• reduce the effects of daily stress;
• overcome the physical impact of periods of high physical activity;
• deal with anxiety and phobias (as outlined in chapter 7);
• help with high blood pressure, migraine, insomnia and asthma (especially in conjunction with biofeedback, as outlined above).

Relaxation is a skill which needs a lot of practice for it to have any impact on our problems. So the key is to encourage clients to practise regularly. Initially, it can take between 30 minutes to an hour to go through the procedure of relaxation, and it usually takes days or even weeks of practice to learn the skill to the level when a client can relax at will quite quickly.

There are numerous methods of relaxation training: here, we briefly describe a method of deep muscle relaxation involving tension and relaxation which we have found to be effective. This method involves the client alternately tensing and relaxing one muscle group at a time, in a particular sequence, so that they can directly experience the difference between tension and relaxation. They do this while imagining a relaxing scene, such as lying by a riverbank on a sunny day. The client is enabled to understand the physical way in which they can relax and to develop the skill of relaxing quickly. The procedure also has an element of hypnosis or suggestion in it, where we repeatedly suggest that they are becoming less tense and more relaxed. We also emphasise that the task is to learn how to become relaxed and alert, not how to fall asleep!

We usually tape-record the first session and ask the client to take the tape home and practise once or twice a day.

Meditation and visualisation
Although there are many forms of meditation, they generally relate to one of two main styles: passive, or dynamic and active. Visualisation,

and techniques associated with this such as the use of images and guided journeys, can be used independently, or in conjunction with, either passive or active meditation.

Passive meditation   In passive meditation our client is asked go somewhere where they can be quiet and relax, so that they can focus upon one element. This may be, for example, their breathing, an idea, image, or special word or phrase – often termed a *mantra* – to which they give their full attention.

The idea is to be relaxed and to concentrate upon this element to the exclusion of all other thoughts, a process of deep concentration. The purpose is to provide a device and a cue or reminder by which the person can substitute thoughts about the mantra whenever they begin to experience stress.

Visualisation   Other forms of meditation such as guided journeys (e.g. into forests, up mountains, into the sky or to the centre of the universe where our clients encounter significant events or people) are also powerful ways of intervening and working with body.

Clearly, meditation and visualisation skills take time to develop, so it is important to encourage clients to persevere. We all have busy minds that are hard to quieten; even experienced meditators continue to have intrusive and distracting thoughts. In spite of this, the benefits can be far-reaching.

Dynamic or active meditation   In contrast, dynamic or active meditation is physically active and exhausting. One form, developed by the followers of a guru named Bhagwan Shree Rajneesh, involves sequences of physical movement accompanied by music: shaking arms, legs and bodies in a rhythmic movement, followed by dancing, then relaxation and a final phase of returning to the speed of normal life.

In the course of this activity, which lasts about an hour, the client finds that their concentration shifts from the task of performing to simply being involved in the dancing and movement to the point where they are completely in touch with their thoughts and feelings, all of which are focused upon the physical movements. It is an effective way of losing oneself in one's body and of emptying the mind of stress and anxiety. It is a meditation exercise precisely because the person loses the social self in the inner self.

The repeated use of this procedure on a daily basis for up to one month has led some clients we have worked with to claim that dynamic meditation was a kind of indoor jogging and relaxation training combined. With practice, these clients reported that they could reduce their stress by remembering the experience of dynamic meditation.

Engaging in almost any activity, however mundane, in a meditative and reflective way, can be a powerful form of active meditation; for example, focusing on the experience of walking to the exclusion of everything else or performing household chores in a reflective and meditative manner. T'ai Chi is another form of active meditation. If as counsellors we can develop some knowledge, expertise or even personal practice, we can encourage our clients to use these techniques.

In both forms of meditation we need to be mindful of the physical nature of dynamic meditation: those who are physically unwell or who have muscular or cardiovascular problems should be encouraged to choose gentler forms such as yoga, meditative walking or T'ai Chi.

There are also many more body-orientated techniques and therapies, such as yoga, which are related to meditation.

Massage

Massage is rarely used in counselling relationships since it can involve clients in undressing and intimate contact. In addition, massage has not been well researched in terms of its efficacy in reducing stress. While those who practise massage claim that it is effective in reducing stress and tension at the time of the massage, it is not clear whether massage affects stress levels afterwards. However, in cases where one is working physically with clients and their bodies, it can be a useful technique.

Again, as with relaxation and meditation, there are many different styles of massage. One method which we have found to be useful involves relaxing our client (see above) and then applying gentle but firm rhythmic pressure to the muscles of the neck, shoulders, back, hips, legs, chest and face such that the pressure tenses the muscles which then relax.

Massage can also be a valuable vehicle for a guided fantasy in which we take the client through the situations they find stressful and encourage them to imagine themselves being unstressed in the same situations. By combining massage with such a fantasy the person can be encouraged to associate non-stressful self-talk with pleasant experiences (few suggest that massage is unpleasant!), and so develop their coping repertoire.

Complementary therapies

A wide range of so-called complementary therapies can also be used in work with the body, including shiatsu, acupressure, acupuncture, reflexology, aromatherapy, Alexander technique, ayurvedic therapy, cranial sacral therapy, rolfing, focus on diet and so on. Whether or not we wish to use any of these methods, it is important to be aware of them, and to note the growing range that is now available. A number of these are based on eastern systems of health, such as Chinese or Indian medicine, using meridians and energy fields to diagnose and treat clients. Many counsellors also take courses in some of these methods, recognising the need to understand and work with the link between mind and body.

When Not to Work with the Body

As briefly discussed in the previous section, it is important to not pursue a focus on the body if a client is unwilling or unable to use this. It may be a question of timing, such as introducing bodywork too soon in the helping relationship, or it may simply not be a style of helping that a particular client can respond to. We cannot stress enough that care and sensitivity needs to be shown when working with a focus on the client's body.

There are a variety of reasons why people may not wish to focus on bodily techniques:

- In British culture people are often not comfortable with the idea of touching or of being touched (often called the British reserve).
- People from many other cultural backgrounds are uncomfortable with being touched by anyone other than their intimates.
- Bodywork of any kind can be particularly sensitive for individuals who have a history of abuse. It is therefore important to check this out carefully.
- As mentioned earlier, some people may experience relaxation training as stressful in itself.

PRACTICAL EXERCISES

Focusing

Bring to mind an important experience or event. Focus on your body, noticing any areas of tension, discomfort or unease. Just stay with the feelings and sensations you become aware of, noting where they arise in your body.

As you do this, let an image emerge that represents these sensations for you, taking note of subtle bodily reactions and changes which may be going on as you work with the image. Have crayons and paper available to draw the image(s) that arise when you are ready to do so.

When you have done this, take some time to reflect on your drawing, asking yourself, 'What might this be telling me about myself? What meaning is there for me in this?' Sometimes it is helpful to explore this with another person, particularly when you find it difficult to make any connections between body and feelings.

Linking

If you are having any persistent problems with your body you may want to ask yourself:

- How is what is happening in my body descriptive or expressive of what is happening in my life?
- When I look at what is happening to my body, under what circumstance in my life is this also being reflected in my attitudes, my thoughts or my emotions?
- What is my body telling me about what needs to happen differently in my life and what I need to do about it?

Reflect on these questions and see what thoughts, words, images and sensations arise. You may want to record this in your Learning Journal to help you with your own personal journey.

SUMMARY

This chapter has covered:

- A brief outline of the approach of working with people's bodies and its underlying principles:
  - The body is a neglected feature of counselling.
  - There is a wisdom in our body's language. It is important to become mindful of the body's language and what it might be signalling to us.
  - Anyone who seeks to help people with stress, anxiety and other forms of distress needs to accept that the body is a vehicle by which distress can be worked with and reduced.

- ○ A person's body can show signs or symptoms of the difficulties they experience; their bodies can be the focus of their presenting problems.
- *A wide variety of skills and techniques* are helpful in working with people through their bodies and how they present themselves, including mirroring, reflective questioning, exaggeration, using biofeedback devices, relaxation training, meditation, visualisation, massage and other physical activities, and complementary activities. These can reduce distress in the short and long term.
- Those of us wishing to use these methods should be encouraged to develop our skills and abilities, provided we are mindful of the ethical issues they can give rise to.
- When not to work with feelings.
- Some practical exercises.
- As with all the chapters on these different approaches in Part II of this book, we have focused here on the techniques we can use to help our clients change what they do. *How* we introduce and help our clients to utilise these techniques is also vital: the core skills of developing a collaborative counselling relationship, and understanding and using the core processes of counselling, which we described in chapter 3 have to be at the heart of everything we do if we want to be effective as counsellors.

11

Helping People with their Unconscious Processes

Man's task is to become conscious of the contents that press upwards from the unconscious. (Jung)

This chapter will focus how we can help people by working with their unconscious processes. The obvious point about unconscious processes is that they are . . . unconscious! But although people are unaware that these unconscious processes are at work, they may be the cause of many difficulties, especially within personal, social and work relationships.

These unconscious processes have a major impact on how we behave, think and feel. An important task, and a particular focus within some areas of counselling, is helping people to become aware of and to understand their inner unconscious life, so that they can begin to exert some control over it.

In this chapter, we first give an outline of the background to this approach and what counsellors and psychologists mean by *unconscious processes*. We then look at some of the common problems with the unconscious, and some key skills and techniques which we as counsellors can use to help people to recognize and change these processes.

Background to Helping People with their Unconscious Processes

Although the term *unconscious* had been in use for a long time, the particular meaning associated with counselling and psychotherapy began with the work of Sigmund Freud, who towered over this field between the late 1890s until his death in 1939, and those who initially worked with him and later developed alternative theories based on the same ideas (Jung, Adler, Klein, and many more). The therapeutic side of their work became termed *psychoanalysis*.

Psychoanalytic theory is hugely complex and beyond the scope of an introductory book. However, the following are the key ideas that psychoanalysts believe.

- As well as the thoughts and feelings we are aware of, which influence our behaviour and which we deal with on a day-to-day basis, there are also thoughts and feelings which are unconscious. They influence what we do and how we do it, but we are not aware of them or of how they influence us.
- These unconscious processes are usually laid down in childhood and are often related to our selfish childhood wants and needs. As we grow up they are overlaid with conscious processes which are more related to living in a social world. But these early processes do not go away – they simply slip into the unconscious.
- These unconscious thoughts and feelings are often in conflict with our conscious ones, leading us to act in ways that seem to be irrational, even to us sometimes.
- If they can be brought into consciousness, we can work with them with our conscious mind and hence resolve the conflicts, or at least control them.

Freud referred to the unconscious as 'mental processes or mental material which have no easy access to consciousness, but which must be inferred, discovered and translated into conscious form'. His theory suggested that aspects of ourselves which are in conflict with our consciously held beliefs or ideals may be denied or suppressed, and hence become unconscious. This, though, suggests an all-or-none quality to the unconscious, but in fact most theorists now believe that we are not completely unconscious of some things but are aware of them on the periphery.

The impact of the unconscious on our thoughts, feelings and behaviour

As counsellors we need to be aware of the impact of the unconscious on behaviour, thoughts and feelings, an impact that can cause repeated problems or conflicts for our clients. These can often lead to repeated unhelpful or even destructive patterns of relating.

Paula, whom we met in chapter 1, had a chronic fear of rejection. She desperately wanted to be included in activities and complained that people never invited her to social events. But as we went over her life in more detail, it became clear that people did invite her but that she refused their invitations, out of a fear that she had nothing to say, that they would find her boring and therefore not want to include her any more. However, because she constantly turned down invitations, friends gave up asking her, which led to Paula feeling rejected.

As Paula's counsellor we commented on what appeared to be going on: how she was setting herself up for rejection. This was a new idea for Paula – she honestly did believe that nobody wanted her to be their friend, and she did not see how what she was doing was creating the very problem she was seeking help for. Together, we traced this unhelpful (and unconscious) pattern of behaviour over time (seeing how it related to her father deserting her, and to her early experiences of having no friends at school) and in her current life.

When working with the unconscious, we may wish just to help people to see current repeating patterns, or we may also want to link this with similar patterns from childhood. Childhood experiences, particularly with significant people such as parents, are seen to be crucial from a psychoanalytic perspective. To do this, of course, means that we need to explore childhood experiences with the client: in Paula's case, childhood experiences of rejection. This is a very different approach to others we have looked at, where our counselling is much more focused on the here and how and oriented towards the future rather than the past.

With **Paula,** she initially told us that she could recall very little from her childhood (often a sign that there are painful memories buried in the unconscious). With careful and gentle questioning, based on the development of a warm and trusting counselling relationship, a number of rejecting experiences at home and school emerged. As mentioned, her father had left the family home for another woman when she was 2 years old. At school she had been shunned from group playground activities and by her 'best friend'. These were memories that Paula had largely forgotten, but which she started to recall during our sessions.

We can see how these experiences can make someone like Paula vulnerable to feeling bad and rejected; and how similar experiences in her adult life may trigger memories of these painful events which are stored in the unconscious. Sensitively enabling clients to bring these experiences into their consciousness can help them to understand their patterns of thinking, feeling and behaviour, and to find alternative, more helpful, ways of relating.

> In **Paula's** case, she had a clearer understanding of why she was vulnerable to interpreting other people's behaviour as rejecting, or setting up events in such a way that she got others to 'reject' her. The awareness of this unhelpful pattern gave Paula the choice to begin to relate in a different way which did not end in rejection. She was able to monitor herself and learn new behaviours that meant she didn't feel excluded or rejected. Paula had to take a risk and ask if she could join her friends at an event. This was not easy and she needed a lot of support and encouragement. As her counsellor, we found that Paula was a 'visual' person, and we suggested that she use pencil and paper to draw this pattern of rejection. This helped her to understand the unhelpful pattern and to develop new ways of relating.

As well of fear of rejection, a client may experience other strong feelings such as sadness, anger or rage, and may not understand why or what is triggering them. Alternatively, a client may experience repetitive thoughts which they can't stop or remove from their mind. The unconscious can also reveal itself in other ways: apparent slips of the tongue, or 'forgetting' to do or say something. (But we need to be aware that there is always a danger of ascribing unconscious motives to chance happenings – sometimes people do just forget!)

In all these instances, tracing experiences from the past and relating them to the current situation can be helpful in developing understanding and leading the client to gain a sense of control. Eventually they are able to choose to think, feel and behave differently.

Problems with Unconscious Processes

Various types of problems relate to our unconscious. We outline three common ones here: repeated unhelpful patterns of behaviour; unconscious conflicts; and defences and resistance.

Repeated patterns of behaviour

As the example of Paula shows, the way our unconscious reveals itself is often through unhelpful patterns of behaviour which we repeat without really understanding why, or sometimes even that we do so. Our unconscious contains thoughts, feelings and conflicts which often were not resolved. They were simply placed into the unconscious, and commonly manifest themselves as these patterns of behaviour, or in our dreams, or as slips of the tongue, as mentioned earlier.

These repeating patterns frequently show themselves in people's relationships, and are often seen within the counsellor–client helping relationship. So, for example, where a client has a pattern of rejection when a relationships starts to become close, the same rejection may occur in the client's relationship with the counsellor. Hence the need to be mindful of the client's feelings, and whether they are legitimate (is it legitimate for my client to be angry with me or to seem so upset by me?) or whether the feelings are being transferred onto the counsellor who reminds the client of someone significant such as a parent. The client may be behaving towards the counsellor in ways that reflect past conflicts with a key figure. In psychoanalytic terminology, this is known as *transference*.

To use the example of Paula again, as her counsellor we became aware of her tendency to see or interpret comments or behaviour as rejection. She saw a need to rearrange an appointment which we had one week, for example, as a direct rejection of her. Her interpretation was that the very fact that we changed the appointment showed that she was not important enough, or that other commitments we had took priority over her.

When this was gently explored, and the behaviour patterns brought into awareness, Paula gained a greater understanding of her behaviour and its meaning and became less vulnerable to interpreting her counsellor's behaviour as rejection. She also became more aware of this pattern operating in other significant relationships in her life. This awareness put Paula in a more powerful position to change her own ways of responding. We will say more about this below, but as counsellors we need to be mindful of these patterns.

It is also important to realise that the same unconscious processes which our clients bring are also at work within ourselves. We need to be aware of our own feelings towards the client and how these change, as they can be useful indicators of these patterns. As counsellors, we too can transfer our unconscious feelings onto our clients, and we can react to their transference in ways which relate to how we have reacted to conflicts in our own pasts. In psychoanalytic terminology, this reacting to the transference of others is known as *counter-transference*. This underlines the importance of regular and effective supervision for all counsellors. These issues were discussed in more detail in chapter 5 under supervision and training.

Unconscious conflicts

Unconscious conflicts usually originate in personal relationships during our formative years, which become internalised and determine the sort of relationships we form. As described above, unconscious conflicts can be repeated within the helping relationship.

Such unconscious conflicts can be manifest as one side of us wanting one thing and another side wanting something else. For example, Paula was attracted to a man she met at work who asked her out for an evening. Paula felt very confused, although she was not sure why, stumblingly refused the date and subsequently avoided him. In counselling, it emerged that one part of her wanted to go but another part did not in case he rejected her. This conflict did not occur in Paula's awareness, but it did create an unconscious dilemma, which she resolved by avoiding him as a way of not having to make a decision. After she became aware of it, she was able to make a more informed choice about what she wanted and how to proceed.

Unconscious conflicts can also manifest themselves via our bodies, as symptoms, as outlined in chapter 10. So, for example, if a child complains of abdominal pain, it might be a symptom of appendicitis or it might be their way of saying 'I don't want to go to school' for some reason that cannot be admitted for fear of adult reactions, or even for unconscious reasons that cannot be expressed.

In Paula's case, it emerged that as a child she often had tummy upsets, which meant she missed school, as a way of avoiding school playground activities and her feared exclusion from games.

Other types of unconscious conflicts often arise because a person has difficulties acknowledging their aggressive or angry feelings. These feelings can be turned inwards, against the self, and manifest themselves in depression, self-harming behaviour such as self-cutting, alcohol problems or psychosomatic symptoms such as hypertension or headaches. Similarly, a bereaved person who has difficulties acknowledging feelings of grief may experience physical symptoms as a result of not expressing their grief in a way that is helpful for them. This is not to say that physical symptoms are *never* caused by physical problems, nor that if they are psychosomatic symptoms they are not *real*. The point is to be aware of the nature and timing of the symptoms in relation to what our client is telling us, and hence to see other possible meanings.

As counsellors working with people through their unconscious processes, we help to make these conflicts explicit and conscious for the client, seeking to clarify the links between the past and present.

Defences and resistance

Two other terms commonly used within psychoanalysis are *defence mechanisms* and *resistance*. These are important concepts but we rarely use these terms with clients, as they may have derogatory connotations: it is important that we never accuse a client of 'being defensive' or of 'resisting'!

Resistance is when a client is unable to acknowledge thoughts and feelings because they are afraid of what will emerge, and of their, or our, reaction. Resistance, which can be conscious or unconscious, is a psychological defence against allowing repressed or unconscious thoughts into conscious awareness. It defends the person against the unbearable upset that they unconsciously know they would feel if they allowed these thoughts and feelings into conscious awareness.

There are many forms of resistance and some are briefly described in table 11.1. A detailed examination of them is beyond the remit of this book, but is covered in the further reading suggestions at the end of the book.

Table 11.1   Some of the forms that resistance can take

Conversion and psychosomatic reactions	Internal conflicts that would give rise to anxiety are instead given symbolic external expression. The repressed issues, and the psychological defences against them, are converted into a variety of bodily symptoms. These may include paralysis, pain or loss of sensory function.
Denial	Refusal to acknowledge painful realities, thoughts or feelings: a person unconsciously rejects some or all of the meanings of an event or situation. Through denial, an individual or even a group of individuals (loved ones, friends, colleagues) avoid awareness of some painful aspect of reality (health, financial or relationship issues) in order to decrease anxiety or other unpleasant emotions such as guilt or shame. Denial is related to repression but denial is more pronounced and involves some impairment of reality. An example of denial would be someone who has had a heart attack telling themselves that eating unhealthy foods will not really affect them.

Table 11.1   (*Cont'd*)

Depersonalisation and confusion	An individual feels detached from their mental processes or body, so that they feel like an outside observer of themselves, or as if they were in a dream.
Displacement	Emotions, ideas, or wishes are transferred from their original object to a more acceptable substitute, often to allay anxiety. For example, in dreams the emotions associated with threatening impulses are often transferred elsewhere, or displaced, so that apparently trivial elements in the dream seem to cause extraordinary distress.
Projection	What is emotionally unacceptable is unconsciously rejected and attributed to (projected onto) others. An example would be projecting elements of oneself that are thought to be bad, such as weakness or homosexual desire, onto someone else 'over there', where they can be condemned, punished, etc.
Rationalisation	An individual attempts to justify feelings or behaviour that would otherwise be intolerable.
Reaction formation	The blocking of desire by its opposite. A person adopts emotions, ideas and behaviours that are the opposite of their own. For example, someone who feels homosexual desire represses that desire by turning it into hatred of homosexuals.
Regression	The partial or symbolic return to earlier patterns of reacting or thinking. This happens when normal desire cannot be satisfied. For example, when a relationship breaks up, a woman starts overeating – she regresses to the oral stage of development – in an attempt to satisfy her needs.
Repression	Thoughts such as unacceptable ideas, fantasies, emotions or impulses are shut out of consciousness. Although not subject to voluntary recall, the repressed material may emerge in disguised form.
Sublimation	Instinctive drives, consciously unacceptable, are diverted into personally and socially acceptable channels. An example is when someone responds to sexual frustration by putting all their energies into a different activity that is not sexual but social, for example sport or politics. Freud argued that this was the way civilisation has been able to prioritise social aims above sexual ones.

Our job is to assist the client in breaking down these defences, and to enable them slowly to accept the unconscious material, in a way that will minimise the pain and anxiety and lead to a successful integration of these unconscious elements into their overall awareness. This process *cannot* be hurried: we need to move at our client's pace, not ours. However, this does not prevent us from acknowledging resistance, as part of the helping process.

> **Susan** had come for help following the death of her husband. She was unable to acknowledge her feelings initially, and persisted in saying she was 'fine'. However, she wasn't sleeping, was unable to concentrate and kept forgetting things. This implied that she was defending herself from the pain that looking at her feelings would bring. As the helping relationship developed, her defensiveness lessened, she became less resistant and she was able to talk about how sad and angry she felt. She also shared an abusive experience that she had been through and had felt ashamed of admitting.

By bringing the resistance itself into awareness, we can help a person to recover the buried or repressed content.

Resistance has to be handled by understanding the reasons for such defensiveness. Only the client can withdraw the resistance, although a sensitive and skilled helper tries to assist the client to understand the reasons for resistance. Working through resistance takes time and the development of a trusting relationship, so short-term work with unconscious processes is usually less effective.

Skills and Techniques for Using Unconscious Processes

There are a variety of methods and techniques which psychoanalysis has developed over the years for working with the unconscious. Some of the best known are:

- *Exploration and questioning*: asking questions, including asking our client to say whatever it is that is on their mind.
- *Clarification*: rephrasing and summarizing what our client has been describing.
- *Confrontation*: bringing resistance or a defence mechanism to our client's attention.

- *Interpretation*, of which there are a number of types, for example, explaining:
  - ○ that being 'too nice' guards against guilt for ever saying upsetting things;
  - ○ how a past event is influencing the present, or how our client is resisting and avoiding their problems;
  - ○ how transference is occurring – how old conflicts are arising in current relationships, including that with the counsellor.
- *Dream interpretation*: obtaining our client's thoughts about their dreams and connecting this with their current problems.
- *Reconstruction*: suggesting what may have happened in the past that may have helped to create a current difficulty.

We will now look at some of these in more detail.

The helping relationship

The helping relationship itself is the most important tool when working with the unconscious. As counsellors we need to be mindful of our relationship with the client, and what both it and we represent to them. We also need to be mindful, as we saw earlier, of our thoughts and feelings towards clients and how they change both within a session and over the course of the helping relationship itself. Supervision is crucial in developing our awareness and understanding of these issues, and in helping us to work effectively with them.

For example, as Paula's counsellor we felt irritation and anger towards Paula at times, because she continually avoided acting on things she said she might do. Through supervision it became clear that some of these feelings were to do with Paula: her unconscious feelings of anger and anxiety, which she was unable to express directly, but which she transferred to us, her counsellor. But it also became clear that our irritation as her counsellor was also related to our own feelings about what Paula represented to us and how unconsciously she reminded us of other, similarly irritating, people in our past lives. Making these conscious by discussing them within supervision enabled us to stop experiencing these feelings in the same way.

Acknowledgement of issues arising within the helping relationship

Explicitly acknowledging issues is a way of *making the unconscious conscious*. It requires counsellors to watch for how clients present themselves, to see if they repeatedly demonstrate a difficulty in expressing uncomfortable or conflicting feelings and if so, to bring them to conscious awareness. We need to be mindful of a client's repeated patterns of thinking, feeling and behaving, in order to make them explicit, acknowledge them and work with them, as we did with Paula.

Additionally, tracing these unhelpful patterns of behaviour onto a diagram, as we did with Paula, can be a powerful way of aiding and increasing understanding of the unconscious patterns. Clients can also use the diagram visually to look for ways out, exits or alternative ways of feeling, thinking or behaving. This in turn means that we can help a person to take more control of their lives.

Difficulties, conflicts or feelings often arise within the counselling relationship which mirrors a client's experiences with outside relationships. Again, it is vital to acknowledge these explicitly, and to work though them, thereby enabling our client to see that these are the same patterns of relating and reacting which they have come to discuss in the first place.

Dreams

Dreams were seen by Freud as 'the royal road to the unconscious'. Psychoanalysts believe that dreams always have meaning, and that the content is derived from our unconscious experience, thoughts and feelings. Dreams serve many functions, and working with dreams is a very skilled technique, well beyond the remit of this book. In brief, however, some of the functions of dreams may include wish fulfilment (e.g. dreams of a lost person whom we long to see again), attempts to master unpleasant experiences or to solve problems, or serving as a prophecy or warning.

Although psychoanalysts do interpret dreams (after some years of training), we suggest that, in counselling through using people's unconscious processes, we should *not* seek to interpret our clients' dreams. Instead we should try to help our client to understand the meaning of their dream in their own way, with our help and via our facilitative questioning.

Free association

As with so many techniques in psychoanalysis, the use of free association also has its origins in the work of Freud. The idea again is simple: the client is encouraged to talk about whatever is in their mind, however trivial, irrational or disturbing it may seem. The rationale is that when people say out loud whatever comes into their minds, this material comes from somewhere. Freud and others believed that, initially, what is said comes from our conscious brain, where thoughts, feelings and speech are all censored by our conscious minds. But if we just *talk*, continuing to free associate so that whatever is said next is simply triggered by what was said previously, unconscious elements creep in and patterns emerge which are determined by our unconscious minds. We can also facilitate this free association by asking questions, such as 'What does . . . mean to you'?

In this way, we can help our client to get in touch with experiences that may be outside or on the periphery of their conscious awareness. Once we had worked with Paula for long enough to develop a very trusting relationship, Paula was asked what 'rejection' meant to her, and just to follow where her answer led, saying whatever came into her head. When she did this she was able to get in touch with other forgotten experiences that had left her feeling abandoned and therefore 'no good'. In turn this deepened her understanding of herself and why she was behaving in the way she did.

Keeping a journal and writing whatever comes into our minds for a specific amount of time on a daily basis can also be an effective tool of free association.

When Not to Work through Unconscious Processes

There are a number of key points we would like to stress here.

- As we have said throughout the chapter, any work with unconscious processes needs careful supervision and should not be undertaken unless close supervision is in place.
- Most psychotherapists and psychoanalysts who work with unconscious processes will have been taught to assess whether a client would benefit from this type of approach. For example:

Paul had been feeling depressed since his wife left him for someone else. He just 'wanted the feelings to go away'. He did not want to understand the underlying reasons for his depression. Throughout counselling, he could see no connection between his feelings about his wife, losing his job, or his mother's death when he was a child, nor did he want to see any connections. When someone responds in this way, it is clear that this approach will be unhelpful. Work with Paul therefore took a here-and-now approach that focused on what he could do on an immediate basis (chapter 6), how he was thinking about things (chapter 8) and tactics to 'get Paul through', rather than one that focused on unconscious processes that might have been contributing to his depression.

- It will often be unhelpful to attempt to work with the unconscious at the beginning of a helping relationship, particularly before we have established a good working relationship. Raising these issues may also make a client feel defensive, because they feel threatened by someone working too deeply too soon. This brings us back to an earlier point about the importance of timing when working with the unconscious. To give an example:

Rosie came for help with her panic attacks. Initially she was unable to see any connection between the onset of her panic attack and her husband's affair. As she felt safer and less threatened within the helping relationship, these connections began to make sense to her.

Because working with the unconscious is theoretically and practically complex, we suggest even more so than with the other approaches, that counsellors who wish to use these methods should:

- read much more about it (working with the unconscious is a vast area with a large body of theoretical approaches, psychodynamic history and tradition);
- undertake specific training;
- ensure access to regular and skilled supervision, from a supervisor who uses and understands how to work with the unconscious themselves.

PRACTICAL EXERCISES

Free association

Make yourself comfortable and ensure you will be free from interruptions. Let your mind wander over something that is concerning you and start to talk out loud about it, trying to allow whatever comes into your head to come out, but at the same time trying to listen to yourself to see what thoughts and images arise.

If this is too difficult, do it again but with a tape recorder running: let your mind relax and *just talk* wherever your thoughts lead you. Later, go back and listen carefully to the tape recording to see what thoughts and images arose.

Dreams

Keep a notebook next to the bed, and as soon as you awake, even if it is in the middle of the night, immediately write down as much as you can about whatever dreams you can recall.

Record these dreams for a week to see if there are any themes. In particular, look for any repeating patterns. Do these dreams or patterns signify anything for you?

Defences

In your Learning Journal, spend a week seeing if you can identify any of the defences outlined in table 11.1, either in yourself or in others whom you encounter.

SUMMARY

This chapter has covered:

- A brief outline of what it means to use unconscious elements and some of the underlying ideas:
    - There is a large range of thoughts and feelings about which we are unconscious, which influence what we do and how we do it.
    - These unconscious processes are usually laid down in early childhood.
    - Conscious and unconscious processes are often in conflict, leading us to act in ways that seem to be irrational.
    - If unconscious elements can be brought into consciousness, we can deal with and resolve (or at least control) the conflicts.
- Some problems related to people's unconscious processes, including repeated unhelpful patterns of behaviour, unconscious conflicts, and defences and resistance.
- Skills and techniques for working with the unconscious, including the use of the helping relationship; explicitly acknowledging issues, working with repeating patterns, and using difficulties, conflicts or feelings that arise within the helping relationship; dreams; and the use of free association.

- The importance of the collaborative counselling relationship in working with the unconscious. In all the chapters on the different approaches in Part II, we have stated how important this relationship is. In these other chapters, we have not specifically emphasised it, but we have in this chapter, as it is seen as being a key technique in working with unconscious processes.
- When not to work with feelings.
- Some practical exercises.

12

Helping People with their Spirituality

It is with the soul that we grasp the essence of another human being, not with the mind, nor even with the heart. (Henry Miller)

Simon experienced frequent bouts of depression and had developed multiple sclerosis (MS). He felt stuck, alienated from himself and the world, with few friends he felt he could confide in. He had difficulty making sense of his life and had felt suicidal. What could help him?

His counsellor worked with him from a spiritual perspective, helping him to explore the meaning of experiences in his life and to evoke a sense of his highest potential. This enabled him to connect with a deeper, wiser part of himself that he could trust. It moved him beyond his everyday experience of himself and helped him to see a wider perspective. He felt part of something greater than himself and uplifted. This, in turn, made him feel less alienated from himself and others. He began to trust others more and started seeking friendships.

Why should spirituality be important in counselling and helping work? And what do we mean by *spiritual*?

Although this area has tended to be ignored within the counselling literature, recently a growing number of books have included the spiritual or *transpersonal* (as we also refer to it) as part of the helping process. This is because increasing numbers of people are recognising that they have a spiritual (although often non-religious) dimension, and feel that they wish to include this in any help that they receive. As Maslow, a key pioneer in what is called the humanistic movement in psychology, said as far back as 1968:

> Without the transcendent and transpersonal we can get sick, violent, and nihilistic, or hopeless and apathetic. We need something 'bigger than we are', to be awed by and commit ourselves to in a new naturalistic, empirical, non-churchly sense.

For example, most of the self-help groups worldwide which are based on the Alcoholics Anonymous twelve-step philosophy include spirituality as one of their central points. Similarly, within mental health, there has been a growing focus on the whole person, including their spirituality and recovery, as an alternative to the dominant focus on illness and psychiatry. This more holistic approach to health care means that there is more interest in including a spiritual dimension within therapy, and a greater focus on wellbeing rather than illness.

In this chapter we:

- outline briefly what a *spiritual/transpersonal perspective* is and, as with other chapters, we will also look at the assumptions of this approach;
- look at some *key skills and techniques* associated with working from a spiritual/transpersonal perspective;
- examine when and when not to work from a spiritual/transpersonal perspective;
- conclude with some practical exercises and a summary

Background to Working with People's Spirituality

The word *spiritual* is loaded. For many people, it conjures up religious beliefs. Yet there is a different view of spirituality, more in line with the quotation from Maslow above, relating to experiences and states of consciousness which transcend – that is, go beyond – the personal and the present, and which are not religious and certainly not related to organised religion.

Nevertheless, because of the association between spirituality and religion, a group of psychologists in the late 1960s coined the term the *transpersonal*, as a way of focusing on the central element of transcendence while distancing it from religion. There is some debate about the use of the word *transpersonal* but in this chapter we use it broadly, to cover the whole approach.

This way of working arose out of both the humanistic and Jungian fields of psychology in the 1960s. Key figures in the field of transpersonal psychology over the past four decades have identified a sense of something greater, which takes us beyond the everyday self, beyond one's personality, beyond the obvious areas we have covered in the previous building blocks to effective counselling: thinking, feeling, doing and sensing our bodies. This approach contains a sense of mystery, a suggestion of something which is larger than we are; and a sense of expansion, a wider perspective, with a focus on our highest potential – often termed in this transpersonal approach *the Self*: one's inner Self as distinguished from the more surface 'personality self'.

There is also an emphasis on *unitive experience*, where we feel a oneness with the world. The reference to transcendent states and transformative experiences suggests a sense of being lifted up by something larger than the self, and having a sense of purpose. The adoption of a spiritual approach aims to elevate us somehow to an experience that is beyond the five senses.

Some people will understand this immediately. For others it may be more difficult, so another way is to reflect on experiences such as listening to a moving piece of music where we may feel lifted out of ourselves and put in touch with something greater. This experience may also be achieved through a particular poem, or seeing a picture, or being stirred by a beautiful sunset or some other natural phenomenon: anything, really, which moves our experience beyond the personal and the singular towards a sense of a larger body of experiences and sensations, beyond words. Another way of understanding this approach is to think about what we know intuitively: proponents of a transpersonal or spiritual approach would suggest that this intuitive knowing is a manifestation of our unitive experience and the something greater that exists within us, even if we are not aware of it.

Assumptions underlying a spiritual perspective

Our aim in using this approach and working with a person's spirituality is to enable a client to access this part of themselves, and to connect with the transpersonal experience that arises from this, in order to help them understand and move through the problem they came with. The key assumption behind the transpersonal approach is that the solution to problems lies within the person themselves, in the centred, wise part of themselves that many people do not know how to access.

As with other approaches, a spiritual or transpersonal perspective makes certain assumptions about our nature and life path. We list eight key ones here, adapted from the work of Brian Wittine.

- *Our essential nature is spiritual.* Our body, conscious and unconscious thoughts and feelings, and our personality are transitory. However our *essence*, or *what we are*, is beyond this: we are more than what we seem to be. Some eastern philosophies refer to this as our 'Buddha nature', 'Atman'; others refer to it as our 'soul' or 'spirit' or 'the Self'. This essential spiritual nature is seen as beyond time and is both eternal and sacred.

    Jo had lost her son and husband in a tragic car accident. She found that in acknowledging and understanding her essential nature, she was able both to see and to manage her pain in a more helpful way. She started to feel stronger in herself, and began to develop a new understanding of events in her life which helped her to move through her pain and distress.

- *Consciousness is multidimensional.* We are not limited to one aspect or dimension of consciousness but can be in touch with many other dimensions. Helping clients to connect with experiences, such as being stirred by a beautiful sunset, can help to facilitate their experience of another dimension of consciousness.

    Gordon had struggled with anxieties and conflicts about himself for many years, regarding his job and his different relationships. He had found it difficult to appreciate everyday pleasures and held limiting views about where and how his life could develop. Work which connected him to other dimensions of consciousness and with some of the moving experiences in his life helped him: he began to appreciate everyday pleasures and to develop a broader view of himself and his life.

- *Our life and actions are meaningful.* Within our ordinary lives we experience the extra-ordinary and sometimes feel a deeper sense of meaning. Questions such as 'What is life asking of you at the moment?' or statements like 'Get a feel for what is in your heart, listen in this moment' may facilitate the client to touch this deeper sense of meaning, beyond superficial causes. These are questions that we used to help Simon (at the start of this chapter) and Gordon to get in touch with the meaning of their experiences and consequently to start feeling more positive.

- *Crises, difficulties or problems may be seen as calls to awaken and opportunities for growth.* They can be seen as opportunities for reassessment, a chance to reflect and listen to the Self, to listen to our 'wise and knowing heart' (as some writers put it), to be awake.

- *Symptoms may symbolise what needs attention and growth.* We do not disregard the real, painful nature of symptoms but in the transpersonal perspective we do not see symptoms as problems in themselves. They are a gateway, a messenger, trying to nudge the person towards learning something about themselves in order to become more healthy and whole.

  For example, working with **Anthony**, who had severe problems with alcohol and self-harm, we came to understand that his cutting represented for him a way of 'cutting into himself to find something real', his drinking represented his search for a new spirit and his thirst for new meaning in his life.

- *We are on a quest or journey.* The process of change or growth throughout our lives is likened to a quest or developmental journey. We use the metaphor of the seed within us, which grows, develops and gets shaped by forces and experiences. Problems can therefore be seen as part of a larger, unfolding journey in which we learn and grow.

  For **Simon**, whom we met at the beginning of the chapter, seeing himself on a quest or journey helped him to make sense of his experiences, use them in a more constructive way and move forward.

- *Our task as counsellors is to focus on health and not on pathology.* As counsellors using this perspective, we are listening for the health and potential within clients rather than seeking to pathologise them. We are asking the question 'What is right?' – not 'What is wrong?' – with a person. We assume that the client has their own inner wisdom or 'knowing heart' that they need help to connect with and we seek to find ways to evoke this 'wise Self'.

This is not to disregard a client's pain or distress, but to work with it from a different perspective. Our aim is to enable a person to deepen their connection with the Self in this process.

> For example, **Gordon** had just been left by his girlfriend of many years. Not long after this, his father died, and his company reorganised. Gordon's job was in jeopardy. He felt overwhelmed and alienated, and that his life had lost its meaning. His counsellor helped Gordon to make sense of and use these experiences as opportunities for growth, by facilitating his connection with his wise Self.

- *The power of love versus the love of power.* Particularly within transpersonal work, we need to be constantly mindful of whether we are working with the power of love or the love of power. Our clients need to experience us as facilitative and healing; if they do, this will enable them to move on. If, however, we are working with the love of power, we will find that our capacity to truly help another person will be very limited, even counter-productive.

In summary, then, transpersonal or spiritual counselling is focused on:

- encompassing a recognition that our clients' essential nature is spiritual;
- using this recognition to help our clients awaken, connect with, listen to and experience the Self within;
- empowering our clients to journey through their life and helping them to recognise and awaken to their highest potential;
- developing a sense of meaning beyond the everyday;
- working with and through the everyday, to connect to something greater;
- understanding problems and symptoms as symbols that call out for attention and through which a deeper understanding can be reached.

Useful Skills and Techniques

It is our wise and loving heart that holds the key. The answer lies within.   (Sarajane Aris)

General points

There are four general points about the skills and techniques used in a transpersonal approach.

- *Working with the client's Self*: The assumption is that *there is a wisdom within the client that knows best* (even if they do not realise this when they come to see us), and that this wise part of them knows more about their life and their needs than anyone else. Hence when we work from a transpersonal or spiritual perspective, we are trying to work with and facilitate our client's Self, this wise part that knows. All of the techniques discussed below are facilitative ones, aimed at enabling our client to reach a deeper and better understanding of themselves, and at accessing the wise inner Self. Hence when we discuss dreams with a client, we do not assume that the client knows what the dream means, but that their inner wisdom will be showing itself through the dream. The task is to help our client to listen to this inner wisdom.
- *Looking for meaning and purpose in distress*: The skills that are used when working from a transpersonal perspective are the same as those used with other approaches. What is different is the *manner* in which they are used and the nature of our listening and questioning which aims to facilitate the inner wisdom of the Self. We are looking at what is *purposeful* in the distress for the person and what meaning this may hold for them. We see the distress as *signalling something greater*: it is there to move the person towards health and wholeness; it is a way of finding the Self. It is this that differentiates a spiritual or transpersonal perspective.
- *Seeing pain and problems as opportunities for growth*: Transpersonal counselling works with the positive and aims to help a client work with their pain, from a holistic perspective. We start to work with our clients by helping them to identify and use their strengths, which enables them to have the courage to work on their pain and distress from a different perspective. We do not accept the pain and problems at face value: we see the distress signalling something greater, something that requires attention, and as an opportunity for learning and growth.
- *Creating a therapeutic space*: Effective counselling is much more related to *how* we do what we do and how we *use ourselves* in the counselling process than it is to the techniques of *what* we do. This is especially the case when using a transpersonal perspective: in order

to counsel from this perspective we need to be able to apply it equally to ourselves. As counsellors trying to facilitate a therapeutic space for our client to learn and grow, it is vital that we, too, are coming from a silent and centred place within ourselves. We have found that a meditative approach can help.

Specific techniques

Many of the skills and techniques outlined below are ones that we would use with a client once the helping relationship has been established. Although it can be argued that all techniques can be transpersonal, some are more appropriate than others to use when working from a transpersonal perspective. These include:

- reflective questioning;
- imaging and dreamwork, and anchoring these via writing, drawing, painting, sculpting, dancing;
- active imagination;
- guided fantasy;
- visualisation;
- meditation, mindfulness and reflection;
- body work, breath work and voice work;
- Dialoguing with symptoms.

All of these are important but to go into them all is beyond the scope of this book. Here, we focus briefly on five which we think are important for this introductory text. (Others are discussed within the suggestions for further reading at the end of the book.)

Reflective questioning

The questions we use are aimed at helping a person get in touch with their *wise or knowing Self*, and to see another perspective when reflecting on themselves and their lives. Such questions may be:

- What sense do you have of your life and what it might be teaching you at this point?
- What does all of this mean to you?
- When you felt so awful before, what brought you through?
- What sense do you have of your recent experiences? Reflecting on all of this, do you have a sense of how things could be different and what might make a difference for you?
- What makes your heart sing? What gives you joy?

Such exploratory questions ask our clients to reflect in a deeper way on their problems. It is the assumptions behind the question that give it a spiritual perspective. We are inviting a client into a space inside themselves where they can go beyond their surface feelings.

Questions such as:

- What is the feeling of all of this?
- Can you just stay with that feeling about all of this?
- What is . . . telling you about . . . ?

are more likely to evoke a response from the wise Self than questions like 'How did you feel about . . . ?'

The Focusing approach referred to in chapters 9 and 10 can be used in a transpersonal way to enable a connection with our client's Self. Other forms of questioning can also be powerful. For example, we can ask a client whether they feel that they have a wiser part of themselves and then ask them to get in touch with it, or suggest that they see their difficulties from the perspective of their wiser Selves.

Sometimes, particularly when people are not aware of this wise Self and find it difficult to access it, it is useful to ask people to do these things *as if* they had a wiser Self.

> For example, **Julie** was unable to decide what to do next in her life. She was asked what the wise or intuitive part of her Self would say and choose to do. Until then she had not realised or accepted that she had a wise Self but this questioning helped her to get in touch with it and to make a decision that felt right for her.

Imaging and dreams

Working with images is a key tool within transpersonal counselling. Such work can be a powerful approach for clients with a range of difficulties, including anxiety, depression, obsession or eating problems. Images go beyond words and emotions, often creating a playful space which can free up a person to connect with the Self and to find new and unexpected meaning in their problems.

Images can arise from many sources. Some come from different parts of our personality, or from the Self. Some can be drawn from outside, if they have resonances for us. Some images can be archetypal, grounded in myth, legend or history. The more we bring images into consciousness, map them and gather them together, the more we access the Self within. It is also crucial to this approach to ground or anchor these images in writing, drawing, painting, sculpting or even body work, either in the session with our client or by getting them to do it outside, perhaps as a homework exercise.

There is no one way to work with images. What is important is that counsellors listen out for images and identify which ones have the most significance for the client.

Listening out for images takes time. Having invited these images we then suggest that clients reflect on them, and ask their meaning and significance. Questions such as 'What might this image represent for you at this time?' may facilitate a deeper connection for the person.

> **Alison** had problems asserting herself with her boyfriend. She also suffered from panic attacks when eating out. Her counsellor invited Alison to come up with an image for her panic attacks: she came up with an image of a tiger. She was encouraged to engage in a dialogue with that energy which personified itself as a prowling and ravaging tiger, to discover what it was about, why it was prowling, what it wanted to say to her, and to get the feeling of what it was like to be a prowling tiger. Alison drew a picture of this tiger as a way of grounding and anchoring the energy. The process of drawing, and of feeling the energy of this in her body, helped her become aware of the nature of her feelings behind her panics. As she talked with her tiger, it said to her, 'You are strong and can do this if you want to.' She began to explore how she might use her energy differently and embody the 'tiger energy'.
>
> The most important part of working with Alison using this approach was in her transformation from a rather meek individual to one who was strong and visible. Alison harnessed and embodied her prowling tiger energy by being mindful of what caused her panic attacks, dealing with these and learning how to speak up for herself with her boss and her boyfriend. She also bought a small toy tiger that represented and anchored the energy of the tiger for her. It acted as a reminder of her own strength. She carried this energy forward into different parts of her life; her panic attacks became less frequent as she began to assert herself with her boyfriend, for instance, about the frequency and type of restaurants they ate in. The transpersonal work touched her life in a deeper and broader way than the specific issues she brought to the sessions.

When working with active imagination in this way, it is important that we do not interpret images too readily. It is up to our client to see where

images lead; it is important that we as counsellors resist the urge to interpret meaning. We need to follow, not lead, our clients.

Another way to enable people to get in touch with images is by using
dreams. Dreams can be seen as living images that we partake in while
we sleep. The principle of working with dreams is the same as with
non-dream images: we need to let the images in the dream speak for
themselves and help the client to make sense of them for themselves.

Guided fantasy and visualisation

This technique allows our imagination to play and to connect with other
parts of ourselves; it allows a deeper and wider dimension of ourselves
to be explored. The idea is that clients imagine themselves in a scene,
for example a meadow, climbing a mountain or visiting a house. The
person is asked to explore that place (the meadow, the house) and to
say anything about what appears and what occurs. They may be asked
to imagine a wise person or wise energy which may have a message about
what the client needs. This can facilitate access to the transpersonal dimension. When the guided fantasy comes to an end, the client can be invited
to draw, paint or write about their experience. The counsellor may
want to explore what the symbols and images mean to the client, and
whether anything is particularly significant in terms of their current
problems.

Dialoguing with symptoms

The body is a great symbol carrier. As James Hillman, one of the best
writers on the imaginal world, says, symptoms are 'the gateway to the
soul'. The art of transpersonal counselling is to help both clients and
ourselves to listen to their symptoms and hear what the symbols are
saying. Slowly we and they learn the language. We do this by listening
and attending, and by asking helpful questions such as 'What might your
neck pain be saying to you?' or 'Perhaps you could talk to the pain in
your stomach and ask what it wants or needs from you?'

Symptoms are an early warning system signalling a disturbance or imbalance between who the person really is, or who they need to become,
and the current situation they are in. If this can be attended to early
enough it is unlikely that the symptoms will become chronic.

Mindfulness and meditation

Mindfulness is a state of being totally focused on the present moment,
rather than thinking about what's past, or planning or fantasising about
the future. It is both a state of awareness that is brought to the present

moment, and one that facilitates present moment awareness. Mindfulness and meditation techniques are becoming popular, and are used with many approaches discussed in other chapters. Research is beginning to demonstrate the effectiveness of mindfulness training for people experiencing a range of difficulties, such as stress, anxiety and depression, and 'personality disorder'.

Among other things, mindfulness can develop a person's awareness; it can help someone to reflect before they react.

> For example, **Tony** easily lost his temper with his colleagues and his wife. By learning skills in mindfulness, Tony began to react more calmly to situations where previously he would usually have lost his temper. He also began to develop a deeper understanding about himself and the meaning of his life.

Both mindfulness and meditation are aimed at stilling the mind. As the mind becomes still, we are more likely to be able to connect with our higher/wise Self. There are a number of different forms of meditation, some of which are discussed in chapter 10 (on working with the body).

When to work from a transpersonal perspective

There are a number of situations where a transpersonal perspective is extremely useful.

- Many people belong to an organised form of spiritual or religious belief. If they already use these beliefs to make sense of their lives, it is often helpful to utilise some of these beliefs within the overall helping and counselling process.
- There are even more people who hold some form of spiritual or religious belief, or who have had a spiritual experience of one kind or another, but who do not belong to any organised church or organisation. A client who does not belong to an organised religion may still find it helpful to discuss their problems from a transpersonal or spiritual perspective.
- Even if it is not necessarily an important perspective for our clients initially, we may be able to facilitate our client's growth by drawing on their inner being, wisdom or knowing, should they be responsive to this. We would do this by listening to the nature of their attempts to make sense of their experience and asking questions that might

lead them to explore their spiritual beliefs and develop an alternative meaning to their life.

Even if we do not work with a client's spirituality directly, we will wish to create an atmosphere and intention that might facilitate some transpersonal connection for the client.

When not to work from a transpersonal perspective

As with all of the approaches examined in this book, if our client finds the approach unhelpful, then we should not use it. Working with a transpersonal approach involves using language and techniques (imagery, symbols) which some people find problematic. If a client is unresponsive to seeking meaning in their lives through their difficulties, is uncomfortable with using imagery, becomes defensive when we use a reflective type of questioning or finds the language of transpersonal counselling off-putting, the work will be ineffective.

However, it may also be that a person is unresponsive to this approach initially, but that as the relationship with the helper develops, they are able to access this aspect of themselves more readily. As counsellors we need to keep this in mind, and be sensitive to a person's changing readiness to engage with this perspective.

We need to be particularly careful how we use this approach with clients who have very severe problems and are experiencing psychosis, when the use of imagery and fantasy may exacerbate their problems. We also need to be very cautious when working with clients who are suicidal. In both cases it is extremely important to be under the supervision of someone experienced in the transpersonal approach.

Finally, it may also be unhelpful to use this approach when our client seems very comfortable in discussing spiritual and transpersonal issues, images, dreams and so on, but seems to use these discussions as a way of *avoiding* doing anything, or thinking about alternatives or what they can do or feel differently.

PRACTICAL EXERCISES

The aim of all these exercises is to invite you into a space where you can access the Self, thereby allowing the wise Self, that part of you that knows, to speak and say what you need and what your next step should be.

A transforming experience

Remember a favourite piece of music, poem or art. If possible, re-experience it again (listen or read or view it again). See if you feel lifted out of yourself, put in touch with something greater or larger, a sense of expansion; see if you can facilitate a connection to the transpersonal part of yourself.

Imaging / active imagination

Take an imaginary journey through a scene in nature such as a forest, a journey up a mountain, through meadows, along the beach. As you make that journey, ask yourself and reflect upon various questions such as 'What is the feeling of all this?' 'What does all of this mean to me?' 'What sense do I have of my life and what it might be teaching me at this point?'

Alternatively, *become* the tree, river, meadow, and speak from that place and see where it takes you.

Spot imaging

Allow an image of a story, concern or issue to form itself. Sense the quality of this, and where it touches you or has touched you, in a bodily way. Allow the image to speak for itself, for you or for the object or symbol. Stay with the bodily sense of it and see where it takes you.

Take the figures and issues that arise, and reflect on the questions: What is this asking of me? What is the next step I am being invited to take? What is this calling me to do? When you have completed this, draw it.

Be mindful of your gestures, noticing when, for example, you put your hand to your heart. Stay with that movement for a while, and see what comes, and whether an image or feeling arises.

The cushion exercise: body, mind, feelings and the Self

Put five cushions in a circle, one for each of body, mind, feelings, sensations and the Self. Sit on the first cushion of your choice (e.g. body) and let the feeling emerge in its own time of how the body feels about whatever the issue or conflict is for you right now. Then sit on the next cushion, asking the same (of e.g. mind); what does the mind think about it? Move again, to the cushion representing feelings, and ask the feelings what they sense about the issue and the same for sensations. Then move again to sit on the fifth cushion and become the Self, whatever that may be for you, asking the same question.

It can be very powerful to switch cushions or come back to the Self cushion between body, mind and feelings. Sometimes each comes with different things. It can also be helpful and powerful to take notes and/ or draw, either immediately after each part of the exercise or when the whole exercise is completed. This can then be further explored.

SUMMARY

This chapter has covered:

- An outline of the transpersonal approach (that the Self extends and expands beyond the personal, everyday self and time, and is concerned with our highest potential) and its underlying principles:
  - Our essential nature is spiritual.
  - Consciousness is multidimensional.
  - Our life and actions are meaningful.
  - Crises, difficulties or problems may be seen as calls to awaken and opportunities for growth.
  - Symptoms are symbolic of what needs attention and growth within a person.
  - We are on a quest or journey.
  - Our task as a counsellor is to focus on health and not on pathology.
  - Counsellors' motivation must be the power of love, not the love of power.
- Some of the skills and techniques associated with a transpersonal perspective, focusing on:
  - reflective questioning;
  - imaging and active imagination;
  - guided fantasy;
  - dialoguing with symptoms;
  - mindfulness and meditation.
- As with all the other building block chapters in Part II, we have taken as read the importance of the collaborative counselling relationship, and of working through the processes of counselling, which were described in some detail in chapter 3. As we have reiterated through-out, these processes are fundamental and, without working through them, it is unlikely that our counselling will be effective. This is

especially the case using this approach, which requires a very facilitative style, with all the techniques discussed being facilitative ones
aimed at enabling our clients to reach a deeper and better understanding of themselves, and at accessing their wise inner Self.

- We have emphasised elsewhere in this book that effective counselling
  is not a simple technological process where a counsellor uses learnt
  techniques; and this is especially the case with this approach.
  Effective work is much more related to *how* we do what we do
  and how we *use ourselves* in the counselling process than it is to the
  techniques of *what* we do.
- When to work, and not to work, from a transpersonal perspective.
- Some practical exercises.

13

Helping People by Coaching

If we do not change direction, we are liable to end up where we are headed. (Confucius)

Mark is a mid-level executive who hopes to rise within his industry. However, he finds presentations to large audiences difficult and anxiety-provoking, while realising that they are an integral part of the job.

The concept of a professional coach originated in the USA, but unlike many of the counselling approaches we outline in this book, it has no particular founding father, though more recently many leaders in the field have emerged (see further reading and websites at the end of the book). Instead, it is the result of a gentle evolution, which owes much to the developments in the self-help, personal growth and personal development movements, and in particular to coaching within sports and performance.

In the late 1980s, social changes such as the smaller and fragmented family and the rise in divorce rates, together with an awareness of the importance of a holistic approach to problems that had traditionally been regarded and treated as stress- or work-related symptoms, led some therapists and counsellors to review their ways of working. This led to many becoming *coaches*, and to their patients becoming *clients*: the coaching profession was born. It was originally influenced by a holistic approach, where body, mind and spirit are all interlinked, predominantly based on humanistic and transpersonal psychology. It has now developed to incorporate other approaches, such as working with thinking, feeling and behaviour.

Unlike many of the approaches examined so far, the growth of coaching has come almost totally from word-of-mouth recommendation rather than via a major academic or theoretical base. It is also linked to the development both of sports coaching, particularly in tennis, skiing and golf, and more recently of executive coaching. These coaching approaches are based on the idea that if a player (or an executive) can be helped to reduce internal obstacles to their performance and focus on their potential, then their natural ability will flow forth, without the need for much technical input from the coach. Coaching is therefore seen very much as a transformational process. One of the leaders in the field, John Whitmore, talks about coaching being about 'unlocking a person's potential to maximise their own performance. It is helping them learn not teaching them.' This is key to coaching.

This chapter gives a brief introduction to coaching, what it is and is not, and its place in the helping relationship. It distinguishes between coaching on the one hand, and on the other, therapy and counselling, mentoring and consultancy, although it is recognised that the boundaries between coaching practice and therapy can be blurred. The chapter also introduces some coaching methods and skills. We look at when it is and is not helpful to use a coaching approach, and conclude with some practical exercises and a summary.

What is Coaching?

A growing field of helping work

Coaching has developed rapidly over the past few years as an approach to helping, and in particular to improving and maximising performance in both individuals and organisations. It has borrowed ideas and techniques from many other approaches, including brief therapy and an approach known as *neurolinguistic programming*, as well as many of the approaches covered so far in Building Block 2, and many of the more general ideas described in Building Block 1.

Coaching has grown into an increasingly professionalised field with a number of training courses and accreditation bodies, for example the International Coach Federation (ICF), European Mentoring and Coaching Council (EMCC) and Association for Coaching (AC). (For details, see the section at the end of the book.)

Some of the main kinds of coaching that are now available include:

- assessment/feedback coaching;
- performance coaching;
- executive and leadership coaching;
- development coaching;
- coaching for emotional intelligence;
- behavioural coaching;
- career coaching;
- team coaching;
- line manager coaching;
- skills coaching;
- life coaching;
- spiritual coaching.

In this chapter we concentrate on using coaching within the context of a combined approach of assessment/feedback, development, skills and life coaching.

A practical approach to personal development

As presented here, coaching is a completely practical, skills-based approach which can be described broadly as working to facilitate and maximise people's performance, learning and development. When coaching, we guide and facilitate our client towards defined goals, often related to maximising their potential. These may concern relationships and interactions with others, career, self-confidence, problem-solving, financial matters, team-building or a realisation that life has drifted off course or 'There must be something better than this'.

Life coaching in particular is about the now and the future: a holistic approach that looks at the present and both clarifies aspirations and sets goals for a successful future. A life coach enables a person to develop confidence and the ability to move forward positively in the areas of their life where they want to change. Life coaching is about breaking down barriers that prevent this change and creating the ideal environment for positive action.

Ordinary people (like you, the reader, and us, the authors) can do extraordinary things when we have to; for example, people can produce superhuman strength and courage to save their child. Some of this potential can be accessed by coaching, and performance can be sustainable at levels far higher than we generally accept.

Coaching settings

Coaching can take place face to face or, quite often, over the phone at a prearranged time. (As with all counselling and helping work, these discussions are of course confidential, within the usual limits of confidentiality outlined in chapter 4.) These calls can be on a weekly basis, although more commonly they occur monthly, with each one typically lasting half to one hour. Face-to-face sessions tend to last from one to three hours on a monthly basis. It is unlikely that we will achieve significant results in fewer than three coaching sessions, although benefits usually begin after the very first session. It is also unusual for a coaching process to last longer than three months without a break.

Coaching is a highly practical and portable skill that can be tailored to suit us as counsellors and those we are helping. It can be used in a variety of different settings, including businesses. Someone can coach someone else alongside occupying another role – hence a manager or boss can also coach an employee.

Key assumptions

As with the other approaches we have examined in this book, coaching is underpinned by some key assumptions. These are:

- *All of us are born with the ability or potential* to be, do or have whatever we want in life. Coaching is about working with our potential.
- *All of us are naturally creative and resourceful.* For some people this gets blocked: coaching can help to unblock these resources.
- By the time we become adults, many of us have lost touch with this ability. At some point in our adulthood, many of us experience the feeling that our lives are drifting off course and that 'there must be something better than this'. *Coaching aims to facilitate the best in people, enabling them to reach for their potential.*
- *Coaching is holistic,* and therefore addresses all aspects of a client's life.
- *A coach does not try to remove the problems* which clients arrive with, but instead works with them in a creative way. As coaches, we work with our clients to reinterpret these problems as challenges, which then enables our client to overcome them by drawing on resources that they never thought they had. This inspires confidence to face new challenges.

- *The agenda comes from the client*, not the coach.
- The helping relationship between client and coach is a *collaborative partnership*.

What Coaching is Not

How coaching differs from therapy or counselling

There are three significant differences that set coaching apart.

- *Coaching focuses on the present and the future.* In many types of counselling, a therapist or counsellor looks with the client at the immediate or even distant past, as a means to understanding a person's difficulties and developing a solution. In coaching, while there is a recognition that we need to have a good understanding of how the past has created the present, the focus is on where the person is now and where they want to be in the future. Coaching is not primarily about the past and does not dwell on what has happened and why.
- *Coaching focuses on the whole person.* Therapy or counselling may address a single specific issue or problem, such as substance misuse or relationship difficulties. Coaching focuses on the whole person, from an awareness of the interactions between all areas of a person's life. Instead of delving into causes, coaching focuses in a holistic manner on the mind, body and spirit to help achieve the client's objectives.
- *The client identifies their goals and how to reach them.* The coach acts as a catalyst who will do whatever it takes to help their client. Coaching seeks to enable clients to explore their own solutions to their problems. The agenda belongs to the client: it is the clients who define what they want from life and how they will get it. Coaching has no prescriptions, because every situation, every session and every person seeking help is unique.

The main purpose of coaching is to empower the client to take control of every aspect of their life, and to accept personal responsibility which is an integral part of such control. A coach shows the client how to do this and acts as a guide for each step.

How coaching differs from mentoring or consultancy

Coaching is not about mentoring, or consultancy per se, although it may utilise many of the same skills as these approaches. It is a way of encouraging and facilitating the client to identify their own personal challenges, dreams and goals, and of working alongside them to help them achieve (and exceed) those self-defined goals. It may use some of the same core listening skills we use in a counselling relationship, but for a different purpose and within a different type of relationship.

Mentors generally guide and teach someone a specific task or job. Mentoring has its origins in apprenticeship, when an older, more experienced individual passed on knowledge of how a job was done and how to operate in that professional world. Like a sports or physical fitness coach, the mentor has often been there and done that; as such, the mentor will draw significantly on their own experience, pass on short-cuts and the tricks of the trade, and teach their apprentice how to achieve a specified result. The mentor will generally know the answers to a task-related problem, and offer advice and direction to their mentee.

Consultants are invited to investigate a particular work-related situation. They gather facts, diagnose the problem and make proposals (supported by those facts) on how to improve the situation. They may be involved in the implementation of their proposals. As with mentors, their focus is on resolving issues (usually in a work setting), but whereas mentors work at an individual or personal level, consultants work at the organisational level. Often, they advise and recommend solutions at an even more macro level in relation to strategic or cultural issues.

Coaches are different from both mentors and consultants. Effective coaching does not require the coach to have had personal hands-on experience of the client's occupation, though in some situations this can be helpful. (For example, very senior people and leaders may find it important to have a coach who is able to empathise with them by having had similar experiences themselves.) Conversely it can be the very *absence* of this experience that adds to the effectiveness of the coach who, by standing apart, can see (and help the client to see) the wood from the trees. It will, of course, depend on the nature and purpose of the coaching, the coaching relationship itself and the contract agreed in relation to the coaching work. Similarly, a mentor knows the answers, but as coaches we work with people so that *they* discover both the questions and the answers for themselves, not just for a particular task, but also for their life situations.

Increasingly, businesses and organisations are utilising corporate coaching instead of (or as well as) mentoring or consultancy. With their depth and breadth of understanding about attitudes and results, coaches will often achieve benefits that are realised faster and that last longer than those achieved by a mentor or a consultant. Corporate coaching

facilitates another individual's learning, development and performance. Coaching permits and equips people to find their own solutions,
develop skills, modify behaviours and change attitudes. It encourages
people to identify and follow their goals which are achieved more quickly
than when an individual pursues them alone.

What Coaching Is and Is Not: Summary

* Coaching does not dwell on what has happened in the past and why.
  Coaching looks to the future.
* Coaching is not mentoring, but a way of encouraging and facilitating the client to identify their own personal challenges, dreams and
  goals and of working alongside them to help them achieve those goals.
* Coaching is about achieving benefits that are realised faster and will
  last longer than mentoring or consultancy.
* Corporate coaching facilitates another individual's learning, development and performance.
* Coaching permits and equips people to find their own solutions,
  develop skills, modify behaviours and change attitudes in a very
  different style, manner and type of relationship from that of a counselling relationship.

Skills and Strategies of Coaching

The coaching process

The fundamentals of coaching are awareness, listening, curiosity, intuition, action leading to learning, and
self-management. The heart is the client's agenda.
The overall framework is designed to facilitate personal learning, where enabling clients to evaluate
and reflect on their learning outcomes is a crucial
element. A fundamental set of skills at the heart of
coaching is the use of effective questioning to encourage clients to learn
and reflect.

As in any of the approaches discussed in the preceding chapters, the
overall process of counselling that was outlined in chapter 3 still holds:
setting the right conditions and working through the stages are crucial
for success. In coaching, however, there is much greater emphasis on

giving clients feedback, and on facilitating potential solutions using the GROW framework outlined below.

Some basic principles
The following example highlights two important principles of coaching: awareness and responsibility.

Awareness relates to our client understanding the value and importance of feedback, receptivity and perception: seeing, hearing and listening. *Responsibility* relates to the development and cultivation within our clients of self-esteem, confidence, enthusiasm, self-motivation and self-reliance. In this example, coaching is being used in a work setting.

> **Sharon** is working on a task that had been discussed and agreed with her manager the previous week. She has a problem and goes to find her manager.

The following typical interaction involves no coaching:

> SHARON: I did what we agreed, but it isn't working.
> MANAGER: I think you must have done something wrong! I'm sure that if you do it the way that we discussed last week, it'll work.

Here is an alternative interaction, based on coaching principles:

> SHARON: I did what we agreed, but it isn't working.
> MANAGER: I have to go and see Stan for a minute. Could you see if you can find out exactly where and when the blockage occurs, and I'll be back as soon as I can to see if we can find a solution together.
> *Ten minutes later when the manager returns:*
> SHARON: I've got the solution – it's working fine now.
> MANAGER: Great. What did you do?

Sharon explains what she has found. Her manager compliments her and comments on her capacity to find solutions when she puts her mind to it.

Sharon's manager, in her intervention, appealed to Sharon's awareness and sense of responsibility, to find a solution to the problem. This was clearly an effective intervention.

In the coaching role, we also need to be *non-critical* and *non-judgemental*, as illustrated in the second interaction with Sharon: the manager presented herself as a partner.

The GROW framework

A fundamental set of coaching skills are related to the GROW (goals, reality, options, will) sequence. (For other approaches, see the section at the end of the book.) With the GROW approach, we as a coach are consciously providing the client with a set of new skills.

The GROW sequence

- *Goals* relates to goal-setting for the session, as well as short- and long-term goals. The client sets the goals.
- *Reality* relates to exploring and understanding the current situation. What is happening in our client's life? What has happened so far?
- *Options* looks at what is available to help the client move forward, and alternative strategies or courses of action.
- *Will* is about *what* is to be done, *when*, *by whom*, and ensuring there is the *will* to do it.

When tackling a new issue with a client for the first time, it is desirable to visit all four stages in sequence. However, when coaching is ongoing and is being used to monitor progress it may begin and end with any stage.

As we enable the client to define their goals, we also propose specific actions that will move them closer to the results they seek. Each session closes with agreement on the actions that the client will take before the next session. In the subsequent session we review those actions, their results and the client's feelings about them. This immediacy and the need to report back are two of the elements which make coaching so effective.

It may seem counter-intuitive to set goals before examining the reality. Surely, we need to know the reality before we can set any goal? This is not the case in coaching. Goals based on current reality alone are liable to suffer from one or more problems: they may be simply a response to a problem, be limited by past performance, be lacking in creativity or suggest smaller increments than may be achievable. They may even be counter-productive if short-term fixed goals lead away from long-term goals.

On the other hand, goals formed by ascertaining a person's ideal long-term solution, and then determining realistic steps towards that ideal, are generally far more inspiring, creative and motivating. For example, if we try to solve a problem of heavy traffic by working from reality first, we are likely to set goals based solely on relieving the existing traffic flow, such as widening roads or building a bypass. This might actually run counter to a more visionary long-term goal, which would be formed by identifying the ideal traffic pattern for the area at some time in the future, and then looking at the stages needed to move in that direction.

Of course, this approach is never hard and fast: sometimes we may be able to define only a vague long-term goal until we have explored the present reality in some detail. In those cases, it will be necessary to go back and define the goal more precisely before moving forward again. And even a sharply defined goal may be recognised as inappropriate once the reality is clear. Similarly, when listing the options, it will be necessary to check with our client to ensure that they would in fact move the client towards their desired goal.

The goals and options may challenge and stretch the client beyond their comfort zone.

We used this GROW sequence and the principles of awareness and responsibility with **Mark** and his anxiety about making presentations.

We started our work by ensuring that he understood how we would approach the problem, and by building a rapport with him. We then jointly set a purpose for the sessions: to make his anxiety more manageable, and eventually to enable him to look forward to making such presentations.

Giving feedback is highly important in coaching, and we helped Mark become more aware by emphasising with him the importance of feedback, receptivity and perception. We got him to bring us the feedback he had received from evaluations of his presentations, and enabled him to recognise that the feedback was in fact very positive. We helped him to question why he was finding it so difficult to see these positive comments, and that he needed to listen to the positive things that people said to him, thus developing his self-esteem, confidence and self motivation.

We facilitated potential solutions by using GROW: we helped him to set goals about how often he would make major presentations; we enabled him to check reality by examining the feedback he had received; we got him to examine options depending on whether he decided to undertake more presentations or fewer; he agreed to take action (to put himself forward to make more large-scale presentations); and we agreed when we would review progress.

Effective questioning

Another fundamental set of skills within coaching are those around effective questioning, sometimes called *incisive questioning*. The questions we ask are crucial to the effectiveness of coaching. Powerful questions stop clients in their tracks, stop them from being on automatic pilot, create space for them to reflect and cause them to make that reflection.

Table 13.1 outlines a set of powerful and effective questions. We have used these effectively as part of the coaching process, to enable our clients to understand and manage their problems better, and to achieve their goals. They are not definitive, and need to be used as a flexible guide to achieving the desired outcomes. They can and will be elaborated upon in practice. As always in counselling, it is crucial to keep judgement or criticism out of this process.

Here is an example of a coach using questions with a client Paul.

PAUL: I'm just not happy at work.

COACH: What do you want?

PAUL: What I want is to love what I do. I don't feel that way. I thought I did – maybe I did, once, but I don't now.

COACH: What would it be like to really love what you do?

PAUL: I'd wake up in the morning excited about the day. I'd be singing in the shower. I'd go through the day feeling good. The little stuff wouldn't get to me. I'd come home tired but still feeling alive.

COACH: That all sounds great. What would it take to make that happen?

PAUL: It feels like I'd have to change my job.

COACH: What would you be willing to give up in order to have work that you love?

PAUL: I'd have to give up some security . . . or maybe I'd just have to give up complaining about not having the work I love.

COACH: What would happen if you gave up complaining?

The Application of Coaching

When to use coaching

Coaching is especially effective when working with people who wish to:

- identify and work with their own personal challenges;
- reach and exceed their particular dreams and goals;

Table 13.1   Coaching questions

Goal	• What is the issue you would like to work on in this session?
	• What kind of outcome do you want by the end of this session?
	• How far do you want to get in this session?
	• In the long term, what is your goal? What time-frame are we working with?
	• What intermediate steps can you identify, and in what kind of time-frame?
	• What are you saying to yourself?
	• Where do we go from here?
	• How will you know you have achieved your goal? Is there a measurement you can use?
	• Where do you have control or influence with regard to this goal?
	• What is the truth?
	• What do you need to say 'no' to?
Reality	• What is the present situation in more detail? What is going on right now that tells you that you have a problem?
	• What is your concern about it? How great is this concern?
	• Who is affected by this issue other than you?
	• What is missing from your current situation that you would like to have?
	• What is happening now that is good? What do you want to keep happening to help you reach your goal?
	• What have you done so far to improve things?
	• What were the results of doing those things?
	• What resources do you already have to help you to achieve your outcomes? (What skills, experience, qualifications, personal qualities, talents, time, enthusiasm, money, support?)
	• What other resources will you need? Briefly write down where you will get them.
	• Who knows about your desire to do something about it?
	• How much control do you personally have over the outcome?
	• Who else has some control over it and how much?
	• What action steps have you taken on it so far, and to what effect?
	• What has stopped you progressing?
	• What obstacles or challenges are you facing that you need to overcome?
	• What, if any, internal obstacles or personal resistance might get in the way of taking action?
	• What resources do you already have? (What skill, time, enthusiasm, money, support etc.?)
	• What other resources will you need? Where will you get them from?
	• What is really the issue here? What is the heart of the issue?
	• Look back at the goal. Is it still relevant, or has it changed? Make adjustments if necessary. If it still stands, leave it alone.

Table 13.1 (*Cont'd*)

Options	• What are all the different ways in which you could approach this issue?
	• Let's make a list, brainstorming all the alternatives and possibilities, large or small, complete and partial solutions.
	• What are you going to do? List the actions.
	• How will these actions meet your main goal?
	• What else could you do?
	• What would you do if . . . you had more time, were the boss, felt more confident, etc.?
	• What would you do if you could start again with a clean sheet?
	• Would it be helpful if I offered a suggestion?
	• What are the advantages and disadvantages of each option in turn?
	• Which would give the best result?
	• Which of these options appeals to you most or feels best to you?
	• Which would give you the most satisfaction?
Will	• Which option or options do you choose?
	• To what extent does this meet all your objectives?
	• To what extent will it move you forward?
	• What are your criteria and measurements for success?
	• What is the benefit of doing this one thing? Will it make you feel better? Will it mean you will know something new? Will it change your opinion of something? Will it relieve stress? There has to be a clear benefit which you can identify and record.
	• When precisely are you going to start and finish each action step?
	• What could get in the way of your taking these steps or meeting this goal? What are the obstacles or barriers that might get in the way or stop you?
	• What personal resistance, if any, could get in the way of your taking these steps?
	• What will you do to eliminate or overcome these external and internal barriers?
	• Who needs to know what your plans are?
	• What support do you need and from whom?
	• What will you do to obtain that support? When?
	• How could I support you in this process?
	• What commitment do you have (on a 1–10 scale) to taking these agreed actions? What prevents this from being 10? What could you do to raise your commitment closer to 10?
	• Is there anything else you want to talk about or shall we close the session?
	• When will you actually start this option? Be specific – day, time, place – and record it in your diary.

- work with a coach who will help and empower them to achieve and even exceed those self-defined goals.

Currently, coaching is a particularly popular approach with managers and leaders in a range of different settings and organisations, as an aid to professional, organisational and personal development

When not to use coaching

Coaching is not therapy, and therefore is not designed to support those needing help in times of deep crisis, emotional trauma or serious difficulties. It is not designed to help people to overcome, for example, feelings of intense grief or deep depression.

The key is to be mindful of the client's level of distress and the nature of their problems. More serious difficulties need a different approach with more in-depth counselling.

PRACTICAL EXERCISES

These exercises can be used both during a session with a client or personally for your own self-coaching.

Visualisation 1

Imagine you are in a large group of people milling around in front of a stage. Up on stage is your future self. Your future self begins to speak to this large group of people. Suddenly you become aware of a shift that has come over you and the entire audience. Your future self has in some way had a profound impact on you and on the whole audience. You are altered or changed in some fundamental way. Aware of this impact on yourself and others, you leave the room altered for the rest of your life.

Questions

- What was the impact of your future self on you and others?
- How were you and the others transformed?
- Who (and how) was your future self, to have such an impact, and how did you change from who you now are to become that future self?

Visualisation 2

Look at a time in your life when you felt yourself to be a powerful person. (If you think you have never felt powerful, just imagine being someone you know who is a good example of a powerful person.) At the time when you felt powerful, your spine, arms and fingertips were tingling with excitement, and you simply didn't care what anyone thought of you. You were absolutely alive!

Questions

- Where were you?
- What were you doing?
- Who was around you?
- What was happening to them at the time?
- What was your impact on them?

Visualisation 3

You get into a rocket ship. It takes off and you are on your way to an undeveloped, uninhabited planet. You have the power to develop this planet any way you want. When you land, what are you going to make happen – what impact do you want that will make the planet the way you want it to be?

The ship lands on the planet. The door opens. You touch the planet and say, 'It's going to be this way.' What is 'this way'? What does it look like and feel like?

Visualisation 4

Imagine yourself at the age of 95, having had the most wonderful life that you can envisage: the perfect life that you would have if you could design it for yourself. Imagine and visualise this life. Fully associate with it. Write down or draw what comes up for you.

Goal-setting

Set yourself some heart-felt goals and place these, with their action points, within a time-frame. Put a start and a finish date on them. A goal is a dream with a date!

Ask yourself, and reflect upon, some personal coaching questions

- What in life is most important to you?
- What do you feel you have been putting up with?
- Who is most important to you?
- What goals have you set aside as unachievable?
- What personal habit do you most wish to change?
- What things touch your heart?
- What things give you most enjoyment and pleasure?

Summary

This chapter has covered:

- A brief introduction to the origins of coaching and what it is.
- How coaching differs from therapy or counselling, mentoring and consultancy.
- An introduction to the coaching process with some key skills and strategies of coaching, including
  - the important outcomes of *awareness* and *responsibility*;
  - the utilisation of the GROW sequence;
  - the use of effective questioning.
- The application of coaching, including when to work, and when not to work, using a coaching approach.
- Some practical exercises.

Part III
Social Processes

Introduction

In chapter 1 we set out a model of counselling (fig. 1.1) which identified three sets of building blocks to comprehensive counselling. The first was *the foundations and core processes* we outlined in Part I. In Part II, we discussed the second set of building blocks: *the range of styles and approaches* which counsellors use. Eight chapters focused on eight different approaches. In Part III, we now look at the third set of building blocks of counselling: *social processes*.

A great deal of this book so far has looked at counselling from the perspective of the individual person. The previous set of building blocks on the range of approaches focused primarily on a person's internal processes such as thinking and feeling. These are of course important, but so are social processes. People are social beings and do not exist in a vacuum.

Counselling that focuses on internal processes implies that the solution to most people's problems lies within themselves: in the ways they think and feel, in their unconscious processes and so on – their intra-psychic forces.

Internal processes are clearly important, but the chapters in this third building block present another model, one that suggests that most people deal with and solve their problems in interaction with others. It also suggests that therapy or counselling which focuses on improving people's ability to use these social processes is at least as important as a focus on intra-psychic forces. These next chapters therefore focus on social processes.

Chapter 14, 'Helping People to Use their Networks', examines how we can work with people's social networks. We outline why these are so important, and how we can assist our clients to improve the size and quality of them; we also discuss counselling couples and families.

In chapter 15, 'Helping People in Groups', we look at another way of utilising social forces to help individuals: working with clients in groups, where the experience of interaction within the group, and the observations and interventions which other group members make, are at least as important as our work as counsellors.

As with the introduction to Part II, there are a few key points we want to make here. First, dividing our building blocks up between individually focused and socially focused counselling implies an either/or approach, where either we work with an individual's internal processes or we work with their social processes.

In fact, most counsellors use elements of a wide variety of approaches: whatever we consider is in the best interests of our client(s) at the time. Hence, with any one client we may use a group approach, or work with a couple or a family, and at the same time work on developing our client's social networks, while also using elements of the eight more individually focused approaches.

So a key task for us as counsellors as we become more experienced is to integrate these different approaches. However, it is easier to integrate ideas when each one is easily separable, so it is best to learn about each approach separately to begin with. Therefore, although most of us use a mixture in our work with any one client, we have presented them essentially as pure forms in the next two chapters.

Secondly, some of the points we made in the introduction to Part II bear repetition here as well. We do not discuss in each chapter the importance of the foundation and core processes of Building Block 1. This is *not* because they are no longer important – they are – but because we are taking them as read. Each of the styles and approaches we introduced in the chapters in Part II, and each of the methods and approaches we introduce in the following chapters in Part III, rests upon these foundations. Simply applying the skills and techniques in these chapters in Parts II and III without using the collaborative counselling relationship and the core processes outlined in Part I will lead to ineffective counselling.

In Part II we introduced a very wide range of possible interventions, skills and techniques, and we will introduce yet others in the following chapters on social processes. But we want to reiterate that we are not suggesting that a massive amount of technical knowledge is required in order to be an effective helper. Of course all these skills that we discuss are potentially useful, and the more skills each of us has in our kit-bag, the more effective we can potentially be as counsellors. But the key set of skills (the foundations in our model in fig. 1.1) do not require extensive technical knowledge, and these key skills are at the heart of all the other interventions outlined in the chapters in both Parts II and III.

Finally, it is important to stress again that the most important element in counselling is the collaborative counselling relationship, not someone's competence in applying their technical knowledge of how to deliver various counselling techniques. Counselling is not about the application of technical knowledge; it is primarily the use of the core skills outlined in Part I of this book, and especially the use of the counselling relationship. This is true for all of the individually oriented approaches outlined in Part II, and it is equally true of the more socially oriented approaches in the following chapters.

14

Helping People to Use their Networks

The world doesn't change one person at a time. It changes when networks of relationships form among people who share a common cause and vision of what's possible. (Margaret Wheatley)

We believe that counselling individuals can achieve long-term results only if, in addition to the counsellor, there are people in a client's social network who also help. They may be relatives, friends, work colleagues or other helping professionals. In this chapter, we focus on the relationships our clients will have with family, friends and others.

A common problem is that we often work with people who appear to have few close friends or confidants.

Take **Sally**, whom we introduced in chapter 1. She had lost her father in her teens. Since his death, she had found it difficult to confide in people and felt quite isolated. She had no close friends and avoided social occasions when she could. Her anxieties had grown to such a degree that she avoided shopping in her local supermarket in case she met anyone she knew.

This chapter clarifies how we can help clients such as Sally to understand their social networks, and introduces skills and techniques which will enable them to develop and use these networks.

What Social Networks Are

There are many forms of social network. For example, we may hear about job opportunities through other people in employment. We may get children's clothes or equipment from other parents. We get support from others when we are part of an *interest network* such as a reading group, sports club or amateur dramatics society. When we experience a loss – bereavement or the loss of a job, for example – family members, friends and relatives frequently create a network to help us cope. Most of us as teenagers found out about sex from friends rather than parents or teachers – the peer network is effective in providing information and advice for this age group. All these are examples of networks in action.

Most networks are informal – they involve friendships that evolve over time, or relationships in our family or at work, or contacts we make through shared interests. More formal networks are specifically created so that people can make contact and support each other. Examples of these more formal networks include self-help groups such as Alcoholics Anonymous, groups for people who are depressed or bereaved, unemployed or 'back to work' groups, and networks devoted to personal growth and development. Some networks are professional, such as the primary care or mental health services networks: groups of people who link together to offer help to people in need.

Why Social Networks are Important

People need to feel that they have emotional support: that someone cares about them, values what they do and wants to spend time with them. People can also be supported by others providing information or material help when they need it, or helping them physically (giving them a lift, or helping with a DIY job). All of these are *social support*. The main function of social networks is to provide this social support.

We introduced the Stress–Strain–Coping–Support (SSCS) model in chapter 6. This model suggests that stress causes strain. The amount of strain a person experiences (damage, anxiety, physical or psychological symptoms) is mediated by the two factors of how that person copes, and the amount and quality of social support they have (see again fig. 6.1). We looked at coping in chapter 5, and social support is of equal importance.

It has been known for some time that people who have more and better relationships (with e.g. family, friends and workmates) find that stressful events cause them less strain than people who do not have such support networks. Simply feeling socially supported enables many people to cope better. People also use social support networks to share concerns, doubts and worries, which reduces their stress-bearing potential. Research has shown that receiving social support from other people acts as an effective buffer to stress and anxiety. By the same token, unsupportive behaviour can make the stress much worse.

When clients seek help from us, it is often a sign that their own helping networks are not working well. They may be disconnected from their own networks of family or friends, or were never strongly connected in the first place. Or the help from their networks may be inadequate for their problem.

Counselling tasks

So our counselling tasks are to help our clients to:

* clarify who the important people in their networks are, and see if there are sufficient people in these networks;
* understand how they are currently using these people, and whether they are being used to best advantage;
* develop further network members, or develop the functioning of existing members.

Sometimes, clients argue that they have well-functioning social networks when we feel that they do not. A gentle challenge is often extremely helpful, to see whether their networks provide emotional support, guidance, advice and information, and practical help.

Working with Clients to Improve their Social Networks

Helping clients to map their networks

First, we need to work with a client to identify the important people in their networks, and see if there are sufficient people in these networks. Questions we can ask include:

- Who do you live with?
- Do you have close friends? How often do you see them?
- Who is your best friend?
- Who do you talk to most about work-related matters?
- Who do you talk to about your personal worries?
- Whose advice do you consider in making important decisions?

By asking these questions we are able to build a picture of the size of a client's support network. It may include professional helpers: social workers, teachers, nurses, doctors. We often physically map out the client's active support network in three layers (as shown in fig. 14.1). Layer 1 is the person's closest friends and supporters – the primary network. Layer 2 is the network of informal helpers associated with groups the client belongs to – social or cultural clubs or organisations, religious groups, women's groups, etc. The final layer involves more formal helpers: people who are paid to be helpers and supporters.

Setting out what a client has told us in this way tends to trigger more detailed responses to questions about the quality of the network, while at the same time helping us to locate our own role.

Helping clients to understand how they use their networks

We should not be fooled if a client has a large number of contacts: network *size* is not the same as network *quality*. Fulfilling the functions of networks depends on the quality of relationships rather than just the fact that people meet each other.

We can seek to understand the quality of the client's support network across the kinds of issues listed below:

- How many people do you know who could come to see you at any time and wouldn't mind if the house was untidy or if you were in the middle of a meal?
- Are there any people you can rely on to give practical help or emotional support in times of difficulty?
- Are there any people who make you feel valued, reassured that you are a person of worth?
- Is there any one person without whom life would be intolerable? Or of whom you could say, 'If all else fails, I can always turn to X'?
- Which of the people you have mentioned know each other?

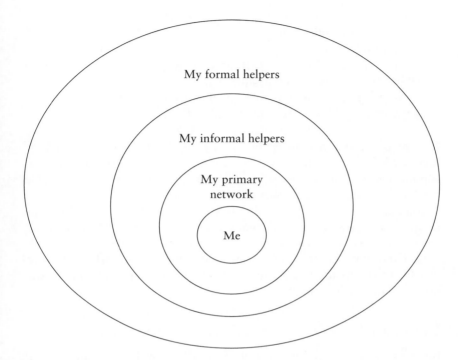

Inner circle: the client
Primary network: core family, other relatives, friends, work colleagues, neighbours
Informal helpers: religious groups, play groups, youth clubs, cultural/artistic/sports groups, community/neighbourhood groups
Formal helpers: primary care, social services, non-statutory agencies (Cruse, Relate, Rethink, etc.), education, police, probation, secondary health services, job centres, benefits agency

Figure 14.1   Layers of social networks

These questions tell us about the quality of the client's support network, and help us to examine the way in which individuals in the network are connected to each other.

Helping clients to develop their networks

The aim of exploring someone's network is to improve their connection with it. Often this can be done by:

- encouraging them to see that people in the network could provide more support than at present;
- suggesting better questions that they can ask network members – in essence, teaching some social or communication or assertiveness skills (as we looked at in chapter 7);
- showing and rehearsing the possible uses of network members, perhaps by role-play or guided exploration.

One of our tasks in counselling is to help clients to get the support they need from their primary and informal networks. Formal and paid support can be immensely useful for people, but a key task is to enable clients to move on so that they do not need it.

Sometimes a good way of doing this is to invite into the sessions one or more key people from a client's network: a spouse, another close family member or a close friend. They can not only hear what is discussed and work in tandem with the counsellor but also offer their own insights or observations. (We say more about working with couples and families later in this chapter.)

Using ourselves to help clients develop their networks

But as we said above, many people do not have well-functioning social networks. In these situations the counsellor may, for a time, become a key person in the client's network. Many books on counselling warn against allowing clients to become dependent on us but we take a rather different view. A major way in which clients can learn how to develop and deal with close relationships is through the development of such a relationship with their counsellor. Hence, we first need gradually to facilitate the client's dependency on us, and then gradually decrease it as we help empower our client to find others who can take on the roles and functions which we have provided.

Many counsellors fear the possibility that they will be sucked into a long-term dependency relationship. This realistic concern needs to be addressed by making explicit how we are using ourselves and the relationship between us, for example, by telling our client:

> Developing a close relationship with me is fine, but we both need to recognise that our relationship is time-limited, and professional. What you need to do (and what I am happy to work with you on) is to become more able to make and maintain close relationships with other people.

Not all of our clients will have limited social networks. Some may have functioning networks but may not feel that it is appropriate to use them for their current problem. For example, a teenager experiencing a personal relationship difficulty may not want to tell parents about it, or older people may be facing up to major decisions which they do not wish their children to be disturbed by.

We may need to act as a surrogate family member in many ways on such occasions, and this is perfectly OK, as long as what we are doing is clear, both to us and to our client. But it is important that we ensure that our client continues to recognise the value of their family for other needs and that they see our intervention as short-term and specific. Sometimes the client makes it clear that they do not yet want their family involved in something which will inevitably be revealed later (such as a teenage girl who is pregnant and plans to keep the baby). In such cases we have a particularly vital role in helping clients to see that they must tell their families at some stage, and working through the advantages and disadvantages of different ways and timings of informing them.

It is also important that we are clear at all times about the time-limited nature of our counselling help, and that there are differences between the type of social support that we can provide and the type that we need to help them acquire from others.

Julia was 76 and very ill with cancer and cardiac problems. Her daughter and son-in-law (her only relatives) knew about her cardiac condition but not about her cancer because Julia did not want them to know. As her counsellor, we helped Julia to get information and support from cancer organisations and to realise the important role her family could play in making her comfortable and giving her support.

While Julia's family did not need to know about her cancer, they did need to know how she felt about them and to be able to share some of their own worries. As her counsellor, we contracted with Julia to assist her to access and receive support for her illness and to act as a trusted person – almost like a nephew who knew how to handle such things – in exchange for Julia talking to her daughter and son-in-law about her feelings towards them.

Though she died five months later, three of these months were happy for her – she felt that she had become closer to her daughter. The last two months were taken up with the process of dying and alleviating pain. As her counsellor, our role changed – the doctor told the daughter why her mother was dying and hence we spent time each week with Julia and her daughter, helping them experience and start to work through their grief.

In this example, the role we played as Julia's counsellor was one of networker within agreed limits, and within a family network.

Working with Couples and Families

  In some situations, we may well see clients as a couple or a family. Couples and family counselling is tremendously interesting and challenging, but like all counselling, it requires training and work with a more experienced counsellor before taking it on. What follows is a brief outline of some of the main points concerning couples and family counselling.

Couples Counselling

To begin with, by *a couple* we mean both heterosexual and single-sex relationships. There is much in couples counselling that is similar to the work with individuals discussed in previous chapters. But there are at least three ways in which couples counselling differs:

- It often involves co-work – working with another counsellor so there are two counsellors as well as two clients.
- The counsellor does less talking and more listening, the main job being to reflect upon and feed back the messages being conveyed.
- The job of the counsellor is to comment on the relationship between the couple, rather than on the two individuals. Thus the process of couples counselling is not to intervene with two individuals at the same time; instead it is to examine what the interplay between the partners implies about the relationship between them.

Developing trust

While the usual stages in the process of counselling (chapter 3) also apply to couples work, the first stage of developing trust can be far more problematic for the following reasons:

- We may already have begun seeing one person before considering couples counselling. This may lead to the 'new' partner feeling that we are siding with the existing client; or the existing client may fear that their close relationship with the counsellor will be broken, or that something might be said which could show up the story in a different light.
- Gender issues will arise, especially if we are working with a heterosexual couple. We may be placed in the 'paragon of virtue' role by the opposite sex partner – 'If only you (the partner) could be like X (the counsellor), life would be wonderful'; or we may be accused of conspiring with the same-sex client to form an alliance – 'It's just like men (or women) to stick together.'
- Once couples counselling has started, many other issues may arise, such as rivalry over the counsellor's interest and attention, jealousy, competition or exclusion.
- We may have difficulties in developing trust when we are immersed in trying to relate to two, possibly arguing, people at the same time. Often one or both partners may attempt to form an exclusive relationship with us, while we are trying to relate to them as a couple.

We need to be on our guard against these common problems, so that we can take evasive action which might include:

- openly discussing the ways in which our previous relationship with one of the couple might complicate matters, and suggesting solutions;
- addressing the couple jointly rather than individually;
- balancing the attention given so that both have equal amounts (although what might be good for one partner might be too little for the other);
- having a co-worker (of the opposite sex if we are working with a heterosexual couple) who is new to the couple to balance both gender and previous knowledge issues.

Major areas addressed in couples counselling

Once trust is established, major areas which are commonly addressed in couples counselling include:

- *Communication*: Here it is important to ensure that couples devote sufficient time to communicating, and have the skills to do so. Couples may communicate, but in ways which do not match the needs of the other partner, for example, 'You never say you love me!' 'But I give you flowers!'

- *Empathy*: Many couples, although they do communicate, cannot see the world from each other's viewpoint.
- *Secrets*: These may be secrets shared within the relationship but not outside, or secrets which one partner feels must be kept from the other.
- *Sex*: Issues here include sexual difficulties, and one or both partners having or having had affairs.
- *Goals*: both generally in life, and currently within the relationship.
- *History*: What are some of the major things which have happened in their lives over the course of their relationship? This links in with other historical issues, both within the relationship and before: Why did they choose each other? Are there links or repeating patterns related to previous relationships, or to parental ones?

Related to these areas are:

- differences in the model of a relationship which each party may have, for example, from believing it is best to do everything together, to believing it is important to do lots of things apart;
- equality issues, where the two partners each want a different type of relationship;
- breach-of-contract issues, where one party (or both parties) thinks the other has breached the agreed contract.

All these issues can be summed up by asserting that a good relationship requires four components – the four Cs:

- *Contract*: Both parties need to be clear about what they want from a relationship, and that their partner wants the same things.
- *Contact*: In order for a relationship to work the partners need to spend time together.
- *Communication*: The partners need to discuss and share their evaluations of how their aims about the relationship are being met.
- *Commitment*: The partners need to be committed to making their relationship work, and hence to undertaking the other three components.

Steps in couples counselling

There are a variety of tasks that a counsellor working with a couple ought to pursue. The first – listen to their concerns – is identical to the first task of individual counselling, but thereafter there are some additional tasks, as well as the ones covered in chapter 3, including:

- get them to talk to each other, not to us;
- get them to listen to each other;
- clarify that there are communication difficulties, and why these exist;
- reformulate or reframe, which means that when two clients have two different perspectives on a problem, our job is to help them to see it in different ways.

Helping to reformulate or reframe

First, we might try to show that the two views are different angles on the same cycle of events.

> For example, **Jane** says that she is worried because her husband **Pete** is often late back from work. She questions him when he comes home, but is met with what she feels to be indifference or evasion. Pete for his part might says that things go quite smoothly until Jane has one of her 'jealous turns' and starts persecuting him with unreasonable questions (of course he is late – he has a demanding job). A major row finally erupts.

Second, problems often arise from natural stresses which occur at different stages in the normal life cycle. For example, both partners in the couple may have to cope with having a baby, adolescent children, ailing parents, retirement – all of which require adjustment on both of their parts. There may also be unexpected changes which can have the same effect. Enabling the couple to reformulate these events as 'normal' life crises normalises the distress they feel, and reduces their feelings of guilt.

Useful techniques

Analyse their time together

The tasks here are:

- to clarify whether the partners are spending enough time in contact with each other for shared activities and satisfactory communication to occur;
- if this is not happening, to pinpoint why these necessary contact and communication activities are absent. For example, is there a failure to express what is wanted, or a lack of shared interests and activities?

In the first instance, we often ask clients to do this as a homework task.

Increase rewarding activities

Work out ways of increasing rewarding activities together. Often clients do not realise that even simple things such as giving flowers, a kiss, a compliment, or a special meal are important currency that improves relationships with little effort.

Train couples in negotiating, problem-solving and communicating

This needs to include the concepts of exchange, flexibility and contracts; and the communication skills of listening, non-interruption, reflection and so on. It is often necessary to help clients to clarify the differences between assertion and aggression, negotiation and confrontation. For example, 'You never take my feelings into account, and I'm not going to stand for it any longer' is confrontational and may sabotage any attempt at negotiation.

A useful technique which can enable a client to see the world from the other partner's perspective is to ask clients to reverse roles. This could be in the session, with one acting out what they think the other would say or do in response to a given comment or action; or outside of the session, where one partner might perform the roles and tasks commonly performed by the other.

Encourage them to engage in bonding activities

Because many clients become relatively estranged from one another, it is important for them to do more things together, to talk more and to disclose more.

Help to reassess the relationship

Many clients have unrealistic expectations of what a relationship involves. For example, many are surprised that a relationship needs open communication: 'In an ideal marriage, people should know what their partner is thinking without needing to talk'!

Clients often have to be introduced gradually to the notion of being specific about their needs. 'You never take my feelings into account', a general complaint, is very different from 'I need to feel an equal part of this relationship; please would you consult me before doing things which commit both of us to doing something', which is far more specific and suggests action the other partner can take.

Challenge unrealistic expectations
Other examples of unrealistic expectations might be couples who do not realise that conflict is inevitable in a relationship and does not imply the failure of the relationship, or that relationships pass through good and bad patches. Many clients need to gain an understanding that relationships evolve and change. The task is to try to ensure that the evolution is in a direction which is desired, or at least acceptable, to both partners.

Family Counselling

Family counselling is similar to couples counselling in that the focus is not on the individual client but the set of relationships between those attending. However, key differences are that there are more people participating and it is a more varied field theoretically, with a huge variety of influential ideas.

Useful considerations

It is useful to consider the following when seeing a family.

- *Family structure*: issues such as who has the power; who does what (e.g. who deals with finance, discipline); what are the age and sex boundaries (e.g. who is allowed in the bathroom with whom).
- *Family processes*: Where are the alliances? Where is the hostility? Families usually have a state to which they return if events knock them off balance, which is known as *homoeostasis*.
- *Family history*: For example, is there a history of problem drinking or other excessive behaviour? If there is, how is it influencing the family's reaction to their current problems?
- *Family patterns of communication*: Who talks to whom, about what, and when? Who keeps secrets from whom? Who has alliances with whom and about what?
- *Family functioning*: What does the family find easy or difficult to do together?
- *Family life cycle*: The family will be at a particular period in its life cycle. For example, a baby may recently have been born, children left home, or a parent died. How has this affected the problem, and why has the family sought help at this point?
- *Family crisis*: Is there a crisis? How has this crisis affected the family, and why has it led them to seek help at this time?

Useful techniques

Try to understand how the family works

This is best done by a mixture of asking questions relating to the issues above, and observing how the members respond and react to each other.

We can ask questions in a variety of ways. One is to ask for explanations of differences, for example:

- *Between relationships*: 'Is your wife closer to Gavin or Tracey?'
- *Between perceptions or beliefs*: 'When people cry, is it to get their own way, or because they are in pain?'
- *Between time periods*: 'Is there more fighting now than before your mother's stroke?'

These questions can help to elicit an understanding of family alliances and processes, which can give a picture of the problematic issues.

Try to facilitate change

Due to the process of homoeostasis, families have proved to be notoriously resistant to change; yet by intervening at the family level we are utilising a model which suggests that the family needs to change to enable the individuals within it to alter their behaviour.

Among the techniques we might use to try to encourage a family to develop new ways of functioning are *reframing* and *reflexive circular questioning*.

- *Reframing* enables clients to see the situation in a different, more positive, way. We gave one example above about how a husband and wife could see their different views as different angles on the same events. Besides facilitating change in the ways family members perceive each other, these interventions create pauses in the repetitive cycle the family has built up, which can be used to alter feelings and responses.
- *Reflexive circular questioning* uses questions to trigger a change and to off-balance participants, rather than to explore issues. An example might be to ask the child, in the middle of an argument between parents in an interview, 'When your parents argue at home, is it more or less intense than it is here?'

Other ways of helping the family to move on use ideas which have been discussed elsewhere: they include goal-setting, empowering clients to engage in new behaviour and clarifying communication between participants.

Using Professional Helping Networks

 To be maximally effective as a counsellor we need to know about other resources available to the client, the resources to which we could refer that person and other organisations' views about co-working (as all our clients are also being seen by other helping professionals, even if that only includes their GP).

This involves finding out about:

- the range and quality of services available to the client from other agencies;
- who is available within these agencies – it is better to get to know a named person rather than just the name and phone number of the organisation;
- what links the individuals within each of the organisations to others – this is a way of extending our own networks;
- how we can collaborate with these other helpers without changing our work in a way that we do not wish to.

These points strongly suggest that we need to get to know other helpers as people, rather than as professionals or organisational representatives. The effort is worth it. Knowing the people in the local helping network in this way will enable us to:

- refer those in need to appropriate sources of advice and guidance;
- obtain advice that will help us to help others;
- understand how best to maximise the help that our clients receive if they are being helped by more than one person or organisation;
- ensure that we see our work in the context of the *range* of helping services available in the community in which we are placed.

Three words of advice about developing such a network of contacts for our own use.

- Don't be territorial. Just because we like to work with (say) couples' problems does not mean that we are the only people who should do so.
- Don't assume that just because a person works in an agency dealing with drink problems this is all that they can help with – recognise their interests and skills as general qualities.

- The best way to get to know others in the formal helpers' network is to collaborate, cooperate or work with them in some way. Doing something with someone is a good basis for getting to know them as individuals.

Conclusion

As counsellors we need to recognise that our own work is a part of a larger canvas of helping within the community. The less connected we are to local networks, the more likely it is that the client is being restricted by our own ignorance of available services. The question we need to ask ourselves when someone seeks our help is: 'Am I the best person to help this individual right now, and if not, do I know who could help them most effectively?' This is not to say that the person seeking our help will always be willing to be referred to someone else, but if we really feel that we are not best able to help, then we need to say so, and to encourage and enable a referral to whoever is best able to help.

One final point: we have responsibilities which go beyond those which we have towards the client. Some of these relate to the discussion in chapters 4 and 5 on confidentiality and when it needs to be breached. But others relate to the psychological and social well-being of our community. Some examples are the effects of parental problems on children, the impact of drug and alcohol problems on communities, and physical and sexual abuse in families. We may also have to comment on the way in which we and other helpers (social workers, policemen, lawyers, doctors) are responding. We must not shrink from the implications of our work for the social institutions designed to serve our clients.

PRACTICAL EXERCISES

Helpful (supportive) and unhelpful (unsupportive) people

The amount of help you get can have a big impact on how you respond to difficult or stressful things in your life. This exercise will help you to think about people who could or do give you support and to find the support that helps you most. It will help you to look at how people around you are helpful and unhelpful, and how this makes you feel.

Exercise 1   Helpful and unhelpful people

Person	How this person is helpful	How this person is unhelpful	How I feel about this person
e.g. A friend at work	He listens to me and we go out to lunch regularly	He tells me that I should leave my wife	It helps to have someone to talk to but it is frustrating that he tells me what I should do
e.g. My wife	She tries to understand my problems with my boss, and is very sympathetic	Because she has never worked in my environment, she can't really understand, so lots of what she says isn't helpful	It's nice that she tries, but she's not really on the same wavelength
e.g. My father	He is always willing to come over to help me with my DIY jobs	I can't talk to him about any of my problems – he just switches off	He's great if I have a DIY problems, but not for much else!
A person in your network			

Source: as for table 6.1.

Do it a few times, with different people and different issues or problems. Reflect on what you have written:

- Are there people who you use a lot, or who you find more or less helpful?
- Are some people helpful for some issues but not for others?

Do I need more support?

This exercise will help you think about whether you need more support to help you deal with problems. Using your responses to Exercise 1, think about what you could do to increase your support.

Exercise 2   Do I need more support?

Question	*Answer*
Who is helpful to me at the moment and what do they do that I find helpful?	
What could I do to get more help from this person?	
Who is unhelpful to me at the moment and what do they do that I find unhelpful?	
Is there anything I could do to change this?	
Who do I need support from?	
What am I going to do to try and get help from them? Give examples.	

Source: as for table 6.1.

SUMMARY

Key ideas in this chapter are that:

- Counselling can achieve long-term results only if there are other people in a client's social network, in addition to the counsellor, who help: relatives, friends, work colleagues or other helping professionals.
- There is a range of types of social networks, formal and informal, including ones which provide information, emotional support and material help.
- Networks are vital because people need to feel (and be) supported, and networks provide that support. They reduce the amount of strain people experience in response to stressful events.
- Our tasks as counsellor include helping people to map out, understand, use and develop their social networks.
- When we work with couples or families our main job is to reflect upon and feed back the messages being conveyed between the parties, to comment on the relationships and to use a variety of techniques to improve the relationships.
- When working with social networks, we also need to know about other services and organisations to which we could refer our clients.
- Finally, we have a responsibility to bring issues which arise out of our work to the attention of the wider community.

15

Helping People in Groups

None of us is as smart as all of us. (Japanese proverb)

The whole is greater than the sum of its parts. (Aristotle,
Metaphysica*)*

So far we have focused on working with individual clients or with
couples or families, but a great deal of counselling and helping takes
place in groups. Group work is highly skilled, different from individual
and even couple or family counselling, and comes in many forms, with
varied philosophies, aims and techniques.

In this chapter, we aim to introduce some of the basic ideas, concepts
and issues relating to counselling people in groups.

Why Should We Work in Groups?

First, counselling in groups can suit individuals who need to:

- learn to understand others better and the way that others see and
  understand the social world;
- learn deeper respect for others, especially people who are different
  from themselves;
- develop and refine skills, such as assertiveness or social skills;
- experience belongingness through sharing experiences with others,
  for example widows, women who have been abused, people with a
  debilitating illness;
- come to terms with certain issues such as sexuality, death, loss or
  unemployment;

- benefit from the reactions of others to their views and concerns;
- begin their counselling in a group before moving on to individual work, or vice versa.

When we establish a group, we need to be clear which of these reasons apply, since it will affect who attends and the style and nature of the group's work.

Second, a group can be an effective and economical way of working because a number of people can be seen in the time it takes to see one. This applies to groups such as assertiveness training, groups dealing with a specific issue such as stress management, or groups focused around a particular segment of society such as high-risk offenders.

Third, the group members themselves can be the main change agents, the source of that change being the group dynamics and processes.

Finally, groups can also be a powerful and effective means of feedback, particularly as an educational aid when people practise new techniques and develop skills. They can also be a place of information exchange.

> **John** was socially quite anxious, often felt very stressed and frequently became depressed. His counsellor thought he would benefit from group work because he would meet other people, and be able to practise his new skills in a safe environment.
>
> He attended a group for 10 weeks, during which he learnt a variety of stress management and anxiety reduction techniques, and (equally importantly) met a number of other people with similar problems. He recognised that some other participants had more severe problems, which helped him to reassess his own problems positively; and he also made a friend whom he now meets regularly outside of the group.

The Aim and Purposes of a Group

A group can have a variety of aims and purposes, depending on who the group is being run for. We therefore need to ask ourselves a number of questions, such as:

- Who is this group for? (Is it being run for women with alcohol problems, managers with stress-related problems?)
- What is the group trying to achieve: what are its specific aims, goals and purposes? Does it aim to:

- use many of the procedures outlined throughout this book in a group setting, in order to effect some specific or general change among participants, or for skills and learning purposes;
- provide emotional and practical support to participants, or opportunities for reflection;
- explore dynamics and issues that are created within the group as part of a development process?

For example, a group such as Alcoholics Anonymous or Weight Watchers has particular targets for members' behavioural and psychological change, and may also provide support for members. Sometimes these groups have a facilitator who provides guidance, but they also have an important mutual-help function.

Other groups, such as those dealing with assertiveness, anger management or stress management, have specific skills-training functions as well as an educational component, and provide support for their members. On the other hand, a group working in a psychodynamic way will focus on the relationships between its members, using its own group processes.

Establishing a Group

 When establishing a group it is important to be clear and specific about its aim and purpose, and to ensure that this is made explicit to potential participants. For example, there is a considerable difference between attending a skills-training session on stress management and exploring one's own experience of stress and its underlying causes and associated pain. Some of the difficulties in groups occur because participants are not clear about the function and purpose of a group or the intended style of working.

Therefore, when we establish a group, we need to be as explicit as possible about the answers to the following questions:

- What is the group's aim and purpose?
- How is it intended to achieve these?
- Who can become a member of the group and how will membership be determined?
- Is it an open or closed group?
- What will be expected of group members – will they be asked to disclose something about themselves or can they be passive?

- Under what circumstances can a person end their membership of a group, and having once left can they later return?

Such questions certainly need to be answered by those who intend to run a group. But they are also useful questions for those who intend to participate.

Framework

As group leader, we need to be clear about the framework within which we wish the group to work. The following questions require us to have a clear philosophy and assumptions about group work:

- How do we envisage the group operating? What assumptions are we making about the value of personal contributions, the place of self-disclosure, the role of participants as confronters and providers of feedback to others?
- What role will we have – initiator, supporter of others, trainer, educator, director of the group (making sure it 'goes the right way'), or simply a facilitator (letting the group choose its own way of working and its own development)?
- Are we also going to take the role of enabler and motivator, encouraging a high level of motivation among group members both before and during the life of the group? (This role would necessitate being relatively more proactive and directive.)

Selecting group members

In most cases, groups involve some pre-selection screening, usually an interview. For example, in forming a group for people wishing to stop using minor tranquillisers, we screened those who expressed an interest in terms of:

- the extent to which they were motivated to attend;
- their willingness to accept that the group might require them to share their feelings and thoughts;
- the degree to which they were seen to be able to fit in with other members;
- the degree to which group work was seen to be more effective for them than individual work.

Whereas these criteria and the selection process are not very scientific or precise, it is essential to screen out those who might have found the group format too problematic, or who might have been too disruptive.

Although not all groups involve such pre-selection, in our experience it helps to prevent problems arising and we strongly advise using some selection process and criteria.

Enabling participants to make the most of group experiences

As group leader we can usefully offer help to participants about how to get the most out of being in the group. Suggestions for pre-group briefing include the following:

- Realise that the group is a means to an end, not an end in itself: while the group may be important to you, don't lose sight of why you joined and what you intended to gain.
- You will learn most from this group by trusting yourself to make decisions and by trusting others.
- You will get most from a group by participating in it and least from merely observing – if you wish to benefit, become involved.
- You are responsible for your own disclosures – decide for yourself how much you would like to tell people, and do not disclose until you are ready to do so.
- A great deal of learning in a group will involve discomfort and sometimes pain – this is normal when you are being asked to examine your well-established ways of thinking and feeling critically, so expect this to happen.
- Don't expect the changes that you are looking for to occur quickly and effortlessly – it will take time and may be frustrating, but it is worth persisting.
- Expect to discover things about yourself that you did not know, especially when others start to give you feedback and support.
- You must decide what you are going to do with what you learn – you take the responsibility for using or not using your learning.
- Listen and attend to others as you would wish them to listen and attend to you – be discriminating in your listening and look for the value of other people's talk, both for them and for you.
- If you have a persistent feeling during a group session, such as pleasure, frustration, uncertainty, doubt or fear, express it.

- Think for yourself – your needs and your thoughts are what matter to you.
- Pay attention to consistent feedback and decide what to do with it.
- Don't pigeon-hole yourself and don't let others categorise you – you are a complex person whom others can only ever partly know. But do listen to the way in which others comment about you: you can learn a lot.
- Don't be afraid to enjoy the experience of discovery and exploration.

Supplying participants with these observations before the group begins presents the group with a basis for a contract and helps the leader to prevent distress by referring to the features of behaviours and relationships in this list.

Leadership in Group Counselling

Leadership style

Different types of groups need different kinds of leadership. For example, if we were the facilitator or workshop leader of an *educative* group, we would need to be offering educative material, have an explicit training function and a variety of skills, and be more directive in leadership style. Hence the term *trainer* is often used for this type of group leader. In contrast, if we were the facilitator of a *support* group, we would work using a non-directive style in order to create an environment of mutual trust and respect, so that all participants felt safe to make statements and examine issues which might be difficult to explore in places other than the group. Our style as a *psychodynamic* group leader may also be more indirect and interpretive, helping participants to understand the unconscious nature of their interpersonal relationships and conflicts, and focusing on the group's process.

Questions for group leaders

There are several features of this leadership role which we need to consider before establishing a group. The first has already been addressed – what is the underlying reason for creating or developing a group in the first place? Further questions we need to address before recruiting the first member are:

- Why is this group something that we wish to undertake – what are our own motives and likely gains?
- What problems might arise in the group and how will we deal with them?
- How will we evaluate the group's progress and success?

Creating the right conditions for the group

Once the group starts there are other issues that concern us as group leaders. The first and most critical is: how to create a group environment that is safe and confidential. The core conditions of counselling individuals that we looked at in the early chapters of this book, such as empathy, warmth, genuineness, feedback, self-disclosure and so on, are needed just as much in a group setting. So we need to:

- establish the parameters of the group by encouraging a group to negotiate a contract about what its concerns are and how it is to operate;
- develop a set of formal or informal guidelines for a particular group that include rules about confidentiality;
- give direct and personal attention to each person there and show that we are concerned for the welfare of the group both as a whole as well as individual group members;
- encourage members to accept and validate each other, offering feedback or challenge in a manner that respects the recipient – the group can develop and achieve its aims only in a climate of mutual trust and support.

To help create these conditions, there are a variety of activities which, as leader, we can use. These include 'ice-breaker' activities which are intended to promote trust, group cohesion and contact between members. Such activities need using carefully: people need to be informed that this is going to happen and given a rationale for it; otherwise such 'games' can be a huge turn-off for people.

What is most critical is that, as leaders, we understand that our actions will largely determine the way that the group develops. We must model how we want the group to behave. Hence we must display trust and confidence in the group, resist overplanning, and permit the group to have its own life. We must accept that, while we have a specific role, we are also a member of the group and should be subject to the same rules as other members. These points apply even when it is intended that the group leader should teach some skill, such as assertiveness.

One final point: beginner group leaders, like beginner individual counsellors, often feel more responsible for the experience of group members
than they need to. Group members are able to take responsibility for
their own actions and for their own well-being and do not need to be
rescued unless they specifically ask for our help. We need to ensure that
group members know that they can ask for our help, but we need not
thrust it upon them because of our concern to make sure that everyone
has a good group experience. We need to allow the members of our group
to be themselves.

Problems in leadership

An examination of some difficulties in leadership behaviour can tell us
more about the nature of the leader's role.

- *Having goals which we do not disclose to the group*: An example of
  this might be if we wish to use the group as a case study of how a
  group develops over time, but do not share this goal with the group.
  This tends to lead to the group feeling that there is another agenda
  at work which it does not know. We should therefore be explicit
  about our own goals and should encourage others in the group to
  be explicit about theirs.
- *Directing a group in unwanted ways*: For example, we might say
  'Right, we've spent enough time on this. Let's . . .', when the issues
  raised by group members actually need more time and energy.
  Directing a group in a way that is insensitive to the needs of participants will impair its development.
- *Seeking to judge the success of a group by the level and expression
  of feelings*: For example, one group leader commented that his
  group 'hadn't expressed any real deep feelings yet'. Groups have their
  own life and dynamics, which need understanding and accepting. A
  group does not need to have major outpourings of feelings – crying,
  shouting – to be successful. What matters most is that the group
  provide an environment where participants feel able to express
  themselves however they wish and where they can develop.
- *Time taken up with leaders exploring themes that particularly
  interest them*: This is in contrast to listening out for themes that the
  group wishes to explore. It may indeed be appropriate for the group
  leader to focus on a particular theme, but it is the *group's* themes
  that are critical.
- *Over-interpretation*: As leader, we may over-interpret or offer too
  many interpretations of the actions of participants: for example, 'You

are saying that because . . .' or 'What this tells me about this group is . . .'. This can lead to group members feeling constricted because their every action is interpreted. It can also set up an unhelpful power dynamic, with the group leader perceived as always knowing better than the participants. A related difficulty occurs when we *tell* group members how they are feeling or what is going on instead of asking them for their opinions.

- *Lack of spontaneity and responsiveness*: Genuineness and spontaneity are critical ingredients in the success of groups. Participants wish to feel that this is *their* group, not just any group, with us as their leader responding to the people in the room genuinely and spontaneously. The more we are seen to be sticking to established formulas and routines, the less likely it is that the participants will feel that we are being genuine.
- *Inappropriate leadership style*: Difficulties can arise when our leadership style is inappropriate for the type of group, for example, if we try to be directive when the group needs an exploratory style, or if we use an exploratory approach when a skills-based response is called for.

Risks and responsibilities

A section on leadership would not be complete without some reference to the ethical and personal responsibilities of the leader. Leadership is necessary in a group in order to protect individuals from psychological or physical harm from other group members, so it is important that we:

- check for signs of participants who are experiencing stress in the group;
- make clear, as part of setting initial group ground rules, what the limits of particular behaviour are in the group;
- intervene whenever we feel that a person is at more risk than is appropriate.

These are difficult and sometimes risky decisions to make. They involve us modelling risk-taking as the group facilitator or leader. The ability to do so comes from experience, understanding group-work issues, and carefully working through our philosophy of group work. The best training for leadership is:

- being an active participant in groups before leading one, and attending a variety of groups run by others;

- observing other counsellors' leadership styles and skills, and discussing their philosophy of group work with them;
- reading about group work;
- examining and reflecting on our own behaviour as a group member.

Stages of Group Development

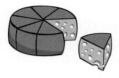 Groups have their own dynamic – that is, they develop a life of their own. There are common patterns which can be seen as stages of group development, although groups do not always follow these sequences and participants do not necessarily experience development as a series of steps which build upon each other. Nonetheless, thinking about group development in terms of stages is helpful in illuminating why and how group behaviour can change over time. It also helps us as group leaders to be aware of what kinds of leadership responses may be appropriate for each of the particular stages.

These stages of group development are commonly known as:

- norming;
- forming;
- storming;
- reforming;
- mourning.

They tend to occur within all types of group, although their expression may be different in, say, a skills-learning group as opposed to a psychotherapy one.

Norming

This is the first stage, during which people try to understand and create the group's *norms*: to get to know each other and the rules of the group. At the early stage group participants are reluctant to make commitments to each other or to self-disclose; they are simply concerned to make contact.

As the group develops, this stage becomes one of resisting personal expression of thoughts and feelings, coupled with a reluctance to explore new thoughts and feelings – participants play safe when asked to describe themselves and their experiences; they look for similarities between themselves and others; they seek to minimise personal risks resulting from self-disclosure, wanting to appear 'normal'. To help participants at this stage, we as leaders need to show that we accept that participants may experience difficulties; therefore we seek to create an enabling climate within which these difficulties can be talked about and worked with.

Forming

Once some progress has been made in developing trust, which encourages participants to disclose more of themselves, they are more likely to begin by describing past feelings. This is because the group has *formed* so people feel safe to talk more honestly and openly. At this stage the group's vocabulary can therefore be more emotion-focused and full of 'I used to feel . . .', or 'I have often thought . . .', or 'Sometimes I feel . . . but at other times I feel . . .'. When this begins to occur it is often useful to help the group to be aware of the language being used and to suggest some language rules for the group. Some of the discussion we had in chapter 9 (on working with feelings, around getting clients to talk differently) may be useful to clarify the sorts of language which are more or less helpful.

Storming

This stage is reached when the group begins to speak about the present rather than the past. It is here that group members most typically express negative thoughts and feelings. These include negative thoughts about self ('I will never understand . . .'), or disillusion with the group ('Where is all this getting us . . . ?'). Group members may even absent themselves from the group for a few sessions. This stage is often necessary so that clients can unburden their immediate thoughts and feelings and move on to being more open to new ideas and exploring feelings. It is crucial that we resist responding to negative comments about the group as if they were a personal attack upon us.

Reforming

Once the negativism in the storming phase has passed, participants seem to free themselves to accept, explore and express personally meaningful material. Such disclosure often leads to expressing more feelings about the group. We as leaders can be most effective here by validating and accepting comments and encouraging acceptance, feedback and confrontation by other members. In doing so, we need to be mindful that the group is extremely sensitive and that individuals remain vulnerable about the extent and nature of their self-disclosures.

Once the group members accept that self-disclosure leads to challenge and feedback which they see as constructive (even if painful), then the potential for self-change and development is considerable. Also, group members provide support for each other and can take their own steps to heal any wounds, reduce pain and increase enjoyment. At this phase, we as leaders need to be especially sensitive to the risks which individuals take when opening themselves to others. The critical task of the leader is not to rescue an individual being challenged or experiencing pain but to ensure that the group's overall quality remains supportive and sustaining.

Mourning

This is the final stage in a group's process, when participants become aware of the ending of the group and the loss that this will mean. Leaders need to be mindful of the impact that endings can have on members, particularly vulnerable or isolated individuals.

Skills and Strategies to Manage Problems in Group Work

Even with the most careful preparation, difficulties may arise simply because of the interactions between group participants and between participants and leaders. In this section we examine nine specific problem behaviours and make suggestions for leadership action. This is not an exhaustive list, but it provides a basis for thinking about other problems too.

Silent group members

The first problem is when members do not participate or contribute unless they are pointedly asked to do so. This can give the group the feeling that some people are not on board, and the attempt to involve them can distract or weaken the group. We need to trust the group to solve such problems. Often a non-participating member will be challenged by the group; our role will be to ensure that such a confrontation is sensitive to the needs of the person.

Monopolisers

A person can monopolise a group by talking a lot, drawing attention to themselves or always adding to comments made by others. As leader we can seek to deal with the issue in the group or, preferably, because the group needs to learn problem-solving skills, wait for the group to deal with it themselves. We can sometimes assist the group by naming difficult behaviours in the first place and asking the group if they are happy with them.

Have you heard . . . ?

This story-telling problem happens when a person simply rambles through anecdotes and stories irrelevant to others or seeks to top a story offered by another: 'A similar thing happened to me . . .', or 'Yes, but worse than that . . .'. Again we can deal with this by naming the problem directly, or we might suggest that the group needs some rules about language such as talking about experiences in the here and now and using 'I/me' kinds of statements rather than 'you/them'. The real problem is usually that the group as a whole is engaged in story-telling, hence the need to teach some language skills pertinent to self-disclosure.

We have ways of . . .

This is known as the interrogation problem – it occurs when a person uses a disclosure by another to interrogate and push that person beyond what they are willing to disclose. For example, here is an extract from a group session in which Tony was interrogating Christine:

> CHRISTINE: The first thing was I didn't feel that I could deal with him being so, I don't know, aggressive . . .
> TONY: You mean you don't know whether he was aggressive?
> CHRISTINE: Well, I mean, I think he was aggressive, yes.
> TONY: You think he was aggressive, but you don't sound sure. It sounds to me like the only thing you're sure of is that you felt weak whenever he was around.

CHRISTINE: You're making a lot of assumptions there . . .

TONY: Are you getting upset now . . . do you see me as being aggressive, am I like the person you were talking about? Christine, what are you afraid of?

One person pushing another can be a valuable aid to their development when there is mutual respect and trust, genuineness and warmth. The tone of Tony's comments was chilled and not genuine and so Christine felt that Tony's questions were like an interrogation. In this case we intervened and asked Christine to tell Tony how she felt about the way Tony was asking these questions – to comment on the process rather than the content of the questions. This led to the group becoming concerned with and discussing genuineness and warmth. Tony explained that he was trying to help Christine to see her problems as residing within herself rather than in others. This leadership intervention – calling attention to the process and providing a positive connotation (a re-framing) to the person who was giving rise to concern – can be an effective strategy for dealing with this issue.

Hostilities

There are occasions in a group when two people become enemies, which affects the group's work. Often the issue is dealt with by the group, who seek to ensure that hostilities occur outside the group. But if necessary we, as leader, can intervene by having a private talk with the people concerned, by explicitly raising the issue within the group or by asking one or both of the hostile people to leave.

If I were you . . .

Another problem is giving advice. Sometimes this is appropriate: a therapy or counselling group may provide a forum in which people can and should offer advice and suggestions. The problem comes when this inhibits people from finding their *own* solutions to their own difficulties. There is a simple intervention which usually resolves this difficulty: a member wishing to offer a suggestion or advice first checks out whether that individual is willing to accept it.

Rescuing

This happens when someone who is experiencing distress or anxiety is rescued by another group member whether or not they wish to be.

Significant learning often involves personal pain, so rescuing a person who is struggling to learn from their distress prevents that person from learning. If rescuing is a repeated feature of the group, a useful strategy is to draw attention to it and to suggest a helpful ground rule: that rescue is *only* appropriate when the person requests help.

Leader over-dependency

A group can quickly become dependent upon its leader. As discussed in the previous chapter, some dependency is appropriate, and this is as true in a group setting as in one-to-one counselling. But such dependency can develop within the group to the point where the group is disabled or impaired by it. Where it is an issue, we need to share that we feel we are being depended upon, and we need to renegotiate the contract, paying special attention to the leader's role.

I think, therefore . . .

The final problem is intellectualising personal and emotional experiences. This can occur when group members are searching for universal rules, models and concepts with which to understand what is happening. The uses of language mentioned in the exchange between Christine and Tony and in chapter 9 are again useful here, as are interventions aimed at ensuring that individuals do not over-generalise experiences. Some of the activities suggested in chapter 9 for work with individuals at the level of feeling (exaggeration, the empty chair, sculpting, reversals) are also useful here to clarify the difference between intellectual statements about thoughts and feelings and the direct experience and expression of thoughts and feelings. Likewise, strategies can be taken from chapter 10 (on working with the body) to deal with such intellectualising.

These are some of the problems those of us wishing to run a counselling group are likely to experience. They are also common problems in other kinds of groups. As leaders, we can generally deal with these issues well, once we have developed a clear philosophy of group work for ourselves.

When Not to Work with Groups

Group work is not necessarily the most appropriate way forward for some people; for example, when:

- a client is feeling too anxious or too self-conscious to be part of a group and needs some initial one-to-one help, after which they may be ready to attend a group;
- a person's problems cannot be dealt with by group work – for example, Kelly's serious social problems meant that she would benefit more from individual than group work;
- clients seem cut off from the reality most of us inhabit, and especially when they are highly suspicious of others (however, there have been recent reports of successful group work with people who suffer from psychosis).

It is also dangerous for us to set up any kind of group without having researched carefully what we are doing, and thinking through the many aspects of group work highlighted in this chapter. We recommend attending a course on running groups, co-running a group for the first few times with a more experienced colleague, and ensuring that we have regular supervision while running any group, particularly early on in a group leadership career.

Practical Exercises

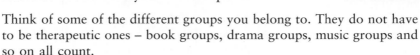

Exercise 1: monitor your own experience

Think of some of the different groups you belong to. They do not have to be therapeutic ones – book groups, drama groups, music groups and so on all count.

- Observe and monitor your own style of running groups and of participating in them, and ask for feedback.
- If the groups have leaders, watch what they do. Look at their individual styles, what seems to work and not work. Write these down and compare them to some of the issues within this chapter.

Exercise 2: look at media representations of groups

Look at films and TV, and find examples of led groups. Note how these groups function. Be aware of and try to identify different types of groups and their leadership styles.

SUMMARY

In this chapter we have covered:

- The reasons for working with clients in groups, and the aims and purposes of groups.
- Important issues when we establish a group, including the framework within which the group will work, how to select members and how to enable participants to make the most of group experiences.
- Leadership issues, including different types of leadership for different types of groups, our own motives for running groups, how to create the right conditions for group members and how to deal with leadership problems.
- Typical stages in group development – norming, forming, storming, reforming and mourning – which can illuminate how and why groups develop over time and the leader's role during these stages.
- Skills and strategies to manage problems in group work, such as people who do not participate or who dominate or give unwanted advice.
- When it is not appropriate to use a group setting to help a client.
- Practical exercises.

16

Summary and Conclusions

A painting is never finished – it simply stops in interesting places.
(Paul Gardner)

Summary

Our ethos of counselling

As we said in the introduction to this book, our underlying approach
to counselling, our overall ethos, has two main parts.

The first is that counselling is fundamentally about *enabling* people
to *take charge of their lives* and *to feel empowered to make changes*.
As the preceding chapters will have made clear, there are, of course, many
ways of enabling and empowering people. We have also argued that it
is important for prospective counsellors to realise that there is no one
right way to counsel all people, and that there is no one theoretical
perspective which has all of the counselling answers. We do, however,
believe that there are some fundamentals, and the second part of our
overall ethos relates to this: *the fundamental importance of the collab-*
orative counselling relationship. While a wide range of approaches and
counselling techniques are introduced and outlined in the book, we believe
that creating and maintaining an effective counselling relationship is at
the heart of all counselling interactions. Counselling is not just a series
of interventions and techniques that are used with (or on) clients.
None of the interventions described in Parts II and III are likely to be
effective in the absence of a collaborative relationship between client and

counsellor. A strong collaborative relationship is the essence of effective counselling and helping.

The building blocks to effective counselling

We have introduced in this book a multistage model of the counselling process, using the idea of sets of building blocks. Our idea is that these building blocks do exactly that – they build upon each other.

Hence there are some core areas of counselling without which it is extremely difficult to counsel someone effectively. These are covered in the set of building blocks within Part I, 'Foundations and Core Processes for Counselling and Helping'. We believe that all counsellors need to learn these fundamental and core skills. Key among them are the creation and maintenance of the collaborative counselling relationship, and the use of the core processes of counselling, of change and of maintenance of change.

Then there are a wide 'Range of Styles and Approaches' and of specific techniques which different counsellors sometimes use, and these are covered in the set of building blocks within Part II. When we use any of the skills and techniques outlined in this block, we still need to use the core skills outlined in the foundation block – these are not alternatives to them but *added* skills which overlay the core ones. However, unlike the core or foundation skills, which we believe *all* counsellors need to learn, we do not suggest that all of us need to learn all of the skills and techniques outlined in the second building block. Our view is that each counsellor needs to find an approach which is right for him or her. The way we look at many different approaches in this book is intended to help you to explore your own preferences and to decide on which approach or combinations of approaches most fits your interests and orientation.

The set of building blocks in Part III, 'Social Processes', introduces another dimension. We believe that counselling individuals in one-to-one sessions about their inner lives (thoughts, feeling, motivations, behaviour, etc.) is not enough. People live in a social context, and this has to be brought into our counselling. Bringing in our clients' social context can occur in different ways:

- sometimes in terms of discussing clients' social contexts with them;
- sometimes by inviting members of that context to join our clients in their sessions;
- sometimes by having the context itself take centre-stage in the counselling (i.e. by counselling couples or families);

- sometimes by seeing groups of clients together and using that context to help them acquire new skills of social interaction which they can use outside, in their real lives.

Again, the skills that we use as counsellors to explore our clients' social contexts, and to empower them to change within these contexts, are not alternatives to the skills used in the sets of building blocks in Parts I and II. They are added skills, which overlay the ones learnt in the previous two sets of building blocks.

Integrating approaches

Dividing our building blocks up between core processes, individually focused counselling and socially focused counselling implies that these are all rather discrete. It might imply (for example) that one either works intra-psychically or through the use of social processes. Although for ease of explanation we have looked at these individually and socially focused ideas as separate, the reality is that most of us as counsellors use elements of a wide variety of approaches to help our clients: we use whatever we consider to be in the best interests of our client(s) at the time we are seeing them. Hence we may well use a group approach, or work with a couple or a family; we may at the same time be working on developing our client's social networks; and we may also use elements of any number of the eight more individually focused approaches within the previous block as part of what we are doing. So, it is quite likely that we will, at times, use these all together and alongside the foundation of relationship formation and maintenance and the core processes of counselling.

We argue that a key task for us as counsellors as we become more experienced is to integrate these different areas, but the best way to get to know about each of these different tools is to see them separately in the first instance: it is easier to integrate ideas when each one is easily separable. So, although most of us as counsellors use a mixture of techniques and ideas from a number of approaches in our work with any client, we have presented them here essentially as pure forms.

Conclusions

Our key messages are these:

- Counselling is fundamentally about enabling people to take charge of their lives, and to feel empowered to make changes.

- There is no one right way to counsel all people, and there is no one theoretical perspective which has all the counselling answers.
- It is important to make explicit to our clients how we work and what we are doing. If we are obscure or vague with our clients or keep secrets from them, they will find it difficult to trust us.
- We must be sensitive to our client's immediate needs and at the same time aware of their long-term needs and of any longer-term problems. We also need to be aware of what is happening between us within our counselling relationship.
- We need always to be clear that our task is to enable our client to get to the stage where they can get on with their own lives without us.
- There are some core areas of counselling without which it would be extremely difficult to counsel someone effectively, and all counsellors need to learn these fundamental and core skills. These are primarily about developing a collaborative counselling relationship, and working through the core processes of counselling, of change and of maintenance of change.
- And then there are a wide range of approaches, some more individual, some more focused on social processes, all of which have useful ideas and important techniques associated with them: a key task is to integrate knowledge from these different areas.
- Crucially, counselling is not about the implementation of intervention techniques in a technically competent way (although intervention techniques are very useful). Counselling is fundamentally about the utilisation of the core or foundation skills covered in the building blocks within Part I.

Research into the experience of clients has shown that there are seven features of helping which are most valued by those who have been helped:

- *The client feeling that the core conditions are present (these include warmth, empathy, genuineness, commitment, active listening)* – it is the extent to which the client feels that they are understood, accepted and reacted to genuinely by us, their counsellor, that is key.
- *Ventilation and expressiveness* – the opportunity to speak about their problems, issues, thoughts, feelings, in depth and at a level which is rare outside of this situation, in a safe and neutral atmosphere.
- *Sensitive challenge* – being with someone who does not just accept what they say, but who pushes them (sensitively and warmly) to explore areas which they shy away from.

- *Increased awareness* – being encouraged to increase self-understanding and to learn more about the ways others see them.
- *Open communication* – an appreciation of the openness and warmth of our (their counsellor's) communication, even when we are challenging them.
- *Recognition of similarity* – being shown how similar they are in many respects to others, something especially important to those who seek help precisely because they feel out of touch with others.
- *Self–other perception* – being made aware of how others see them.

These seven points express succinctly much of what has gone before, in two ways:

- First, they emphasise that what is important in counselling is to *see the process through our client's eyes*: this is what our clients value, so this is what we should strive to provide.
- Second, these seven ideas sum up much of what it is that we need to do as counsellors. We do have to be ourselves, but within that, we have to *engage in the helping process with a high level of energy and commitment*. By engaging in this way, *we act as a model for the client to follow*.

Our prime function as counsellors is to empower our clients. To do this, we engage with our clients and encourage them to discover options which they had not considered or which they had previously discarded, either because the option was too threatening or they did not have the skills or the confidence to try it. Counselling is about empowering people in need: our clients.

Notes

PREFACE

1   R. Velleman (2001), *Counselling for Alcohol Problems* (2nd edn), London: Sage. Portions of chapter 3 of this present book are based on chapters 3 and 5 that book; and portions of chapter 14 are based on chapter 10 of that book.

CHAPTER 2

1   Statutory organisations are ones like the NHS, Social Services, Probation, etc., who provide services because they have a statutory (i.e. legal) duty to do so; non-statutory organisations (which are also called voluntary organisations, or sometimes NGOs – non-governmental organisations) are ones like Age Concern, Childline, CRUSE, or SANE, which exist without any statutory duty to do so, but which have been formed in response to a locally or nationally recognised need.

CHAPTER 3

1   A *lapse* here means a single event (e.g. a person who gets depressed feeling low, or someone with a drink problem having a single drink, or a dieter having a single biscuit); a relapse is if this lapse then goes on to become a full-scale return to problematic behaviour or feelings.

CHAPTER 5

1   Others do not share our view: some counselling courses now expect trainee counsellors to undergo personal therapy, and some forms of counselling or psychotherapy (such as psychodynamic counselling and some other in-depth counselling approaches) view ongoing personal therapy as a prerequisite.

Further Reading, Websites and Organisations

PART I: FOUNDATIONS AND CORE PROCESSES FOR COUNSELLING AND HELPING

Two series of concise, well-written, informative and accessible books about specific aspects of counselling are:

- The Counselling in Action series (published by Sage), where each book covers one from a wide range of different kinds of counselling areas such as cognitive-behavioural, feminist, Gestalt, rational emotive behavioural, and many more.
- The Counselling in Practice series (published by Sage), where each book covers one particular problem area such as anxiety, alcohol, depression, eating disorders, post-traumatic stress disorder, adults who were sexual abused as children, etc.

There are also many individual books on counselling. Among the best are:

De Board, Robert (1997) *Counselling for Toads: A Psychological Adventure*. London: Routledge.

Dryden, Windy and Feltham, Colin (1995) *Counselling and Psychotherapy: A Consumer's Guide*. London: Sheldon.

Egan, Gerard (2006) *The Skilled Helper: A Problem-Management and Opportunity Development Approach to Helping* (8th edn). Andover: Thomson Learning.

McLeod, John (2003) *An Introduction to Counselling*. Buckingham: Open University Press.

Nelson-Jones, Richard (2003) *Theory and Practice of Counselling and Therapy*. London: Sage.

The following slightly more specialised books look at a variety of issues within counselling.

In health-care settings

Rollnick, Steve, Mason, Pip and Butler, Chris (1999) *Health Behaviour Change: A Guide for Practitioners*. Edinburgh: Churchill Livingstone.

With couples and families

Carr, Alan (2000) *Family Therapy: Concepts, Process and Practice*. Chichester: Wiley.

Dallos, Rudi and Draper, Ros (2000) *Introduction to Family Therapy*. Buckingham: Open University Press.

Gilbert, Maria and Shmukler, Diana (1996) *Brief Therapy with Couples*. Chichester: Wiley.

O'Leary, Charles (1999) *Counselling Couples and Families: A Person-Centred Approach*. London: Sage.

With gay, lesbian, bisexual and transgender clients

Davies, Dominic and Neal, Charles (eds.) (1996) *Pink Therapy: Guide for Counsellors Working with Lesbian, Gay and Bisexual Clients*. Buckingham: Open University Press.

Davies, Dominic and Neal, Charles (eds.) (2000) *Therapeutic Perspectives on Working with Lesbian, Gay and Bisexual Clients (Pink Therapy)*. Buckingham: Open University Press.

Neal, Charles and Davies, Dominic (eds.) (2000) *Issues in Therapy with Lesbian, Gay, Bisexual and Transgender Clients*. Buckingham: Open University Press.

Perez, Ruperto, DeBord, Kurt and Bieschke, Kathleen (eds.) (2000) *Handbook of Counseling and Psychotherapy with Lesbian, Gay and Bisexual Clients*. Washington DC: American Psychological Association.

With minority ethnic groups

Hays, Pamela (2001) *Addressing Cultural Complexities in Practice: A Framework for Clinicians and Counselors*. Washington DC: American Psychological Association.

Lago, Colin (2006) *Race, Culture and Counselling: The Ongoing Challenge* (2nd edn). Buckingham: Open University Press.

Ponterotto, Joseph and Cass, Manuel (1991) *Handbook of Racial/Ethnic Minority Counseling Research*. Springfield, IL: C. C. Thomas.

Ponterotto, Joseph, Cass, Manuel, Suzuki, Lisa and Alexander, Charlene (2001) *Handbook of Multicultural Counselling* (2nd edn). Newbury Park, CA: Sage.

Shaikh, Zaibby, with Reading, John (1999) *Between Two Cultures: Effective Counselling for Asian People with Mental Health and Addiction Problems*. Hounslow: Ethnic Alcohol Counselling in Hounslow (EACH).

Wing, Su Derald and Sue, David (2007) *Counseling the Culturally Diverse: Theory and Practice.* Chichester: Wiley.

On the experience of being a client

Howe, David (1993) *On Being a Client: Understanding the Process of Counselling and Psychotherapy.* London: Sage.

On supervision

Dryden, Windy and Thorne, Brian (eds.) (1991) *Training and Supervision for Counselling in Action* (Counselling in Action series). London: Sage.
Hawkins, Peter and Shohet, Robin (2000) *Supervision in the Helping Professions* (2nd edn). Buckingham: Open University Press.
Holloway, Elizabeth and Carroll, Michael (eds.) (1999) *Training Counselling Supervisors: Strategies, Methods and Techniques.* Buckingham: Sage.
Spouse, Jenny and Redfern, Liz (eds.) (1999) *Successful Supervision in Health Care Practice.* Chichester: Wiley.

Books and articles referred to in Part I

Prochaska, J. and DiClemente, C. (1983) 'Transtheoretical therapy: Toward a more integrative model of change', *Psychotherapy: Theory, Research and Practice,* 19, 276–88. See also DiClemente, C. (2006) *Addiction and Change: How Addictions Develop and Addicted People Recover.* New York: Guilford.
Rogers, C. (1961) *On Becoming a Person.* Boston: Houghton-Mifflin.

PART II: THE RANGE OF STYLES AND APPROACHES

Chapter 6: Helping People to Cope

Cheevers, Peter (2007) *Coping with Family Stress: How to Deal with Difficult Relatives.* London: Sheldon.
Davis, Martha, Eshelman, Elizabeth Robbins and McKay, Matthew (2000) *The Relaxation and Stress Reduction Workbook* (5th edn). Oakland, CA: New Harbinger.
Elkin, Allen (1999) *Stress Management for Dummies.* Chichester: Wiley.
Orford, Jim et al. (2005) *Coping with Alcohol and Drug Problems: The Experiences of Family Members in Three Contrasting Cultures.* London: Taylor & Francis.
Palmer, Stephen and Cooper, Cary (2007) *How to Deal with Stress.* London: Kogan Page.

Tyrer, Peter (2003) *How to Cope with Stress* (2nd edn) (Overcoming Common Problems). London: Sheldon.

Chapter 7: Helping People to Do Things Differently

Dickson, Anne (1982) *A Woman in your Own Right: Assertiveness and You.* London: Quartet.

Havelin, Kate (2000) *Assertiveness – How Can I Say What I Mean: Perspectives on Relationships.* Mankato, MN: Capstone.

Kanfer, Frederick and Goldstein, Arnold (eds.) (1991) *Helping People Change: A Textbook of Methods.* London: Allyn & Bacon.

Lindenfield, Gael (1986) *Assert Yourself.* London: Thorsons.

Rollnick, Steve, Mason, Pip and Butler, Chris (1999) *Health Behaviour Change: A Guide for Practitioners.* Edinburgh: Churchill Livingstone.

Rosqvist, Johan (2005) *Exposure Treatments for Anxiety Disorders: A Practitioner's Guide to Concepts, Methods, and Evidence-Based Practice.* London: Routledge.

Chapter 8: Helping People with their Thinking

Casey, Andrew, Dryden, Windy, Trower, Peter and Fokias, Dene (2004) *Cognitive-Behavioural Counselling in Action* (Counselling in Practice series). London: Sage.

Dryden, Windy and Neenan, Michael (2004) *Rational Emotive Behavioural Counselling in Action* (3rd edn) (Counselling in Action series). London: Sage.

Greenberger, Dennis and Padesky, Christine (1995) *Mind over Mood.* New York: Guilford.

Mace, Chris (2007) *Mindfulness and Mental Health: Therapy, Theory and Science.* London: Routledge.

Simos, Gregoris (ed.) (2002) *Cognitive Behaviour Therapy: A Guide for the Practising Clinician.* London: Brunner-Routledge.

Wilding, Christine and Milne, Aileen (2008) *Teach Yourself Cognitive Behavioural Therapy.* London: Teach Yourself Books.

Chapter 9: Helping People with their Feelings

Brantley, Jeffrey (2007) *Calming your Anxious Mind: How Mindfulness and Compassion Can Free You of Anxiety, Fear and Panic.* New York: Guilford.

Clarkson, Petruska (1999) *Gestalt Counselling in Action* (Counselling in Action series). London: Sage.

Duncan, Shannon (2003) *Present Moment Awareness.* Novato, CA: New World Library.

Faupal, Adrian, Herrick, Elizabeth, and Sharp, Peter (2003) *Anger Management.* London: David Fulton (now Routledge/Taylor & Francis).

Gendlin, Eugene (2003) *Focusing: How to Open Up to your Deeper Feelings and Intuition*. London: Rider.

Gilbert, Paul (2009) *The Compassionate Mind*. London: Constable.

Glouberman, Dina (1995) *Life Choices, Life Changes: The Art of Developing Personal Vision through Imagework*. London: Thorsons.

Harbin, Thomas (2000) *Beyond Anger: A Guide for Men*. New York: Marlowe (now Perseus).

Kabat-Zinn, Jon (2006) *Mindfulness for Beginners*. Audio CD. Louisville, CO: Sounds True Inc.

Lindenfield, Gael (1993) *Managing Anger*. London: Thorsons.

Williams, J. Mark, Teasdale, John, Segal, Zindel and Kabat-Zinn, Jon (2007) *The Mindful Way through Depression: Freeing Yourself from Chronic Unhappiness: Guided Meditation Practices for the Mindful Way through Depression*. New York: Guilford.

Chapter 10: Helping People with their Bodies

Many of the books listed for chapter 9 will also be relevant here.

Caldwell, Christine (1997) *Getting in Touch: A Guide to New Body-Centred Therapies*. Wheaton, IL: Quest.

Dethlefsen, Thorwald and Dahlke, Rudiger (2004) *The Healing Power of Illness: Understanding What your Symptoms are Telling You*. London: Vega.

Downing, George (1998) *The Massage Book*. New York: Random House.

Fontana, David (1992/1998) *The Meditator's Handbook: A Comprehensive Guide to Eastern and Western Meditation Techniques*. Shaftesbury, Dorset and Rockport, MA: Element Books.

Gawain, Shakti (1998) *Creative Visualisation*. Novato, CA: New World.

Kern, Michael (2006) *Wisdom of the Body: The Craniosacral Approach to Essential Health*. Berkeley, CA: North Atlantic.

Staunton, Tree (2002) *Body Psychotherapy* (Advancing Theory in Therapy). London: Routledge.

Chapter 11: Helping People with their Unconscious Processes

Bateman, Anthony, Brown, Dennis and Pedder, Jonathan (2000) *Introduction to Psychotherapy: An Outline of Psychodynamic Principles and Practice* (3rd edn). London: Routledge.

Hughes, Patricia and Riordan, Daniel (2006) *Dynamic Psychotherapy Explained* (2nd edn). Oxford: Radcliffe.

Jacobs, Michael (2004) *Psychodynamic Counselling in Action* (3rd edn). London: Sage.

Jacobs, Michael (2005) *The Presenting Past: The Core of Psychodynamic Counselling and Therapy* (3rd edn). Buckingham: Open University Press.

Chapter 12: Helping People with their Spirituality

Lines, Dennis (2006) *Spirituality in Counselling and Psychotherapy*. London: Sage.

Marshall, Hazel (2006) *Journey in Depth: A Transpersonal Perspective*. Wimborne, Dorset: Archive Publishing.

Moore, Judith and Purton, Campbell (eds.) (2006) *Spirituality and Counselling: Experiential and Theoretical Perspectives*. Ross-on-Wye: PCCS.

Pargament, Kenneth (2007) *Spiritually Integrated Psychotherapy: Understanding and Addressing the Sacred*. New York: Guilford.

Rowan, John (2005) *The Transpersonal: Spirituality in Psychotherapy and Counselling* (2nd edn). London: Routledge.

West, William (2000) *Psychotherapy and Spirituality: Crossing the Line between Therapy and Religion* (Perspectives on Psychotherapy series). London: Sage.

Chapter 13: Helping People by Coaching

Downey, Myles (2003) *Effective Coaching* (2nd edn). London: Orion Business Books.

Fortgang, Laura Berman (1999) *Take Yourself to the Top*. London: Thorsons.

Gallwey, Timothy (1986) *The Inner Game of Tennis*. London: Pan.

Hawkins, Peter and Smith, Nick (2007) *Coaching, Mentoring and Organizational Consultancy: Supervision and Development*. Buckingham: Open University Press.

Megginson, David and Clutterbuck, David (2005) *Techniques for Coaching and Mentoring*. Amsterdam: Elsevier Butterworth Heinemann.

Passmore, Jonathan (2006) *Excellence in Coaching*. London: Kogan Page/ Association for Coaching.

Simmons, Annette (2008) *Quantum Skills for Coaches*. Evesham, Gloucestershire: Word for Word.

Stober, Dianne and Grant, Anthony (2006) *Evidence Based Coaching Handbook: Putting Best Practices to Work for your Clients*. Chichester: Wiley.

Whitmore, John (2003) *Coaching for Performance* (3rd edn). London: Nicholas Brealey.

PART III: SOCIAL PROCESSES

Chapter 14: Helping People to Use their Networks

Brown, George and Harris, Tirril (1978) *Social Origins of Depression*. London: Tavistock.

Levine, Murray, Perkins, Douglas and Perkins, David (2005) *Principles of Community Psychology: Perspectives and Applications* (3rd edn). Oxford: Oxford University Press.

Orford, Jim (2008) *Community Psychology: Challenges, Controversies and Emerging Consensus*. Chichester: Wiley-Blackwell.

Rappaport, Julian and Seidman, Edward (eds.) (2000) *Handbook of Community Psychology*. New York: Kluwer Academic/Plenum.

Scileppi, John, Teed, Elizabeth and Torres, Robin (2000) *Community Psychology: A Common Sense Approach to Mental Health*. Upper Saddle River, NJ: Prentice Hall.
See also the material on couples and families and minority ethnic groups above.

Chapter 15: Helping People in Groups

Chesner, Anna and Hahn, Herb (eds.) (2001) *Creative Advances in Groupwork*. London: Jessica Kingsley.
Cohen, Marcia and Mullender, Audrey (eds.) (2003) *Gender and Groupwork*. London: Routledge.
Doel, Mark (2005) *Using Groupwork*. London: Routledge.
Jaques, David *(2000) Learning in Groups* (3rd edn). London: Kogan Page.
Yalom, Irvin and Leszez, Molyn (2005) *The Theory and Practice of Group Psychotherapy* (5th edn). New York: Basic Books.

WEBSITES AND ORGANISATIONS

The British Association for Counselling and Psychotherapy (BACP) and the British Psychological Society (BPS) websites have a lot of useful information on accreditation and qualification.

United Kingdom

British Association for Counselling and Psychotherapy (BACP), BACP House, 15 St John's Business Park, Lutterworth, Leicestershire LE17 4HB, United Kingdom. www.bacp.co.uk/
British Association for Behavioural and Cognitive Psychotherapies (BABCP), Victoria Buildings, 9–13 Silver Street, Bury BL9 0EU, United Kingdom. www.babcp.com/
The British Psychological Society (BPS) (Counselling Psychology Section), St Andrews House, 48 Princess Road East, Leicester LE1 7DR, United Kingdom. www.bps.org.uk/dcop/dcop_home.cfm
NICE (National Institute for Health and Clinical Excellence) Guidelines, online at: www.nice.org.uk
Relate, Premier House, Carolina Court, Lakeside, Doncaster DN4 5RA. Relate offers advice, relationship counselling, sex therapy, workshops, mediation, consultations and support face to face, by phone and through their website. www.relate.org.uk/

Canada

Canadian Counselling Association (CCA)/Canadian Counselling and Psychotherapy Association (CCPA), 16 Concourse Gate, Suite 600, Ottawa, Ontario K2E 7S8, Canada. www.ccacc.ca/home.html

United States of America

American Counseling Association (ACA), 5999 Stevenson Avenue, Alexandria,
VA 22304, USA. www.counseling.org/
American Psychological Association (APA), 750 First Street NE, Washington,
DC 20002–4242, USA. www.apa.org/ and Division of Counselling Psychology
www.div17.org/

Australia

Australian Counselling Association (ACA), National office address: Thomas Street,
Grange, Queensland 4051, Australia. Postal address: PO Box 88, Grange,
Queensland 4051, Australia. www.theaca.net.au/
Australian Guidance and Counselling Association (AGCA) www.agca.com.au/
Australian Psychological Society (APS), Level 11, 257 Collins Street, Melbourne,
Victoria 3000, Australia. Postal address: PO Box 38, Flinders Lane, Victoria
8009, Australia. www.psychology.org.au/ and www.groups.psychology.org.au/
ccoun/ and www.psychology.org.au/community/specialist/counselling/

New Zealand

New Zealand Psychological Society (NZPsS), PO Box 4092, Wellington, New
Zealand. www.psychology.org.nz/
The New Zealand Association of Counsellors (NZAC), PO Box 165, Waikato
Mail Centre, Hamilton, 3240, New Zealand; and Level 3, Federated
Farmers Building, 169 London Street, Hamilton, 3240, New Zealand.
www.nzac.org.nz/

International

International Association for Counselling (IAC): www.iac-irtac.org/

Other organisations

Positive psychology
www.authentichappiness.sas.upenn.edu/Default.aspx
www.ppc.sas.upenn.edu/
www.centreforconfidence.co.uk/pp/
www.positivepsychology.net/

Coaching
Coaching and Special Interest Group, British Psychological Society:
www.sgcp.org.uk/cpinfo.cfm

Association for Coaching: www.associationforcoaching.com/home/index.htm
The European Mentoring and Coaching Council: www.emccouncil.org/uk/about.htm
International Coach Federation: www.coachfederation.org/ICF/
Coaching resources (articles, magazines and books): www.peer.ca/coachingnews.html#magazines
The Coaches Training Institute (CTI), founded by Laura Whitworth and Henry Kimsey-House, 1879, Second Street, San Raphael, CA 94901, USA: www.thecoaches.com

Index

Note: page numbers in italics denote figures or tables